EXTRAORDINARY ENCOUNTERS

Methodology and History in Anthropology

General Editor: David Parkin, Fellow of All Souls College, Oxford

Just as anthropology has had a significant influence on many other disciplines in recent years, so too have its methods been challenged by new intellectual and technical developments. This series is designed to offer a forum for debate on the interrelationship between anthropology and other academic fields but also on the challenge that new intellectual and technological developments pose to anthropological methods, and the role of anthropological thought in a general history of concepts.

Volume 1
Marcel Mauss: A Centenary Tribute
Edited by Wendy James and N.J. Allen

Volume 2
Taboo, Truth and Religion
Franz B. Steiner
Edited by Jeremy Adler and Richard Fardon

Volume 3
Orientpolitik, Value, and Civilization
Franz B. Steiner
Edited by Jeremy Adler and Richard Fardon

Volume 4
The Problem of Context: Perspectives from Social Anthropology and Elsewhere
Edited by R.M. Dilley

Volume 5
Religion in English Everyday Life: An Ethnographic Approach
Timothy Jenkins

Volume 6
Hunting the Gatherers: Ethnographic Collectors, Agents, and Agency in Melanasia, 1870s–1930s
Edited by Michael O'Hanlon and Robert Welsch

Volume 7
Anthropologists in a Wider World: Essays on Field Research
Edited by Paul Dresch, Wendy James, and David Parkin

Volume 8
Categories and Classifications: Maussian Reflections on the Social
N.J. Allen

Volume 9
Louis Dumont and Hierarchical Opposition
Robert Parkin

Volume 10
Categories of Self: Louis Dumont's Theory of the Individual
André Celtel

Volume 11
Existential Anthropology: Events, Exigencies, and Effects
Michael Jackson

Volume 12
An Introduction to Two Theories of Social Anthropology: Descent Groups and Marriage Alliance
Louis Dumont

Volume 13
Navigating Terrains of War: Youth and Soldiering in Guinea-Bissau
Henrik E. Vigh

Volume 14
The Politics of Egalitarianism: Theory and Practice
Edited by Jacqueline Solway

Volume 15
A History of Oxford Anthropology
Edited by Peter Riviére

Volume 16
Holistic Anthropology: Emergence and Convergence
Edited by David Parkin and Stanley Ulijaszek

Volume 17
Learning Religion: Anthropological Approaches
Edited by David Berliner and Ramon Sarró

Volume 18
Ways of Knowing: New Approaches in the Anthropology of Knowledge and Learning
Edited by Mark Harris

Volume 19
Difficult Folk? A Political History of Social Anthropology
David Mills

Volume 20
Human Nature as Capacity: Transcending Discourse and Classification
Nigel Rapport

Volume 21
The Life of Property: House, Family, and Inheritance in Béarn, South-West France
Timothy Jenkins

Volume 22
Out of the Study and Into the Field: Ethnographic Theory and Practice in French Anthropology
Edited by Robert Parkin and Anne de Sales

Volume 23
The Scope of Anthropology: Maurice Godelier's Work in Context
Edited by Laurent Dousset and Serge Tcherkézoff

Volume 24
Anyone: The Cosmopolitan Subject of Anthropology
Nigel Rapport

Volume 25
Up Close and Personal: On Peripheral Perspectives and the Production of Anthropological Knowledge
Edited by Cris Shore and Susanna Trnka

Volume 26
Understanding Cultural Transmission in Anthropology: A Critical Synthesis
Edited by Roy Ellen, Stephen Lycett and Sarah Johns

Volume 27
Durkheim in Dialogue: A Centenary Celebration of The Elementary Forms of Religious Life
Edited by Sondra L. Hausner

Volume 28
Extraordinary Encounters: Authenticity and the Interview
Edited by Katherine Smith, James Staples and Nigel Rapport

EXTRAORDINARY ENCOUNTERS

Authenticity and the Interview

Edited by
Katherine Smith, James Staples and Nigel Rapport

berghahn
NEW YORK · OXFORD
www.berghahnbooks.com

First published in 2015 by

Berghahn Books

www.berghahnbooks.com

© 2015, 2018 Katherine Smith, James Staples and Nigel Rapport
First paperback edition published in 2018

Library of Congress Cataloging-in-Publication Data
Authenticity and the interview / edited by Katherine Smith, James
Staples, and Nigel Rapport.
     pages cm. -- (Methodology and history in anthropology ; volume 28)
  Includes bibliographical references.
  ISBN 978-1-78238-589-9 (hardback) -- ISBN 978-1-78238-590-5
(ebook)
  1. Interviewing in ethnology. I. Smith, Katherine, 1979- editor of
compilation. II. Staples, James, 1966- editor of compilation. III. Rapport,
Nigel, 1956- editor of compilation.
  GN346.3.A87 2015
  305.8--dc23

                                                        2014033562

British Library Cataloguing in Publication Data

A catalogue record for this book is available from the British Library

ISBN 978-1-78238-589-9 (hardback)
ISBN 978-1-78533-817-5 (paperback)
ISBN 978-1-78238-590-5 (ebook)

CONTENTS

THE INTERVIEW AS ANALYTICAL CATEGORY

James Staples and Katherine Smith

In the social sciences, publications about research methods all too often confine their discussions to issues of data collection and analysis, without exploring in much depth knowledge traditions and claims to understanding. There are, of course, some notable exceptions, including Jonathan Skinner's work (2010, 2012) on the ways in which an anthropology of the senses should be extended to the data-gathering side of ethnography; Jenny Hockey's (2002) questioning of the general perception in the social sciences that participant observation must pragmatically encompass interviews as a seamless, holistic ethnography; and Janet Finch's (1984) early work on the impact of ethical and political decisions of the social researcher in interview situations. The chapters collected in this book likewise make an important departure from the more general trend in 'how-to' publications, attempting to capture, ethnographically, the particular moments when social and personal life is imagined, discussed, documented and seen as the emerging outcome of complex personal and collective histories, rather than as mainly defined by the specificities of interview questions.

For all of the descriptive promise and analytical potential that ethnography offers, the interview itself has made relatively little theoretical impact on the ways in which anthropological methods play a part in the representation of ethnographic details. The assumption may be widespread that the interview offers uniquely privileged data, grounded in biographical experiences and social contexts, and yet the presentation of the knowledge acquired from conducting ethnographic interviews continues to raise hoary questions concerning the relations between subjects and objects, and things as they are against things as they might be (Strathern 2004). Writing is much more than the recording of facts and observations (ibid.: 7), in short, and the interview is much more than a means by which to collect them.

The interview is a social event that requires continual attention because of the way in which it garners the interest of researchers and research subjects alike. An elemental part of modern social practice is the reflection and realisation of human ideas and subjectivities, and their detachment from the moment of experience as ideas are discussed in conversation with others. Within the context of ethnographic inquiry, the interview itself may, then, play a crucial role in eliciting information that would otherwise not be discussed in everyday life and conversation. People may become easily analytical about their own and others' experiences in an interview situation. The interview may be seen to provide a space for the detachment and envisioning of subjectivities at a particular moment in time, and in a particular moment of experience. As the anthropologist explains the role of the interview as the furtherance of respect and awareness of other ways of life, individuals may choose to resist or disagree with social norms and expectations as they carve out new ways of communicating particular, perhaps personal, views and imaginations that, in the interview, may take precedence over wider social expectations. Jenny Hockey (2002: 214) points out that, 'interviews are situated moments in which people engage with aspects of life which may not surface elsewhere. [Interviews] allow past and future to be accessed via the present and create space for what has been left unsaid and what remains invisible'. Here, we explore the interview as a medium through which to express a variety of lived experiences and imagined futures.

Each of the contributions to this volume approaches the ethnographic interview both as a method and as an analytical category. It is seen as an essential part of the ethnographer's 'toolkit' in order to collect data and gain a particular kind of knowledge and understanding in fieldwork, as well as a vague construction based on the field researcher's experience of immersion in fieldwork and their own academic training. 'The interview is not over-determined socially or culturally, but is a matter of point of view' (Rapport 2012: 57–58). The interview in ethnographic writing, as support and demonstration of thoughts and knowledge accrued in fieldwork, embeds what we see here in this volume as an extraordinary encounter in what is commonly considered 'ordinary' in ethnographic practice (Rapport 2012: 57). Therefore, the following chapters offer ethnographic examples that allow for 'an interrogation of what difference it makes to an analysis of human social life to re-situate our focus on the interview' and how the interview is experienced and imagined as a particular kind of space within which personal, biographic and social cues and norms are explored and interrogated, and as a space for mutually constructed reflection and analysis, providing direction and awareness for future encounters. Collectively, the chapters offer a powerful new appreciation of the interview as a space of extraordinary encounters that, at the same time, inform everyday social relations. Considerations of the interview thus accompany broader discussions and debates concerning how social science might apprehend unique events and experiences alongside those that are more general, patterned and conventional in social life. The interview as a theme brings to the fore methodological issues of authenticity and also provides a fruitful focus on how the everyday is continuously constructed through moments of reflection and authorship.

Collectively, the following chapters demonstrate how the interview represents a different context to everyday conversation and interaction, a context that can elicit a different kind of response. Existing social relations are reflected upon, new ones are developed, and in reflecting upon the particularity of the interview and its different kind of response, the chapters in this volume, taken together, show what this means for our ('authentic') data and our contributions to the production of knowledge. We show that in the telling of a life story, in the exchange of knowledge in the context of the interview and in writing, personal lives are related to the lives of others; thus, as Brian Roberts explains, 'there is both autobiography and biography' (2002: 163).

Ethnographic examples make possible a critique of those accounts that assume the interview to be a second-rate choice in relation to participant observation (see Hockey 2002). At the same time they allow for an interrogation of those analyses in which the interview is deemed to be less effective or 'authentic' because research subjects and researchers experience the interview as a context situated outside everyday life, or talk about personal and social issues in different ways in an interview context. Looking at how the interview in ethnographic research is organised, conducted and explained provides in-roads to problematising the idea that our research participants can be represented as homogeneous, with a shared set of interests.

Critical reflection on the interview allows us to come to terms with the various ways in which the study of 'others' is not always and simply the study of the powerless (see for example Shore and Nugent 2002) but is about the realisation, reflection and expression of self, society and culture. The recounting of the interview can add to the dramatic portrait of personal engagement with the field, with people and with ideas (Rapport 1994). Tracking and documenting ideas that become paramount in the interview context, and what sorts of shifts in perspective are recounted and how, shows that there is a rupturing of the illusory experience of wholeness and the consistency between the self and the social and cultural setting (cf. Sökefeld 1999).

In sum, the interview should be seen as a special, productive site of ethnographic encounter. It is less to be distinguished from ethnography than explored as a site of a very particular and important kind of knowing: one which allows those we learn from a unique opportunity to reflect, comment upon and interpret their own actions and the world around them in their own terms. It is the co-creation of the interview as a space within which the personal reflections, memories, life stories, embellishments and justifications for actions and ideas are discussed that make this context an 'active' (Holstein and Gubrium 1995) and 'relational' (Tietel 2000) reinforcement that at once focuses and expands both the interviewer's and interviewee's experiences and senses of self. Interviews can be considered as building blocks for the construction of an image of the self that may otherwise come in and out of focus in everyday life.

In the following introductory pages we begin by problematising the notion of the interview per se, exploring it both as a methodology and, subsequently, as an analytical category. In setting out what we hope to achieve by bringing together the chapters of this volume we also situate the collection amid what we identify as the various genres of publications on the interview. Finally, we turn our attention to the individual chapters to explore the connections that bring them together as a whole, revealing the many ways in which interviews are, as our title has it, indeed 'extraordinary encounters'.

A Fresh Interrogation of the Interview in Ethnographic Practice

From the combative radio or television interview aimed at extracting the 'truth' from an expert interviewee – a politician or industrialist – well versed in the arts of political spin, to the cosier, sofa-style interviews with actors and pop stars that dominate the evening schedules and fill consumer magazines, interviews are, after all, everywhere. Police officers undertake interviews to interrogate their suspects – which, even if we are not arrested, we can witness versions of in the surfeit of docudramas and serials that fill our screens – while barristers draw out information pertinent to cases in similar fashion. Counsellors, in particular, but increasingly other health professionals, offer care through talk therapies that might likewise be classified as particular kinds of interviews.

Indeed, such is our familiarity with the interview as a format that television interviewers – from the likes of David Letterman in the United States to Michael Parkinson and Jonathan Ross in the United Kingdom – are as famous, and often more so, than the celebrities to whom they pose their questions. Audiences across the industrialised West – academic or otherwise – are well used to the interview as a medium for unearthing a person's story or hearing their point of view: as a method of 'unfolding the subject's lifeworld', to borrow a phrase from Skinner (2012; see also Kvale 1996).

The utility of the interview in ethnographic research and writing traditionally involves taking notice of the use of interviews, and mentioning their importance becomes a 'fundamental section of the intact chapter, providing that foundation, in quantitative terms, assuring that all bases have been covered' (Thomas 1991: 308). The interviews themselves may take the form of 'structured', 'semi-structured' or 'unstructured' exchanges that may be recorded on audio devices, laboriously transcribed, reflected upon, selected and analysed. Interviews, as things to be dealt with, are the data that contribute to the 'knowledge', as opposed to 'information', which we as ethnographers use to think with. So why, given that interview techniques – unlike the more elusive anthropological method of participant observation – are hardly shrouded in mystery, should we need even one book, let alone another addition to the many that already exist out there, devoted to 'the interview'?

There are, of course, many possible answers to that question. The first is that precisely because of the interview's ubiquity in everyday life, we need, as social scientists, to be consciously aware of, and to reflect upon, the interview's provenance – to ask why it is such a powerful tool for mining subjective information – if we are to use it effectively and ethically as a research tool. We need to be able to see beneath the surface of the interview, whether presented for our light entertainment, news or as a source of data. It might look very simple: one person poses a question, another one answers it, and so it goes on, each interlocutor in turn, until the interviewer terminates the encounter. Like the properly functioning body (Leder 1990; see also Haraway 2004), the interview is sufficiently unremarkable and commonplace that, unless we make a special effort to attend to it, it disappears from view. But attending to what is behind a question – what the interviewer has at stake in asking the question, and what is going to be changed by someone answering it – might tell us more than the raw data collected by the interview itself. To quote Hobart: 'Descriptions do not occur *in vitro*, but are produced on occasions when someone plans to assert the status quo, find a reason for doing nothing or change something' (1990: 98). Replace 'descriptions' with either 'questions' or 'answers' and the point is as valid in respect of scrutinising the presuppositions that might underpin a particular interview context.

We also need to remind ourselves that, despite living in what Atkinson and Silverman (1997) call 'the interview society', interviews are not taken-for-granted facts of life everywhere, and nor is every interview the same kind of thing. Asking someone a series of questions in rural South Africa about their disease status, as one of our contributors does (Niehaus, this volume), is not likely to produce the same results as asking a similar set of questions to, say, an 'expert patient' (Department of Health, 2001) in the British National Health Service (NHS), who, we might assume, is well versed in certain kinds of interview, and briefed in how to respond to questions about their conditions. Likewise, interviewing fellow anthropologists whose ethnographic practices one has some acquaintance with, as Okely (this volume) does, is a very different proposition to questioning those from profoundly different cultural or intellectual traditions. So, for all its apparent simplicity – someone asks a question, an interlocutor responds to it and so on – the outcome of any interview is heavily influenced by the contexts in which it takes place.

The State of Play

Books on the Interview

The use of the interview in other disciplines, most notably in sociology, has involved its extensive examination and structuring as a particular kind of 'science' (see Skinner 2012: 8). And until recently, anthropology's relationship with the interview has been dominated by the general acknowledgement that interviews, while expected in any credible ethnography, are the important means by which to demonstrate the long, sustained and transformative knowledge gained in fieldwork. As might be expected for a research method as established and variable as the interview, there are a number of existing books alongside which this volume might sit comfortably on the bookshelves of scholars and field researchers. Much of the existing material out there – some of it very good – fits into one of three categories. What we set out to do with this particular book is something a bit different. This book attempts to go beyond each of them.

The first category consists of critical work by sociologists, in particular, to which our volume provides a valuable anthropological counterpart. Given the relative lacuna of work from an anthropological perspective, this gives the current volume an obvious appeal to social anthropologists, but it also provides a body of material with which sociologists and other social scientists will also be able to engage in productive conversation. The book might be said to form, if you will, part of an 'inter-view' (Finch 1984), and a focused conversation with these other social science disciplines about a shared practice. Holstein and Gubrium's (1995) work is a good example of this category of critical sociological reflection on the interview, and we build here on their lead by taking further the notion of activity and agency that they introduce. Most significantly, in relating the interview to the social relations and processes that surround it – in breaking down the distinction between the occasion of the interview and the moments of social exchange of which it is part – the activity and agency of the interview can be seen to be part of the intentionality of social life. As an extraordinary encounter and the expression of non-conventional voices and identities, the interview is also to be seen as evidencing those powers of individual meaning-making by which cultural forms are everywhere animated. Here the anthropologist is able to draw on more extensive knowledge of the interviewee – gained from fieldwork – so as to put the interview in a wider and fuller context.

The second of the three broad categories is of books written and edited by anthropologists, but which only focus on the interview, if at all, as one of a much wider range of ethnographic methodologies (e.g., Bernard 1994; Clair 2003; Emerson, Fretz and Shaw 1995). Anthropologists can also be rather dismissive of the interview as an ethnographic technique. As Hockey (2002) notes, interviewing is often characterised as a second-rate methodological choice compared to the anthropological pièce de résistance of 'participant observation'. By contrast, while in this book we do not shy away from the richness of the data that may be created through engaged interviews, we aim to address some of the lacuna such approaches identify by focusing specifically – and critically – on the interview from the anthropologist's perspective. In a tradition of anthropological knowledge production, we recognise that the danger in approaching the interview as simply a practice that is shared and recognisable with certainty, is that interviews serve as a means to an end while the persons we learn from become fixed in contexts not of their own making.

The third category includes the plethora of how-to textbooks (e.g., Rubin and Rubin 2005; Kvale and Brinkmann 2009; Kvale 2007; King and Horrocks 2010; Weiss 1994; Galletta 2013; Seidman 2013). Between them, these volumes (and many more besides) offer a forensic exploration of everything from recruiting interviewees to the recording, transcription and analysis of interview data and its final publication. In addition to advice on the practicalities of interviewing – from expressing and ordering questions in the most effective way to using computer software packages to code the material gathered – such books also invite their readers to reflect on ethical dilemmas and to develop strategies to prevent themselves being cast in the role of therapist. This book, by contrast, is less of a step-by-step guide and more an examination of the nature of the data that interviews offer, and the ways and extents to which this data is different from what might be gained from participant observation alone. It is also an examination of the nature of the consciousness of the interviewee (and interviewer), their intentions and world views, and the way in which an appreciation of this by the interviewer affords insights into how the interviewee and others can be seen to be responsible for the everyday construction of order and sense in their lives (Rapport 1993). It works from the idea that the importance of the interview is affected by the ambivalence in social science research of what constitutes a 'good' and 'useful' outcome of the interview process. This collection of case studies, and reflection on them, sets out both to challenge and renew the ways in which the ethnographic interview is seen as a constellation of objectives in which all participants come to know, through imaginative investigation, the social worlds in which they live. Equally, by addressing the ways in which the interview may be conducted, recorded and used, our book provides useful examples for readers to anticipate and negotiate their own extraordinary encounters in fieldwork and with research data.

The Interview as Analytical Category

Examination of the complex ways in which people's inner states reflect lived experience within everyday worlds as well as within temporary spaces and transitions can disturb and enlarge presumed understandings of what is socially possible or desirable. The interview, then, is both an empirical reality and an analytic category, as each explores the agonistic and practical activity of engaging identity and society, patterned and felt in historically contingent settings, and mediated by institutional and academic processes and cultural forms.

The literary or rhetorical turn in anthropology continues to produce a substantial body of work aimed at raising an awareness of the discursive construction of knowledge and textual modes of representation (Clifford and Marcus 1986; Marcus and Fischer 1986; Geertz 1988). The contextualisation of the interview in ethnographic writing raises the question of how 'data' is made relevant after the interview. If the goal of research is to produce 'useful and credible information' (Pelto and Pelto 1978: ix) that is 'authentic' and 'relevant', and that informs a wider view of social networks and relations, who sets the terms for this? Is the interview that explores personal and biographical views and stories really more 'authentic'? How can an interview tell us about new kinds of 'public-private involvements' (Hockey 2002: 214) when participants can contradict themselves, each other and the researcher's contributions and interpretations of social life? Biographical accounts gained in this context supply information that is often counter-intuitive and non-conventional, whilst at the same time providing information that is generalisable beyond particular social and cultural contexts. Other selves and ideas are searched for: the interview elicits information that may not be discussed or discernable in everyday social interaction. Memories, life stories, embellishments and justifications for actions and ideas at once focus and expand both the interviewers' and interviewees' experiences. An anthropology that explores methodological traditions in new ways can bring balance to, as well as complicate, more quantitative analyses that do not necessarily anticipate the value of the relations that are recalled, forged and maintained beyond the interview setting.

The Ethnographic Examples

In this introduction we have aimed to 'set the scene' by addressing the idea that an elemental part of modern social practice is reflection, and

that the interview provides a space for re-imaginings and re-articu-
lations of personal and social practice. Each of the following seven
chapters should be read both as interrogations and reflections on the
interview in their own right, as well as parts of an integrated whole.
The epilogue reviews what the volume can be seen to have achieved.

In the first three substantive chapters, Pat Caplan, Isak Niehaus and
James Staples offer up data on their research methods that would have
otherwise been absent in their published work, and on which, in some
cases, they had not themselves openly reflected. In their chapters, they
take that knowledge and apply it in pursuing in-depth, biographic
or life-history type interviews. In doing so, they each challenge the
findings of case studies that follow more conventionalised narrative
structures by exploring – contra Henige's (1988) view that life-history
interviews teach us little about the wider socio-historical context –
how one person's experience can shed light on social relationships,
institutions and norms in the telling of a life story. The dialectical
structure of the interview – the to-ing and fro-ing between a
researcher and informant – is sometimes mirrored in the scaled-up
dialectic between the informant's account and consideration of the
wider literature.

In the first of the case studies, Pat Caplan begins by questioning
whether her encounters with Mikidadi, the biographical subject of her
chapter, can be considered interviews at all: Mikidadi's untimely death
meant he was not physically there when she began pulling together
the components of his story, and much of her material relies on other
sources, such as past correspondence with him, diaries Mikidadi kept
for her, and memories of a relationship that dates back more than
thirty years. If, however, we think of interviews in the broader sense
that we have outlined earlier in this introduction, we would argue that
even in the absence of the subject, as in Caplan's case, the exchange
between the anthropologist and the informant shares more than
enough of the same characteristics of the interview to be considered
as such. Interviews do, after all, have 'a life of their own', as Caplan
points out, and although she has not sat down and constructed a list of
questions to be posed in a particular order, she has, over a long period,
asked questions – by various means – of her interlocutor and recorded
the answers. The data, then, arose naturally from conversations, later
recorded in her notes, and from sources like the diaries Mikidadi kept
for her. The conversations might not, at the time, have had a purpose –
in the sense that Robson (1993) defines – but, defined retrospectively,
they were certainly utilised towards a purpose. They also, importantly,
throw up information about Mikidadi's life that it would not have

been possible to gather from participant observation alone, even if the latter – in all the cases elaborated in this book – was a prerequisite to being able to ask, and then to interpret, the appropriate questions.

In Niehaus's account, the story of Reggie Ngobeni, who has been diagnosed HIV- positive, is enhanced and interpreted through recent material on HIV treatments and narratives about public health education in respect of the syndrome. At the same time, however, his stories allow for a more nuanced, critical reading of the literature. In capturing the texture of social relationships and of subjective experience, Niehaus argues, convincingly, that a biographical interview is particularly well placed to explore the complex, multifaceted questions posed by responses to AIDS/HIV – and can help us to understand, in ways the contemporaneous participant observation alone cannot, why ordinary South Africans are often so ambivalent towards the antiretroviral (ARV) drugs that could, on the face of it, ameliorate their suffering. As Niehaus puts it, 'the capacity of biographies to capture the unfolding of shifting, indeterminate and contradictory meanings in individual lives, make them an extremely valuable addition to studies of social and cultural phenomena of a more public nature' (Niehaus, this volume).

Something of the same process is also detectable in Staples' account of the life of his research assistant Das, where a close examination of one man's life throws new light on the more general regional ethnographic literature on institutions such as caste, Hinduism, and Indian notions of purity and pollution. In both these accounts it is difficult for the researchers concerned to discern where the boundaries between the 'interview' and other methods of research, such as 'participant observation', might lie. Niehaus's telling of Reggie's story, for example, is informed by conversations with others – including Reggie's cousin – and his wider ethnographic knowledge of the context in which Reggie lives. The same could also be said of Staples' account, whose 'interviews' include taking Das back to significant places that emerge through his stories and observing his interactions with others in those places. His telling is also informed (as is Caplan's) by informant diaries, field notes and letters, which are clearly different but not entirely separable from that which might be more recognisable as an interview: a social context in which the researcher poses questions to which the informant responds.

The following chapters explore interviews of particular kinds and as spaces not just for revelation, but also for the co-production and exchange of information and knowledge between participants. Katherine Smith's encounters with members of the ladies' darts

team in 'Starlings' – a northern English working men's club – also
show the interview as a very privileged kind of space in which both
interviewer and interviewee can interrogate and make sense of their
more informal exchanges, the meanings of which might otherwise
remain unintelligible, at least to the outsider. In the incidents Smith
describes, for example, she interviews the women about their practice
of 'having a barter' – a quick-fire exchange of apparently derogatory
banter – which, taken at face value or heard in another context,
might be read as an act of verbal aggression. The interview, however,
provides a bracketed context in which the women concerned can
reflect on their utterances and articulate what they meant by them. In
this way, through the interview, data that otherwise remains implicit
can become unambiguously explicit for, in many cases, the first time:
again, it provides a place for reflection for the interviewee as well as
data for the interviewer.

The Catalonian children who feature in Àngels Trias i Valls's
chapter are likewise very aware – surprisingly, perhaps, given their
youth – that the interview is a very particular kind of exchange,
distinct from the other verbal encounters of everyday life. In a
painstaking analysis of her video recordings of interviews with
children about the gifts they were hoping to receive over the
Christmas season, Trias i Valls demonstrates that children, some as
young as three, were fully capable of dropping in and out of the
interview context, moving aside when they became bored (to argue
with a sibling or to ask a parent a question), and shifting back into a
distinctive interviewee mode – focused and direct – when they were
ready to return to the formal interview, a space in which information
that might otherwise be left unsaid can be conveyed.

The subsequent chapter, in which Judith Okely reflects on the
experience of interviewing fellow anthropologists about their own
research methods, appears, on the face of it, to take our discussion in
a different direction. Here, Okely attacks what she terms the 'banality
of formulaic methods', drawing a marked distinction between the
interview as a fixed, highly structured and, ideally, objective encounter
– in which all respondents are asked the same questions regardless of
their responses and, in many cases, are offered only a limited range of
possible responses – and the more meandering, open-ended interviews
described by most of the contributors to this volume, and which she
herself undertook with more than twenty anthropologists. Although
the interviews she conducted were, as she points out, of a particular
kind – drawing both on personal acquaintance and shared disciplinary
knowledge as the basis on which the exchanges take place – there are

also some striking resemblances between her interlocutors' responses and those of the Catalonian children and members of the Starlings' darts team described by Trias i Valls and Smith. As was the case in the other interviews, the anthropologists Okely interviewed – largely because of the open, discursive context in which their exchanges took place – reflected on their research practices in ways they might not have done previously, particularly in their published work.

There are parallels here with how the UK sex workers that Ana Lopes interviews come to understand their experiences in new, previously unexplored ways, often by self-consciously appropriating the interview format. In her chapter, Lopes discusses how, in the process of conducting 'action research' (Reason and Bradbury 2001) with these sex workers, she came to understand the interview not simply as a tool through which to elicit data for her own ends, but as a structure that might also be appropriated by interviewees to construct a better understanding of their own situations. Her interviews with sex workers came to constitute, as she puts it, 'a process by which individuals perform in-depth analysis of their own realities' (Lopes, this volume). By talking about their work, their feelings towards it and their problems in organising themselves collectively, Lopes's interlocutors were often articulating these issues openly for the first time and, in doing so, were able to order and make sense of them in their own terms. The interview context formed the basis for action – in this case for establishing a trade union.

Collectively, these chapters demonstrate the matter of perspective inherent in the interview and its utility in ethnography. They explore the construction of biographical accounts in ethnographic research and writing, addressing the ways in which life stories address concerns beyond the individual, whose life is studied in ways that are both grounded and accessible, as well as the ways in which the (dis)organised interview elicits a particular kind of information and knowledge that is unique to the interview context. What then, one might ask, distinguishes a biographical interview and the other, more routine anthropological methods – such as participant observation – into which it frequently merges? For one thing, as Douglass (1992) points out, in reality participant observation tends to be either participation or, more often, observation: watching events unfold, and maybe asking questions about them. The distinction between the two practices may, however, not always be so clear-cut and require continual attention (Smith 2012). Biographies – in common with interview data more generally – mostly require more than the contemporaneous recording of events: we need to find out, usually by asking questions, what happened a long time before the events we are observing. Such questions might be recognisable as what we would think of as interview questions, a more or less chronological documenting of events, from the relatively banal (for example, 'When and where were you born?') to a more complex probing of the data being offered. Often, however, the questions will not be asked in a structured sense. Interviewees, once asked to tell their story, might need very few interjections at all, even though the presence of the researcher is still required in order to justify the telling of the story and to record it – a role analogous, perhaps, to that of the therapist. It is the interviewer, even when silent, on to whom the interviewee's commentary is projected. When interviewers do interject, as Staples (this volume) points out, such interjections might only take the form of prompt words, which, as in his case, make little objective sense when transcribed. He writes, for example, of one lengthy, recorded interview in which, aside from a scene-setting comment at the start to identify the period that he wanted Das to recount, his only interjections were single word prompts along the lines of 'And?', 'So?' and 'Then?', showing that there is more to the successful interview encounter than the actual words uttered.

What it means to witness and be a part of the 'ongoing reconstruction of experience' (Ginsburg 1989, cited in Rapport, this volume) of social life vis-à-vis the interview context is what Nigel Rapport, our co-editor, discusses in the epilogue of this collection. He draws out the different components and key themes of each of the contributions to this volume and revisits the notion of an interview's extraordinariness. He also introduces us to his own experiences of interviewing Ricky Hirsch, an 84-year-old Canadian, and survivor of the Holocaust, whose narration of his personal history was episodically ruptured in the interview so that he moved from the vivid personal accounts of his past experiences to detailing what sorts of feelings and emotional responses he was experiencing in the moment of recounting his past. It is this momentary tension between being-in-a-life and adopting an ironising stance in regard to it that the context of the interview can hope to elicit, Rapport contends. The interview allows for a space within which we 'can and do stand outside the experiential flow of our lives and call ourselves honestly to account' (Rapport, this volume).

Conclusion

Conducting interviews and carrying out participant observation are cross-disciplinary methodological decisions for many types of social investigations. This collection is a response to the shared task of understanding human experience, making the invisible visible. Rapport has argued elsewhere that always and everywhere, individuals are prone and able to 'detach themselves', to question the value and justification of the roles and practices in which they are currently implicated, and to envision themselves with different relationships and preferences (Rapport 2002: 153). Engaging with such 'detachments' during fieldwork animates the fact that pre-designed research methods, such as conducting interviews, become of secondary significance, as they are dependent on the researcher's ability to generate trust and establish meaningful relationships with informants (Kalir 2006: 235). Indeed, even the ever-controversial notions of introspection, reflexivity, 'self-study' and 'participant objectivation' (Bourdieu 2003; Douglass 1992: 131), which formulate the thick descriptions of participant observations in fieldwork, may not produce the desired clarity of language, through a lack of being surrounded by a variety of influences, and without the shared information of those with whom we live, work and learn from in 'the field'; hence the 'conjunctural' nature of all ethnography (Piña-Cabral 2000: 341).

The interrogation of what to know and how to know, and specifically the 'interview' as a part of our anthropological toolkit, poses theoretical and methodological challenges for anthropology: a discipline long since concerned with issues of epistemology, reflexivity, representation and power, and a discipline with a particular focus on ethnography. By subjecting the interview to a similar spectrum of analytical discussion as participant observation, it can be shown that the interview elicits information that is at once specific and generalisable, personal and social, pragmatic and conceptual, extraordinary and insightful of the everyday. The interview, approached as a particular kind of experience and a particular kind of space, is something imagined and experienced in personal ways, and yet shaped by circumstances, by personal and social histories and imagined futures. Both interviewer and interviewee may be transformed by the occasion, and so the interview is located at the cusp of remembering and re-authoring personal and shared identities, and may be responsible for making new kinds of public-private involvements.

References

Atkinson, P. and D. Silverman. 1997. 'Kundera's Immortality: The Interview Society and the Invention of the Self', *Qualitative Inquiry* 3(3): 304–25.

Bernard, H. 1994. *Research Methods in Anthropology*. Oxford: Altamira Press.

Bourdieu, P. 2003. 'Participant Objectivation', *Journal of the Royal Anthropological Institute* (N.S.) 9: 281–94.

Clair, P. 2003. (ed.). *Expressions of Ethnography: Novel Approaches to Qualitative Methods*. Albany: State University of New York.

Clifford, J. and G. Marcus (eds.). 1986. *Writing Culture*. Berkeley: University of California Press.

Department of Health. 2001. *The Expert Patient: A New Approach to Chronic Disease Management for the Twenty-First Century*. London: Department of Health.

Douglass, W.A. 1992. 'Anthropological Methodology in the European Context', in J. de Piña-Cabral and J. Campbell (eds), *Europe Observed*. Oxford: Oxford University Press, pp. 123–32.

Emerson, R.M., R.I. Fretz and L.L. Shaw. 1995. *Writing Ethnographic Fieldnotes*. Chicago: University of Chicago Press.

Finch, J. 1984. '"It's Great to Have Someone to Talk to": Ethics and Politics of Interviewing Women', in C. Bell and H. Roberts (eds), *Social Researching: Politics, Problems*, Practice. London: Routledge, pp. 70–87.

Galletta, A. 2013. *Mastering the Semi-Structured Interview and Beyond: From Research Design to Analysis and Publication*. New York: New York University Press.

Haraway, D. 2004. *The Haraway Reader*. London: Routledge.

Henige, D. 1988. *Oral Historiography*. London: Longman.

Hobart, M. 1990. 'The Patience of Plants: A Note on Agency in Bali', *RIMA*, 24.

Hockey, J. 2002. 'Interviews as Ethnography? Disembodied Social Interaction in Britain', in N. Rapport (ed.), *British Subjects: An Anthropological Britain*. Oxford: Berg, pp. 209–22.

Holstein, J. and J. Gubrium. 1995. *The Active Interview*. London: Sage Publications.

Kalir, B. 2006. 'The Field of Work and the Work of the Field: Conceptualising an Anthropological Research Engagement', *Social Anthropology* 14(2): 235–46.

King, N. and C. Horrocks. 2010. *Interviews in Qualitative Research*. London: Sage Publications.

Kvale, S. 1996. *InterViews: An Introduction to Qualitative Research Interviewing*. London: Sage Publications.

———. 2007. *Doing Interviews*. London: Sage Publications.

Kvale, S. and S. Brinkmann. 2009. *InterViews: Learning the Craft of Qualitative Research Interviewing*. London: Sage Publications.

Leder, D. 1990. *The Absent Body*. London: University of Chicago Press.

Marcus, G. 1995. 'Ethnography in/of the World System: The Emergence of Multi-Sited Ethnography', *Annual Review of Anthropology* 24: 95–117.

Marcus, G. and M. Fischer. 1986. *Anthropology as Cultural Critique: An Experimental Moment in the Human Sciences*. Chicago: University of Chicago Press.

Pelto, P. and G. Pelto. 1978. *Anthropological Research: The Structure of Inquiry*. Cambridge: Cambridge University Press.

Piña-Cabral, J. 2000. 'The Ethnographic Present Revisited', *Social Anthropology* 8(3): 341–48.

Rapport, N. 1993. *Diverse World-Views in an English Village*. Edinburgh: Edinburgh University Press.

———. 1994. *The Prose and the Passion: Anthropology, Literature and the Writing of E.M. Forster*. Manchester: Manchester University Press.

———. 2002. 'Post-Cultural Anthropology: The Ironisation of Values in a World of Movement', in V. Amit (ed.), *Realising Community: Concepts, Social Relationships and Sentiments*. New York: Routledge, pp. 146–64.

———. 2012. 'The Interview as a Form of Talking-Partnership: Dialectical, Focussed, Ambiguous, Special', in J. Skinner (ed.), *The Interview: An Ethnographic Approach*. ASA Monographs 49. Oxford: Berg, pp. 53–68.

Reason, P. and H. Bradbury (eds.). 2001. *Handbook of Action Research. Participative Inquiry and Practice*. London: Sage.

Roberts, B. 2002. 'Sociological Lives and Auto/Biographical Writing', in K. Milnes, B. Roberts and C. Horrocks (eds), *Narrative, Memory and Life Transitions*. Huddersfield: University of Huddersfield Press, pp. 163–70.

Robson, C. 1993. *Real World Research: A Resource for Social Scientists and Practitioner-Researchers*. Oxford: Blackwell Publishers.

Rubin, H. and I. Rubin. 2005. *Qualitative Interviewing: The Art of Hearing Data*. London: Sage Publications.

Seidman, I. 2013. *Interviewing as Qualitative Research: A Guide for Researchers in Education and the Social Sciences*. New York: Teachers College.

Shore, C. and S. Nugent (eds). 2002. *Elite Cultures: Anthropological Perspectives*. ASA Monographs 38. London: Routledge.

Skinner, J. 2010. 'Leading Questions and Body Memories: A Case of Phenomenology and Physical Ethnography in the Dance Interview', in P. Collins and A. Gallinat (eds), *The Ethnographic Self as Resource: Writing Memory and Experience into Ethnography*. Oxford: Berghahn, pp. 111–28.

Skinner, J. (ed.) 2012. 'Introduction', in *The Interview: An Ethnographic Approach*. ASA Monographs 49. London: Berg.

Smith, K. 2012. *Fairness, Class and Belonging in Contemporary England*. Houndmills: Palgrave Macmillan.

Sökefeld, M. 1999. 'Debating Self, Identity and Culture in Anthropology', *Current Anthropology* 40(4): 417–47.

Strathern, M. 2004. *Partial Connections*. Walnut Creek, CA: Alta Mira Press.

Thomas, N. 1991. 'Against Ethnography', *Cultural Anthropology* 6(3): 306–22.

Tietel, E. 2000. 'The Interview as Relational Space', Forum: Qualitative Social Research 1(3). Retrieved 10 January 2012 from http://www.qualitativeresearch.net/index.php/fqs/article/viewArticle/1095

Weiss, R.S. 1994. *Learning from Strangers: The Art and Method of Qualitative Interview Studies*. New York: The Free Press.

Chapter 1

THE TRANSCENDENT SUBJECT?

BIOGRAPHY AS A MEDIUM FOR WRITING 'LIFE AND TIMES'

Pat Caplan

This chapter is about the writing of a biography of a man from Mafia Island, Tanzania, whom I knew for nearly four decades, from my first visit as a Ph.D. student in 1965–67 until his death in 2002 shortly after we had worked together in Tanzania that summer. I begin by considering why an anthropologist should want to write a biography, then move to the nature of the material available in this particular instance and raise some questions and difficulties around the utilisation of this genre by anthropologists. In conclusion I consider what may be learned, and by whom, from such writing.

Why Biography?

Historians make frequent use of biographies, and they are among the most popular kinds of writing for the intelligent lay reader. A historian friend, who has written a number of biographies in recent years, told me: 'This is a good way of writing history for those who would not necessarily read a history book'. So is it a good genre for anthropologists too? Would it attract an audience who would not otherwise read anthropology? But the same friend added firmly that 'what I write are biographical histories, not historical biographies'. In other words, she sees what she writes primarily as history, whereas I see what I am writing as historical biography, where the primary emphasis is on the life of the subject, and the times are the context in which it is lived. The context frames the life, but at the same time, the life also elucidates the historical context.

Most historical biographies are written about people who are considered to be famous for some reason, although there are a smaller number about people deemed to be 'ordinary', especially with the influence of subaltern history (see for example Colley 2003; Anderson 2012). The difficulty for historians in writing about the latter category is that often the documentation is lacking, but anthropologists writing about the subjects of their research have fewer problems in that regard. Yet, as Eriksen has recently remarked, it is puzzling that 'so few anthropologists have written accessible, engaging biographies of people they know intimately' (2006: 19), and goes on to suggest that 'a flourishing of well-written anthropological biographies, or documentary stories, would doubtless raise anthropology's presence in the popular consciousness' (2006: 20).

While anthropologists have rarely used the term 'biography', they have written a number of life histories and personal narratives,[1] and some conflate these two genres, using the terms interchangeably. However, I would suggest that a distinction be drawn between biography on the one hand, and personal narrative or life history on the other. I would offer the following: biographies are ways of writing the story of someone's life through changing historical circumstances; they are thus about 'a life and times'. Life history or personal narrative, on the other hand, as used by anthropologists, while not ignoring the wider historical context, focuses on a particular person's world view, and is thus a way into understanding a particular society and culture.

In 1997 I published a book entitled *African Voices, African Lives*, about a man from Mafia Island whom I called 'Mohamed', using a mixture of materials: his diaries, my diaries, our conversations, his life history recorded on tape, and participant observation – interaction (including the exchange of letters) with both him and members of his family over a period of thirty years. My aim in writing that book was to use Mohamed as a vehicle for understanding Swahili society and culture, and a large part of it was concerned with spirit possession. I would thus see this book as an example of the genre of personal narrative. In accord with anthropological tradition, I disguised the subjects as much as I could, although they are probably recognisable to those who know the area well. However, Mohamed and his family were not very well educated nor did they operate on a stage larger than that of the north of Mafia Island, apart from brief trips to Dar and Zanzibar.

My current biographical project focuses on the life of a man ('Mikidadi') who was also from Mafia, but who was in many ways a rather different kind of person than Mohamed. Unlike the latter, he had received some education and lived much of his life in Dar, although continued to return regularly to the island, sometimes for long periods. Mikidadi was also someone with whom I had a very different relationship to that with Mohamed. It started when, as a boy, he became my adopted 'younger brother' in the village on Mafia, and, as time went on, he increasingly also became my interlocutor.

Given that I did not consider Mikidadi to be a subject or informant in the same way as Mohamed and others, why have I decided to write about him at this stage? One reason is that we had planned to work on a book (a short history of Mafia Island written in Swahili and aimed at a local audience) together, but this project was aborted by his untimely death. The second reason is my view of an unfinished life, that of someone who wanted to 'be someone', but who was largely thwarted by circumstances, even though he struggled against them. In that sense, the biography is a kind of testimony. The third reason for writing such a book is that it is perhaps my last major project on an area I have worked in for forty-five years, and it is thus a way of rounding off, of writing a history of the area as I have witnessed it through the spectrum of a life or lives. My target audience for this book is as much a lay as an academic audience, an African as well as a Western one. I am particularly keen to present his life as that of someone who struggled against the constraints of his circumstances, thereby countering the widespread Western view of Africans as being either victims or villains.

Biographical Material

Given the context of this chapter, in a publication which considers the subject of 'the interview' and its place in anthropology, it is paradoxical that I never formally 'interviewed' Mikidadi. Perhaps because of the closeness of our relationship it never occurred to me to do so. When I think about other areas where I have conducted long-term fieldwork and established particularly close friendships or quasi-familial relations, I find that in such places there are also people I never interviewed in any formal sense and do not usually write about. Perhaps this is because, as Langness and Frank (1981) suggest, by placing people in the context of a formal interview situation, there may be a tendency to objectify and reify, which is the antithesis of friendship and kinship.

Given the lack of formal interviews and the fact that I can no longer ask Mikidadi any questions, I have had to turn to other material: the many letters we exchanged in between my visits, notes on and memories of encounters and conversations, photos and film material. In addition, there are two diaries he kept for me – one in 1966 when he was twelve years old and one in 2002, the last time we worked together just before his death – as well as my own fieldwork diaries. Some of our conversations started with my raising an issue about which I wanted to know more, while others started with his questions. Other interactions might be conducted in a companionable silence, particularly during our long walks along the beach, away from the village, usually in the late afternoon, when we would stop for him to say the maghribi (evening) prayer on the sand, facing the setting sun, or sometimes at night when there was a full moon. I would not consider such interactions to be interviews even in an informal sense, since they rarely had any kind of predetermined agenda. Furthermore, I did not regard myself on such occasions as necessarily 'doing fieldwork' but rather spending time with a friend.

Two Accounts of a Life

In this section of the chapter, I give two accounts of the life of Mikidadi. The first and shortest is his own autobiographical account, the second is my own much longer account and thus biographical. Although the content has many similarities, the tone is different, for reasons that will be discussed.

A Short Autobiography

Mikidadi Tells the Story of His Life

It was the end of the summer of 2002, and Mikidadi and I had worked together for several months in northern Mafia, Dar and Zanzibar. We were both tired, but had gone to Zanzibar to see some members of his family and carry out a few final interviews with some members of his NGO (Non-Governmental Organisation). We had finished what we had had to do, and it was raining non-stop. We sat in the lobby of my hotel and had a meeting with a man from Zanzibar who had once been to London and visited my college. Rather to my surprise, Mikidadi started talking about his life – ostensibly he was telling the story to the local man, but I suspect he wanted me to hear it. These are his words as I noted them down later that evening:

> I came to school here in Zanzibar [c. 1966] and got as far as the first year of secondary. But when my sister, with whom I was living, and her husband moved to DSM [Dar es Salaam], I had to transfer to a Dar school, as I no longer had anyone to stay with in Zanzibar. I was told that I needed T.Sh. 380/- to get a place in secondary school.
>
> So I went back to Mafia and got twenty hens, which I sold at 20/- each, thereby raising T.Sh. 400/-. But this money came two weeks too late and it was not enough for the transfer fee. So I was told I had to go back to primary school, and was sent down to St 6 [the penultimate year of primary school]. I repeated those two years and was always first in my class. Then I was selected to go to Pugu Secondary School, a boarding school which used to be run by missionaries, and there were still some European expatriates teaching there at the time. I eventually got up to Form 4 [(equivalent to O-levels), but not with the support of my father, who only wanted me to have a bit of education and then to get married.
>
> Then I went to Forestry School in Arusha (1975–77) and did a two-year course. Most of the teachers were Canadians, and they kept promising us a trip to Canada, but it never happened. Afterwards I got a job near to Morogoro, and then after a year managed to get a transfer to Dar as a City Tree Officer. I stayed there for six years, but the pay was not very good and I found a better job with a chemical company – I was their Farm Manager. However, my father became ill and I kept taking unpaid leave to go to Mafia and look after him, until I was told that I had to choose between my father and my job. As my father's state was so bad, I decided to leave that job.
>
> Since then I have been unemployed. The worst thing is the loss of colleagues – they cease to be your friends. And people look down on you. My wife was very worried: 'How will we live?' We do manage, but with difficulty. I do odd jobs:
>
> *   I work for people who need follow-ups [in dealing with bureaucracy].
> *   I sit in a shop for the owner when he needs to be away.
> *   I go to seminars – that's the one thing I asked my ex-colleagues to help me with and they have. You get food and attendance allowances.
> *   I cultivate.
>
> So I have no clothes, nothing [that is true – his clothes, and especially his shoes are very shabby], and I got old before my time [that is also true, he looks much older than me, although thirteen years younger, and is regularly called *mzee* – old man]. I have learned to deal quite differently with people and I've succeeded. I try to behave like a retired government officer.

This narrative – with my brief contextualisations – tells of the problems of a man who put his family responsibilities before his career, and the repercussions of his decision. But it also tells a story of agency and survival techniques during a period when life in Tanzania, especially in the city, was very hard, and of attempts to maintain dignity and respect.

Mikidadi's Life as Told by the Anthropologist

Mikidadi was born in 1953 towards the end of the British colonial period in Tanganyika. He was the son of a Koran school teacher in Kanga village, northern Mafia Island, one of the least developed parts of the country. He went to the village primary school and the Koran school run by his father until the age of twelve, when his parents decided to send him to continue his education in Zanzibar, where he lived with his married sister and her family for several years from 1966. Kanga school at that time had only four standards or grades, so if he had stayed on Mafia he would have had to have gone to another part of the island to complete his seven years of primary school. It should also be noted that during that period, many Mafians, like Mikidadi's sister and her husband, migrated for longer or shorter periods to Zanzibar, considered to be the centre of Swahili culture and offering paid work in the clove plantations.

Two years earlier, in 1964, there had been a revolution in Zanzibar[2] and life there became increasingly difficult. Mikidadi's sister and her family eventually moved to Dar es Salaam, and attempted to place him in secondary school. At this point in time, in spite of the recent union of Tanganyika and Zanzibar to form the United Republic of Tanzania, the mainland educational authorities did not fully recognise the Zanzibar educational system, and Mikidadi was forced to wait a year to get into school and then repeat a year. When he finished his secondary school education at Form 4 he was not selected for Forms 5 and 6[3] (the equivalent of A-level) but went on to study forestry at a college in Arusha.

After completing his two-year vocational course, he did his compulsory one year of military service, and then obtained a job as City Tree Officer, working for the council in Dar es Salaam. Mikidadi told me of the frustrations of working in this capacity in a city where people suffered from fuel shortages and often hacked away at street trees. However, this post enabled him to meet important people, including President Nyerere with whom he had several conversations.

He stayed in that job for some years, in 1981 marrying a distant relative, a young woman ten years his junior called Hadiya. She was from a neighbouring village on Mafia, but had spent most of her life in Zanzibar. No sooner had his marriage taken place than his classificatory brother (mother's sister's son) died unexpectedly, and Mikidadi took on responsibility for his six children, several of whom lived with him and his new wife in Dar. Mikidadi often referred to the difficulties with which his new bride had immediately been faced, and how incredibly well she had coped. As I recorded in a 1985 notebook, he recounted as follows:

> My wife is very clever. She manages things well. She has a lot of work. No sooner was she married than the following week my [classificatory] brother died, and some of his children came to live with us. She will be old before her time with so much work. That is what happens to people in Tanzania these days.

Mikidadi and Hadiya soon had two daughters of their own, Amina and Khadijya, to add to the children for whom they were caring. Given the size of his household, Mikidadi decided to seek better-paid work and obtained a job with one of the private companies that had begun to proliferate in Tanzania with the end of the Nyerere period of *ujamaa* (African socialism')[4] and the rise of neo-liberalism in the 1980s.

After only a year in his new post, matters became difficult, as his own father, still living on Mafia, was increasingly unwell, and Mikidadi repeatedly took leave from work to help care for him and manage the family's affairs, including the Koran school. Finally, he had to decide between responsibility for his father and his own employment, so he resigned from his job and went to stay on Mafia until his father's health improved, when he returned to live in Dar. He was never able to obtain work in the formal sector of the economy again. Nonetheless, in spite of his financial difficulties, he also took on the care of several of the children of his older sister, who died in childbirth in 1988 (see Caplan 1995). He also received and housed the children of several Mafia relatives, who wanted them to have a better education. Altogether he had major responsibility for around sixteen children during the 1980s and 1990s. Mikidadi told me that he sometimes got a bit of financial help from the parents of some of these children, saying that 'If I don't push, they won't get a proper education'. This referred not only to finding the necessary money, since fees, books and uniforms were required, but also to dealing with the educational bureaucracy and even convincing sceptical relatives of the value of keeping their children – daughters as well as sons – in school.

To make ends meet he engaged in a number of small income-generating projects (*miradi*), such as selling stationery in the city, and taking to the Dar market products from Mafia, such as dried fish and coconuts from the family's trees. All of this meant that he was unable to continue his own education, as he very much wished to do, and go to university. Instead, he became an autodidact, reading everything he could, and attending the numerous seminars that NGOs, mushrooming in Tanzania at that time, laid on in Dar. It was the accepted practice for participants in NGO seminars to receive a 'sitting fee' (as well as food), and in this way he was sometimes able to supplement his income. His English improved immeasurably, and he also worked on his Arabic so that he could read Islamic texts (some of which I brought or sent him). In the early 1980s, for several years, he was Director of Youth and Camps for the Tanzania Muslim Association,[5] a post which at the best paid a small stipend, but which he hoped would lead to a proper job. He was keen to be involved in Islamic activities, which he considered to be linked with modernisation and development, a trajectory which was to continue throughout his life. Mikidadi became increasingly aware of and frustrated with the state of underdevelopment in his birthplace. In the early 1990s, together with some other Mafians living in Dar, he founded an NGO called 'Chamama' (*Changia cha Maendeleo Mafia* – 'Group for Developing Mafia'), and attempted not only to obtain grants, but persuade people to work together in small cooperatives for their own betterment. The initial task of Chamama was to lobby for a secondary school on Mafia, which was still without one until – at least partly because of their efforts – the Kitomondo School opened near the district capital Kilindoni in 1994. A constant problem for Chamama was lack of funds, and, during my 1994 visit, I witnessed their unsuccessful attempts to obtain funding from a Dutch agency (see Caplan 1998). Later they did succeed in getting some money from the NGO 'CARE' for HIV/AIDS work.

In 1994, after the introduction of multi-partyism in Tanzania, Mikidadi, like other Chamama activists, decided to stand for election to the Mafia District Council. Mikidadi was defeated by a mixture of factionalism and, reportedly, the 'buying' of votes by people holding power whose behaviour he had challenged. Indeed, his political activities sometimes brought him into conflict with local power holders. Mikidadi felt that his NGO operated against the odds, and that its role as a catalyst for change and a challenger of inertia and corruption got its members into trouble. One of his colleagues told me

'Chamama is not an *ehwallaha* (Yes Sir!) organisation' and Mikidadi sometimes found himself in the hot seat (*kiti moto*) with the district authorities. For example, he opposed the sale of beach land to foreign investors proposing to build hotels on Mafia, pointing out to people that this was short-termism, and that they would lose rights of access to the beach ('their workshop') and the sea where they fished. He and Chamama were also believed by the authorities to have been behind the opposition to the setting up of a prawn farm on Mafia Island, although the protests did not succeed and the prawn farm was established (see Caplan 2003). I learned after his death that he had also been under surveillance by the local security services.

Mikidadi's work for Chamama enabled him to move between Dar and Mafia on a regular basis, which he needed to do, since his father had died early in 1994 and he became the head of the Koran school, the largest in the village, with over 100 children. His father had always wanted him to return to the village and take it over, but Mikidadi resisted. This did not mean that he was uninterested – on the contrary, he had ambitious plans for the Koran school and wanted to turn it into an Islamic secondary school which would also offer adult and vocational education. Meanwhile, he installed two teachers and brought in books in Arabic, telling me that the children needed not just to learn the Koran by rote, but to understand what they were reading. The books were mostly from the Africa Muslims Agency,[6] rather than those from Iran, since in his view the latter's books taught a very Shi'ite version of Islam. He himself taught advanced classes to young men when he was on Mafia. He was very keen that all kinds of learning should be available in the village, both what he called 'general knowledge' (politics, economics, science, geography and history) and vocational training (carpentry, for example), as well as a modern religious education. He argued that there was no conflict between Islam and a modern education, and that such a school would be the best way of ensuring both development and the perpetuation of local culture. He succeeded in raising funds to buy some land and building materials, but progress was very slow. I received regular updates by letter, including some written on headed notepaper with the school's name 'Madrasatul el Khairiyah', and with photographs of the bricks he was storing up to construct a new building.

Mikidadi had acted as a researcher for me when he was very young, in the summer of 1966, half way through my first fieldwork, when I had had to leave the village for a month. He wrote an excellent events diary when he was only twelve. More than thirty years later, in 2002, he spent the summer working with me on Mafia, carrying out a variety of mostly independent small projects of his own, and writing another detailed diary.

Shortly after my return to the UK in 2002, Mikidadi died in Dar es Salaam of a stroke, aged only forty-nine, having complained for some time previously of high blood pressure, which was not properly treated. Although he had sought medical help, it is unlikely that all of the necessary investigations were carried out, given the parlous state of the Tanzanian health service.

After his death, Mikidadi's wife Hadiya struggled to make a living for herself, because when she had finished her widow's period of seclusion (*edda*), which lasts for over three months, she was never able to get back the job she had previously held in a flower nursery or obtain any other form of paid employment. She was also grief-stricken, and refused to contemplate a remarriage, which many family and friends urged on her, and which might have made her life more comfortable. Hadiya's older daughter had gone to live in Zanzibar with Hadiya's sister some years before, and now her younger daughter Khadijya also went to live in Zanzibar with another sister, ostensibly to improve her tailoring skills, but probably because Hadiya could not afford to support her.

Hadiya also encountered numerous problems with the inheritance of their house in Dar and land on Mafia. The elders who were in charge, notably the village Imam, tried to insist that all the property be sold and that it be divided between the wife (one eighth), Mikidadi's remaining sister (one quarter) and his two daughters, as well as various more distantly related males. Eventually, in order to retain possession of the family house in Dar, she went to court and successfully defended her rights, but suffered constant bouts of ill health, probably occasioned by depression and grief, and died in 2008 before the estate was settled.

Comparison between the Two Accounts

Mikidadi's own short account of his life has to be seen in a number of contexts. One is the immediate setting: he was tired, he was sad that I was about to leave and that our work together (and the salary it gave him) was coming to an end. Another is the nature of his audience – the young man with whom we were meeting and myself. The former, to whom he ostensibly told the story, had received what Mikidadi craved so much – a university education. He had even saved enough money to make a holiday trip to the UK, and had visited my college. Mikidadi may have felt the need to justify his own relative lack of education by explaining the circumstances that had prevented him from furthering it. He also knew, of course, that I was listening and perhaps felt that he needed to put together in a more coherent way what I had previously only learned in a fragmentary fashion.

There appear to me to be two major differences between our accounts. Whereas Mikidadi's story is a single narrative, my own history of his life, as presented briefly above, is gleaned from a series of fragments – our meetings, his letters, his diaries. There are gaps both in the chronology of events and in my understanding of why things happened as they did. Secondly, Mikidadi's account focuses largely on his education (or lack of it) and the consequences of his onerous family responsibilities. As a result it is also perhaps more downbeat than my own. He saw these aspects of his life as marked by failure and disappointment, whereas I tend to see him both as a survivor and an enabler, one who strategised in a myriad of ways and refused to be a victim. I also see him as someone who took his responsibilities very seriously, perhaps too seriously, given their eventual impact on his health.

Some Problems with Writing Biography

I began this chapter by suggesting that biography is a genre which anthropologists, especially those who are keen to communicate beyond the discipline, might consider writing more often. I also suggested that we need to think through differences, if any, between the genres of biography, personal narrative and life history, as well as differences in some of the kinds of material we might use, such as interviews, conversations and participant observation, as well as texts such as letters and diaries. But these are not the only issues which need consideration in engaging in such an enterprise, and here I briefly discuss some others I have encountered.

Methodological difficulties lie in doing such a project post facto, and especially post mortem – I can no longer ask Mikidadi to elucidate issues, or explain gaps. The subject is deceased, so are his wife, his parents and his older sister, and it is not easy to communicate with other members of his family, friends and colleagues, hence the information is fragmentary. To what extent, then, do I use my own local knowledge to attempt to fill in the gaps? Inevitably, of course, I have done so to a considerable degree.

Then there are a number of ethical issues. How will telling this story affect his family, his community and his own reputation? How much should be included about his family members, some of whom are still alive? Are there some issues which should be left out in case they cause embarrassment to surviving relatives? What about the fact that much of the material I possess was not gathered in quite the usual way, but is privileged information arising out of a close and affectionate relationship? And does this lead to the necessity of introducing myself as both observer and participant, since it is quite difficult to write myself out of it, yet I am mindful of the fact that this is his story, not mine, and part of the reason for writing it is to pass on a testimony to future generations.

Finally, there is the question of whether or not he would have wanted his story to be told to a wider audience. When I wrote a paper about childbirth and the death of his older sister (Caplan 1995), I sent the draft to him to ask if he felt it appropriate to publish it, and he wrote back telling me to go ahead. But in a discussion we had in 2002 when he had read my book *African Lives*, a personal narrative, things were more equivocal:

> Mikidadi: It is clearly Mohamed's language and words, so it is effectively a joint work.
> PC: Who do you think would be able to read it locally?
> Mikidadi: Maybe Secondary Forms 4 to 6 leavers a bit, or teachers.
> PC: Suppose X (a highly educated Mafian) read it?
> Mikidadi: He would know that it's all true. But he would regret that 'things of the inside' have come outside – *mambo ya ndani wako nje* [i.e., secrets have been revealed]. For example, exactly how corpses are buried is not known to women, nor do they know how boys are circumcised. And he would reproach [*kulalamika*] the man who had revealed such secret information to you.
> PC: So would he regret the existence of such a book or be pleased?
> Mikidadi: He would feel both!

In other words, some things are *mambo ya ndani* (things of the inside), they are *siri* (secret), and their revelation can lead to *aibu* (shame), *kuvunja uso* (loss of face) or being scorned or laughed at, and for that reason they should be concealed. In the case of Mohamed, the subject of *African Voices, African Lives*, the decision to publish was a joint one, his and mine, and he was the agent involved in 'revealing secrets'. But in the case of Mikidadi, he has not been party to this decision, and any secrets revealed in this account are through my agency, not his. Yet at the same time, in my view, telling the life of someone who showed agency and such a high degree of responsibility is both an example (*mfano*) for others to emulate, and a form of testimony (*ushahidi*). I thus see work of this kind as not only contributing to anthropology, but also serving as a means of sharing anthropological insights and experience with lay audiences in the West and 'giving back' data and insights to those among whom we have worked.

In short, then, undertaking the writing of a biography is fraught with problems which have to be thought through in different ways for the various potential audiences for such a work: fellow anthropologists, lay readers outside of Tanzania, Tanzanians, and local people on Mafia and its diaspora, including members of Mikidadi's family. Nonetheless, it seems to be a project which is worth undertaking.

Seeking Permission and Filling in the Gaps

In the summer of 2010, I returned to Tanzania to talk to relatives, friends, neighbours and ex-colleagues of Mikidadi. I wanted to know what they thought of the project of writing a biography and how they felt about appearing in it themselves. I also wanted to fill in some of the gaps I had identified when working through the material I had on Mikidadi, and to find out what kind of memories people had of him. As an aid to these ends, I took with me a large collection of photos I had taken of Mikidadi and his family over the years. I spent time in Dar, where some of his family and also members of his NGO Chamama are living; in Zanzibar, now home to both of his daughters; and on Mafia Island, both in the district capital Kilindoni, where Chamama still has a branch, and in Kanga village, where Mikidadi came from, where his younger sister lives and where the Koran school still flourishes.

I talked to many people about the proposed biography, and everyone said that it was a good idea. To my surprise, they also said that it should be published using proper names, not pseudonyms, a view I had not anticipated. This goes against the common anthropological convention that informants are protected by being anonymised, a view against which Fabian has recently argued: 'If there is a rule about withholding names it should be this: In our accounts, ethnographers and interlocutors are both agents; why should the author be named and others remain anonymous?' (2008: 17). While not agreeing that Fabian's view is appropriate in all circumstances, use of proper names does feel right in a historical biography such as this one, if the subjects are willing.

I had hoped that some people would fill in gaps in my knowledge of Mikidadi's life and its aftermath, and indeed some were able to do that. For example, in the 1970s, Mikidadi changed his name for a time. He told me about this in his letters but did not give a reason, and I neglected to ask him. I probably assumed that it was to do with the anger of a neglected ancestor, a not uncommon situation. But in my 2010 trip, I heard from one of my informants that he had changed his name in order to get entry to a school. I also learned from one of Mikidadi's daughters what had happened about the inheritance of Mikidadi's property: Hadiya had finally gone to court and won the case, and after her death, his older daughter made sure to collect all the official documents and ensure that the house and land were properly registered.

I would describe these encounters as 'interviews', in that I had specific questions to ask of particular people, yet, like many interviews, they had a life of their own. Some people were overcome with emotion, especially when they looked at the photos and remembered past times. Some had insights of their own into Mikidadi's life, forcing me to reconsider some of my own ideas. When the first draft of the book was finished, I sent it to Mikidadi's older daughter and to his cousin who had studied in Egypt, as both knew some English. Both said they liked it. They later also received a copy of the Swahili translation.[7]

What Can Be Learned From the Story of a Life?

What emerges from such material as Mikidadi's? The first is the story of the life of someone who wanted to 'be someone', who had a great desire for more education, but who was largely thwarted by his circumstances. One such disadvantage was being born into a poor family in a remote village in Tanzania at a time when formal education was scarce. Another was his acceptance of the heavy responsibilities laid upon him by his kinship obligations, as he saw them.

Secondly, from his life also emerges an understanding of Islam and what it means to be a good Muslim. Mikidadi was the son of a Koran school teacher, and he was strongly influenced both by his own upbringing and also the changes in Islam which have taken place in Tanzania over the last few decades.[8] We sometimes discussed and disagreed about some of the new Islamic practices: the derogation of spirit possession and other 'customary' (*mila*) practices, the changes in clothing (especially for women), the requirements of the *sharia* and how this should be interpreted. But Mikidadi questioned both versions, and in his mind there was no conflict between the practice of Islam on the one hand, and 'development' (*maendeleo*) and modernity[9] on the other.

Finally, Mikidadi's life also enables us to follow the history of his community, Mafia Island, and his country, Tanzania, through the immediate postcolonial period, the Revolution in Zanzibar and its union with Tanganyika, the period of 'African socialism' (*ujamaa*), the rise of neo-liberalism in the late 1980s and the switch to multi-partyism. All of these sweeping economic and political changes in the country which have taken place in the fifty years since independence in 1961, just before I started my own research, had their impact on his own life, those of his family members, and other people on Mafia. While the early period of African socialism afforded him a vocational education and a job in the public sector, the changes of the 1980s – such as structural adjustment – made his life and that of many other Tanzanians increasingly difficult. Yet the effects of historical changes have also been uneven, and Mikidadi was quick to seize the new opportunities afforded by the rise of 'civil society' and NGOs, thereby finding a new niche for his talents and energies.

Mikidadi has also to be seen as an individual who grappled with ideas and saw his responsibilities as extending beyond his family to his community, including his natal village and the island of Mafia. He wanted an improved infrastructure, as well as better schooling and health care, and felt that under the neo-liberal economic and political regimes of the post-Nyerere period these could be achieved only with difficulty and by confronting those in power, including senior government officials.

In telling the story of Mikidadi's life, we may see how aspects of what is glossed as 'globalisation' and 'modernity' percolate down to the lives of ordinary people like him, yet such processes and their accompanying ideologies have uneven effects, and are actively confronted and analysed by those affected. In some cases, such as this one, the subject manages somehow to transcend his difficult circumstances and 'make his own life', albeit, of course, not always in conditions of his choosing.

Acknowledgements

I am appreciative, as always, of Lionel Caplan's reading of several drafts and making incisive comments, and to the ASA panel audience (Belfast) for its questions. A similar paper was also given at the Eighth European Swahili Workshop, and I am grateful to its convener Iain Walker and other participants for their comments. I particularly thank members of Mikidadi's family, his friends, neighbours and colleagues, who in 2010 shared with me their memories of Mikidadi.

Notes

1. See for example Casagrande 1960; Freeman 1979; Lewis 1976 [1959] et passim; Personal Narratives Group 1989; Mintz 1960; Mirza and Strobel 1989; Munson 1984; Shostak 1983 [1981]; Smith 1981 [1954]; Werbner 1991 to mention a few.
2. The Zanzibar Revolution ('Mapinduzi' literally 'overturning') took place in 1964, and resulted in the overthrow of the Sultan, and the coming to power of the Afro-Shirazi Party, which, after the union of Tanganyika and Zanzibar, merged to form the Chama cha Mapinduzi (CCM Party of the Revolution). See Cameron 2004, Larsen 2004, Lofchie 1965, Okello 1976, Clayton 1981.
3. At that time, a very tiny proportion of children continued their education up to Form 6, the qualification needed for university.
4. See Boesen et al. 1977; Coulson 1979; Havenik 1993; Von Freyhold 1979.
5. Tanzania Muslim Association – also known as Bakwata. See Lodhi and Westerlund 1997; Van der Bruinhorst 2009 http://www.islamicfinder. org/getitWorld.php?id=40732. There are also references to BAKWATA on the U.S. government website http://www.state.gov/g/drl/rls/ irf/2005/51499.htm. It is often viewed as linked to the ruling CCM party, and in recent years its authority has been challenged by more radical groups.
6. Africa Muslims Agency is funded from Kuwait but has offices throughout much of Africa, with headquarters in South Africa. See www.africanmuslimagency.co.za. It is engaged in many different kinds of activities, including the provision of aid and relief, community development, livelihood education, setting up schools and universities, and running an educational broadcasting station.
7. The Swahili version of the manuscript has recently been published by Mkuki na Nyota Publishers, Dar es Salaam. A longer English version is currently in press.
8. See Pirio 2005; Larsen 2009; Loimeier and Seesemann 2006; Lodhi and Westerlund 1997.
9. For some discussion of local understandings of development and modernity, see Caplan 2003, 2004a, 2004b, 2008, 2009; Walley 2004.

References

Anderson, C. 2012. *Subaltern Lives: Biographies of Colonialism in the Indian Ocean World, 1790–1920*. Cambridge: Cambridge University Press.

Boesen, J., B. Storgard Madsen and T. Moody. 1977. *Ujamaa – Socialism from Above*. Uppsala: Scandinavian Institute of African Studies.

Cameron, G. 2004. 'Political Violence, Ethnicity and the Agrarian Question in Zanzibar', in P. Caplan and F. Topan (eds), *Swahili Modernities: Culture, Politics and Identity on the East African Coast*. Trenton, NJ: Africa World Press.

Caplan, P. 1995. '"Children are our Wealth and We Want Them": A Difficult Pregnancy on Mafia Island, Tanzania', in D. Bryceson (ed.), *Women Wielding the Hoe: Lessons from Rural Africa for Feminist Theory and Development Practice*. Oxford: Berg Press, pp. 103–20.

———. 1997. *African Voices, African Lives: Personal Narratives from a Swahili Village*. London and New York: Routledge.

———. 1998. 'La Vie Politique en Mutation d'un Village Cotier de la Tanzanie', in F. le Guennec-Coppens and D. Parkin (eds), *Autorite et Pouvoir chez les Swahili*. Paris: Karthala; Nairobi: IPRA, pp. 77–97.

———. 2003. 'Local Understandings of Modernity: Food and Food Security on Mafia Island, Tanzania', Unpublished report presented to COSTECH, the Tanzania Commission for Science and Technology. Retrieved from http://www.gold.ac.uk/anthropology/staff/pat-caplan/project-tanzania-global/.

———. 2004a. 'Introduction' to P. Caplan and F. Topan (eds), *Swahili Modernities*. Trenton, NJ: Africa World Press.

———. 2004b. 'Struggling to be Modern: Recent Letters from Mafia Island', in P. Caplan and F. Topan (eds), *Swahili Modernities*. Lawrenceville, NJ: Africa World Press, pp. 43–60.

———. 2008. 'Between Socialism and Neo-liberalism: Mafia Island, Tanzania, 1965–2004', *Review of African Political Economy* 114: 679–94.

———. 2009. 'Understanding Modernity/ies on Mafia Island, Tanzania: The Idea of a Moral Community', in K. Larsen (ed.), *Knowledge, Renewal and Religion*. Uppsala: Nordic Africa Institute, pp. 213–35.

———. 2014. *Mikidadi ya Mafia: Historia ya Mwanaharakati na Familia Yake Katika Tanzania Tangu Wakati wa Uhuru* (Mikidadi of Mafia: The story of an activist and his family in post-colonial Tanzania). Dar es Salaam: Mkuki na Nyota Publishers.

Casagrande, J.B. 1960. *In the Company of Men: Twenty Portraits of Anthropological Informants*. New York, Evanston and London: Harper Torchbooks.

Clayton, A. 1981. *The Zanzibar Revolution and its Aftermath*. London: Hurst and Co.

Colley, L. 2003. *Captives: Britain, Empire and the World*. London: Pimlico.

Coulson, A. (ed.) 1979. *African Socialism in Practice: The Tanzanian Experience.* Nottingham: Spokesman Press.

Eriksen, T.H. 2006. *Engaging Anthropology.* Oxford: Berg Press.

Fabian, J. 2008. *Ethnography as Commentary: Writing from the Virtual Archive.* Durham, NC: Duke University Press.

Freeman, J.M. 1979. *Untouchable: An Indian Life History.* London: Allen and Unwin.

Havenik, K. 1993. *Tanzania: The Limits to Development from Above.* Uppsala: Nordiska Afrikainstitutet; Dar es Salaam: Mkuki na Nyota.

Langness, L.L. and G. Frank. 1981. *Lives: An Anthropological Approach to Biography.* San Francisco: Chandler and Sharp.

Larsen, K. 2004. 'Change, Continuity and Contestation: The Politics of Modern Identities in Zanzibar', in P. Caplan and F. Topan (eds), *Swahili Modernities.* Trenton, NJ: Africa World Press, pp. 121–44.

———. (ed.) 2009. *Knowledge, Renewal and Religion: Repositioning and Changing Ideological and Material Circumstances among the Swahili on the East African Coast.* Uppsala: Nordiska Afrikainstitutet.

Lewis, O. 1976 [1959]. *Five Families: Mexican Case Studies in the Culture of Poverty.* London: Souvenir Press.

Lodhi, A. and D. Westerlund. 1997. 'African Islam in Tanzania'. Retrieved 3 August 2014 from www.islamicpopulation.com/africa/Tanzania/ African%20Islam%20in%20Tanzania.htm.

Lofchie, M. 1965. *Zanzibar, Background to Revolution.* London: Oxford University Press.

Loimeier, R. and R. Seesemann (eds). 2006. *The Global Worlds of the Swahili: Interfaces of Islam, Identity and Space in 19th and 20th-Century East Africa.* Berlin: Lit Verlag.

Mintz, S. 1960. *Worker in the Cane: A Puerto Rican Life History.* New Haven: Yale University Press.

Mirza, S. and M. Strobel. 1989. *Three Swahili Women: Life Histories from Mombasa, Kenya.* Bloomington: Indiana University Press.

Munson, H. Jr. 1984. *The House of Si Abd Allah.* New Haven: Yale University Press.

Okello, J. 1976. *Revolution in Zanzibar.* Nairobi: East African Publishing House.

Personal Narratives Group (eds). 1989. *Interpreting Women's Lives: Feminist Theory and Personal Narratives.* Bloomington: Indiana University Press.

Pirio, G.A. 2005. 'Radical Islam in the Greater Horn of Africa'. Retrieved 3 July 2014 from http://www.dankalia.com/archive/2005/050202.htm.

Shostak, M. 1983 [1981]. *Nisa: The Life and Words of a !Kung Woman.* Harmondsworth: Penguin Books.

Smith, M.F. 1981 [1954]. *Baba of Karo: A Woman of the Muslim House.* New Haven and London: Yale University Press.

Van der Bruinhorst, G.C. 2009. 'Siku ya Arafa and the Idd el-Hajj: Knowledge, Ritual and Renewal in Tanzania', in K. Larsen (ed.), *Knowledge, Renewal and Religion.* Uppsala: Nordiska Afrikainstitutet, pp. 127–50.

Von Freyhold, M. 1979. *Ujamaa Villages in Tanzania: Analysis of a Social Experiment.* London: Heinemann.

Walley, C. 2004. 'Modernity and the Meaning of Development in Mafia Island Marine Park, Tanzania', in P. Caplan and F. Topan (eds), *Swahili Modernities: Culture, Politics and Identity on the East African Coast.* Trenton, NJ: Africa World Press, pp. 61–82.

Werbner, R. 1991. *Tears of the Dead: The Social Biography of an African Family.* Edinburgh: Edinburgh University Press for the International African Institute.

Chapter 2

USING AND REFUSING ANTIRETROVIRAL DRUGS IN SOUTH AFRICA

TOWARDS A BIOGRAPHICAL APPROACH

Isak Niehaus

Earlier generations of anthropologists often dealt with social and cultural phenomena, rather than with the intricacies of individual lives. From the viewpoint of those interested in social and symbolic structures, biographies had all the drawbacks of one-person surveys. Only rarely did anthropologists reconstruct the lives of key informants (Casagrande 1960). This has been done to unearth complexities that escape conventional social analysis. For example, Mintz (1974) collected the life story of the sugar cane worker Don Taso to understand personal experiences of conversion to a Protestant revivalist sect.

A shift towards diachronic- and practice-orientated approaches has generated greater interest in biographies. Anthropologists such as Crapanzano (1980), Werbner (1991), Brown (2001) and Chernoff (2003) recognise that the compilation of biographies from a variety of different interviews can offer unique insights. They foreground subjective experience and historicity, and have the capacity to capture the texture of social relationships (Bertaux 1981). From the vantage point of individual lives we can also discern the interplay of structures and events, of public and private domains, and of diverse, sometimes discordant and contradictory, discourses (Niehaus 2006). Biographical narratives can also show the disjunctions between different levels of experience, such as representational models, normative notions, and concrete acts (Holy and Stuchlik 1983), and reveal how people's ideals do not match the actuality of their lives (Niehaus 2006).

In this chapter I contemplate how biographical approaches can offer new insights into the complex issues raised by the South African HIV/AIDS pandemic, particularly concerning the use of life-saving antiretroviral drugs (ARVs). Since the first cases of HIV infection became apparent during the early 1980s, the pandemic has rapidly grown. By 2009 one in every five South Africans, or approximately 5.7 million people, lived with the virus (UNAIDS 2010). President Thabo Mbeki's government stubbornly opposed the use of AZT (azidothymidine) and Nevirapine, drugs shown to be effective in reducing mother-to-child transmission of HIV (Nattrass 2007). Only in 2004 did South Africa's health ministry approve a national 'roll out' of HAART (Highly Active Antiretroviral Therapy), protease inhibitors shown to enable remarkable recoveries of persons even in the latter stages of AIDS. But the department consistently failed to meet its own targets. South Africa's health minister commented on the toxicity of HAART and encouraged sufferers to use alternative remedies, such as vitamins, garlic and African potato (Illife 2006: 149). These views were reportedly influenced by those of dissident scientists, who disputed the existence of HIV, and claimed that the pharmaceutical industry promoted ARVs because it had vested financial interests in their use. Commentators see President Mbeki's denial of the sexual mode of transmission of HIV as a reaction to racist renditions of Africans as 'promiscuous carriers of germs' (Posel 2005).[1]

One important question has been whether national political debates resonate with experiences of HIV/AIDS and of ARVs within ordinary village and township settings. In this domain, too, social surveys have shown great ambivalences about ARVs. Many citizens have refused to test for HIV antibodies, and people in need have consistently refused to take life- enhancing drugs. This does not seem to be a simple effect of the absence of political authorisation (Biehl 2007). Workplace programmes, operating independently of government, have failed to achieve desired results. For example, in 2005 only 2,936 (8 per cent) of approximately 33,500 HIV-positive employees of the Anglo-American mining corporation used ARVs: 29 per cent of employees started but then opted out of treatment (George 2006). Resistances have persisted despite the comprehensive campaigns by Aaron Motsoaledi's health ministry to improve treatment for AIDS. People at higher risk of HIV infection were not more likely to get tested, and many only avail themselves for treatment at late stages of infection (MacPherson et al. 2008; Steven et al. 2010).

From Surveys to Life Stories

Qualitative studies gleaned from questionnaires, topic-based interviews and, to a lesser extent, also participant observation (Nachega et al. 2005) unearth reasonable understandings of biomedical perspectives on the transmission of HIV, the symptoms of AIDS, and on the therapeutic potential of ARVs in Johannesburg's townships. They contend that their results are generalisable to other parts of the country.

Other factors, such as the extreme stigma of being labelled 'HIV-positive', seem to be of greater importance than knowledge per se. Stigma incorporates a condemnation of sexual misdemeanours, but also arises from the location of persons living with AIDS in the liminal domain betwixt and between life and death. The latter is a product of different discourses, including those in public health that portrayed AIDS as a fatal, incurable condition. Saying that a person is 'dead before dying' generated a fatalistic attitude towards treatment, and questions about the threat of pollution that the sick person might represent to others (Niehaus 2007). Being on treatment did not greatly reduce such stigma. Dahab et al. (2011: 53–59) found that HIV-infected employees receiving ARVs regularly discontinued treatment due to workplace discrimination and harassment by line managers, who refused to grant time off for clinic attendance.

The plausibility of alternative sickness aetiologies has also undermined effective biomedical treatment. Throughout South Africa AIDS-related sicknesses are seen as symptoms of bewitchment, rather than of a sexually transmitted virus (Ashforth 2002). Attributions of witchcraft are appealing because they shift culpability from the victim, who might otherwise be blamed for contracting HIV and spreading it to others (McNeill and Niehaus 2010).

Gender and financial concerns, too, come into play. Skhosana et al. (2005) and Mfecane (2010) contend that men were less likely than women to adopt the sick role and commonly felt alienated from the proceedings in HIV support groups, which they saw as more accommodating of women's concerns. Extreme poverty also undermined treatment regimes. People with a CD4 count of 200 or less were judged incapable of working and were eligible to receive monthly disability grants, valued at R780 (£68) in 2005. In fear of losing their grant money once their health improved, persons without other sources of income defaulted on ARV treatment to drive down their CD4 counts (Leclerc-Madlala 2006). Others defaulted on treatment due to a lack of money for clinic transport (Dahab et al. 2011).

Against this backdrop, a small number of studies in which authors reconstruct the life stories of people living with AIDS have considered how sickness and therapy might transform their sense of self and also the social networks in which they participate (DiGiacomo 1987). By allowing research participants to speak for themselves and reflect upon sickness and therapy in the context of unfolding life experiences, the anthropologist can avoid prejudging the issues involved and their relative significance. A juxtaposition of the life stories of Magda A and of the well-known disc jockey Khabzela have highlighted the gendered nature of encounters with HIV, AIDS and ARVs.

Fassin, Le Marcis and Lethata (2008) show how testing and treatment have enabled a positive transformation in the life of Magda A. During her childhood in Lesotho and in Natal, she was a victim of sexual violence at the hands of her uncle and stepfather, who brutally raped her. Magda escaped to Johannesburg where she secured accommodation and financial support through engaging in sexual relations with a succession of men. After giving birth in a rural hospital in Limpopo during 1995, she, her partner, Christos, and their child were all diagnosed as HIV-positive. Magda separated from Christos and returned to Johannesburg. This diagnosis enabled her to access a social grant and secure a relatively well-paid position at an NGO (Non-Governmental Organisation) operating in the domain of AIDS awareness. She also became a regular participant in TAC (Treatment Action Campaign) activism for universal access to ARVs. Magda obtained HAART by enrolling for a clinical trail at Chris Hani-Baragwanath hospital, well before the national roll out of these drugs began. She rapidly regained her health. In this manner an HIV-positive status enabled her to attain goals that had been out of her reach. Fassin, Le Marcis and Lethata (2008: 234) contend that through constructing her biography, Magda overcame emotional pathos through storytelling, no matter how terrible the events she evoked.

MacGregor's (2005) attempt to reconstruct Khabzela's experiences, by interviewing members of his primary networks after his death, paints a diametrically contrasting picture. As a disc jockey on Johannesburg's Youth Radio Station, YFM, he secured an audience of 600,000, and lived the lavish lifestyle of a celebrity. Despite marrying a young woman called Sebongile, Khabzela fathered children with five other lovers, and boasted about his sexual conquests on the air. In 2003 he became ill and on advice of his employer tested for HIV antibodies. Although he publicly announced on radio that he was HIV-positive, Khabzela only took ARVs for a short while, and then resorted to alternative remedies. Khabzela consulted several diviners, and used vitamin tablets dispensed by a Christian healer. It is not clear whether he still believed that he was HIV-positive. His family blamed his wife, Sebongile, for bewitching him so that she could claim his inheritance. When Khabzela's immune system barely functioned, South Africa's health minister, Manto Tshabalala-Msimang, dispatched a Dutch nurse, Tine Van der Maas, to treat him with 'African solutions'– a compound comprising African potato, grapefruit seed extract, and olive oil. Khabzela died and was buried as a celebrity. Thousands of mourners attended the night vigil that was held for him at the famous Orlando stadium.

These accounts show the importance of culpability that an acceptance of being HIV-positive implies. Whereas Magda was a victim of sexual violence, Khabzela boasted about his sexual conquests on radio. As such, men's reluctance to test for HIV antibodies and refusal to use ARVs may be linked to notions of shame, and to the possibility that they might have infected numerous others with a potentially deadly virus. This contrast illuminates official figures for 2010, which show national testing rates of 71 per cent for women, and 38 per cent for men (Government of South Africa 2010).

Using ARVs in Bushbuckridge

The Life Story of Reginald Ngobeni

The life story of Reggie (Reginald) Ngobeni provides significant insights into the experience of being diagnosed HIV-positive, and using ARVs, that escape the above mentioned studies. Beyond confirming the importance of culpability at the level of interpersonal relations, it shows the indeterminacy of knowledge. In situations of profound 'medical pluralism' (Janzen 1978), the diagnosis and labelling of sickness frequently involves the consultation of very diverse specialists, such as diviners, Christian healers and different biomedical practitioners; as well as constantly shifting, but nonetheless coexisting, perspectives on sickness.

I first met Reggie in 2005, whilst doing fieldwork in Impalahoek, a village of about 20,000 Northern Sotho and Tsonga-speaking (Shangaan) residents, located in the Bushbuckridge municipality of the South African lowveld.[2] By then Reggie was desperately ill. He saw his symptoms as a sign of spirit possession and was undergoing training as a diviner's apprentice. The next time I met him was in July 2007. Reggie now seemed to be in a perfect state of health. He told me that although he had tested positive for HIV, he did not believe that he had AIDS. Yet Reggie complied with medical advice and successfully used ARVs.

He welcomed company, and was eager to tell my research assistant, who was actually his cousin, and me his life story and also his experiences of sickness and therapy with as little prompting as possible. Our six, two-hour conversations took place over the course of two weeks during July 2007. Reggie's narrative of his experiences seemed to resemble the obituaries constructed at funerals in Bushbuckridge (Niehaus 2013: 183–201) and displayed an acute awareness of South Africa's turbulent political history.

Early Years in the Periphery, 1961–88

Reggie Ngobeni told me that he was born in 1961 in Delhi – a farming area then administered as part of the former Gazankulu Bantustan for Shangaans. He was the third son of his father's first wife, Maria Mathebula. Reggie described his domestic unit as 'nearly wealthy'. By local standards this seems to be an accurate description of their status. Each of his father's wives had sufficient land to keep cattle and goats, and also to cultivate maize, peanuts and sugar cane.

Reggie encountered mystical explanations of misfortune early in his life. In 1961, his father, Ferris Ngobeni, died, and his remaining paternal kin accused his mother of having bewitched him so that she could inherit his property. Maria Mathebula denied this accusation, and she and her sons relocated to her natal family in Impalahoek, a village situated in the Bushbuckridge enclave of what was then the Northern Sotho Bantustan, Lebowa. Here the Mathebula family were part of a sizable Shangaan minority. Reggie grew up with his maternal grandparents, two older siblings (Petrus and Sidney), and two half-siblings (Steven and Aaron). Steven's father was a Usinga man whom Reggie never saw, and Aaron's father was Rexon Ndlovu, who worked as a security guard at a local supermarket. Both Steven and Aaron used the surname, Ngobeni, rather than that of their own fathers. This was to facilitate the equivalence, and also solidarity, of their sibling group (Niehaus 2013: 38–39). In Impalahoek, villagisation had destroyed the last remnants of subsistence agriculture and Reggie's maternal kin possessed no rural resources.[3]

Reggie attended the local primary school, but only from 1971 until 1977. He seemed to have done fairly well in schoolwork, but dropped out during his first year at secondary school. He attributed this to poverty: 'It was really difficult to be without a father. Nobody worked at home. At school I had no books, no shoes and no uniform'. But neighbours alerted me of another reason as to why he quit school. In 1976, the year of the national uprisings, a number of political activists had fled Soweto for Impalahoek to evade the police, and Reggie's grandmother accommodated them in a building in her backyard. Some of the political refugees were renowned football players. Others possessed firearms and were engaged in crime. Reggie was constantly seen in the company of these men and, according to neighbours, assisted them in criminal operations, such as looting general dealer stores, and stealing from white-owned farms.

Reggie was eager to relay how the men from Soweto taught him about politics, and about heroes of the Liberation Struggle such as Steve Biko and Nelson Mandela. Although he did not say a word about crime, he boasted that he was a lucky gambler who once won R1,000 (£83) during a single game of dice. He attributed his success to the use of mystical potions that he obtained from an elderly male relative. Be it from the proceeds of crime or from gambling, Reggie had sufficient money to send his younger siblings to school. Whilst Steven completed high school, Aaron dedicated himself to the political struggle against apartheid. During 1990, Aaron was part of a small group of young men who crossed the Mozambican border to undergo training as a soldier of the ANC's (African National Congress) military wing, MK (*Umkhonto we Sizwe*, 'Spear of the Nation'). Aaron sent two letters home from Zambia, but never returned from exile, and he has been missing ever since.

Reggie enjoyed fairly good health as a young man, but occasionally suffered from excruciating stomach pains. He first experienced these pains in 1980, and felt 'as if there was something hot, burning inside my stomach'. He encountered two contrasting accounts for the nature and origin of his sickness. A diviner attributed his symptoms to possession by fierce spirits from Mozambique, who were calling him to undergo training as a diviner-herbalist. During training the spirit is exhorted to state its demands and, once appeased, could be converted to a benevolent force. In the latter capacity the spirit bestowed its medium with the power to divine, and also to heal various disorders and diseases. A Christian prophet, on the other hand, guided by the Holy Spirit, diagnosed witchcraft. In Lowveld belief, witches (*baloyi*, sing. *moloi*) inherited malevolent mystical power from their mothers, or else purchased harmful skills and substances from urban marketplaces. Witchcraft encompassed diverse activities – cursing, poisoning, the use of potions (called *dihlare*) and the deployment of animals as witches' familiars (*dithuri*) – all intended to harm. Witches reportedly transformed their victims into zombies (*ditlotlwane*), whom they used as servants at night. The Christian healer lit candles and prayed for him.

Reggie learnt to live with indeterminacy. Although he felt relief from his pains, and believed that both healers had made an accurate diagnosis, he failed to identify the precise source of his distress. This contradicts the assumption that health-seekers display an unswerving commitment to a single interpretative paradigm, which is often implicit in social surveys (Helman 1984).

Life, Love and Sex in Johannesburg, 1988– 2004

In 1988, at the age of twenty-seven, Reggie left home to search for work in Johannesburg. He idealised Johannesburg as a place of political power and wealth, but given his poor education, he could only hope to find work on the lower echelons of the city's labour market. At first he secured accommodation in Meadowlands in the garage of Milton Nonyane and his father, who were also from Impalahoek. He paid only R150 (£13) per month for rent and was happy that the garage was 'not too cold'. Reggie later found it more convenient to stay in Soweto with an old man called Matlale, whose son once resided in his grandmother's compound in Impalahoek. He paid no rent, but he regularly bought the old man groceries, meat and home-brewed liquor. Reggie found employment at an engineering company that repaired mining technology. He was very happy with his wage of R250 (£21) per week after deductions, but complained bitterly that the foul smell of the grease he removed from the machines constantly made him feel nauseous.

In Soweto, Reggie fell in love for the first time: with Zanele Maseko, a Swazi woman. Reggie had previously engaged in sexual intercourse in Impalahoek. He said that on a few occasions women had asked him to accompany them home, and invited him to their rooms. But Reggie was anxious of women's company, and feared that sexual intercourse might pollute his gambling potions, and render them ineffective. He also told me that he preferred to choose his own partners. His relationship with Zanele fulfilled his greatest desires: she was beautiful, contributed financially to their endeavours by working at a crèche, cooked for him and cleaned his room. 'She satisfied my heart', he exclaimed.

But the security that Reggie found in Soweto came to an abrupt end. In 1994 Matlale expelled Reggie from his home, for swearing and fighting with others in the early morning hours. Hereafter, he and Zanele rented a room for R150 (£13) per month. But in February 1995 he lost his job at the engineering company. Reggie told me that his technical director fired him because he had become extremely interested in politics, after Nelson Mandela's release from prison in 1990, and regularly attended trade union meetings: 'He said that I was a rotten potato, who made the other potatoes to be rotten'.

In the same year that Reggie became unemployed, Zanele left him for another man, called Findo. There is a definite economy of sexual relations, in which men who are unable to provide resources to their partners find themselves to be in an extremely vulnerable position. Reggie was deeply hurt by the experience of rejection, and began to question his status as a man. Not only did he fail to provide financially for his lover, he also began to doubt whether he had been able to satisfy Zanele sexually. Reggie told me that he might well be infertile; he wanted to father a child and never used condoms during sexual intercourse, but failed to impregnate Zanele: 'Findo took my girlfriend in 1996, and he made her pregnant in 1997. After losing her, I hated everything'.

In July 1997, Reggie found a new position as an assistant and security guard at Cardies – a shop that sold birthday, wedding, Valentine's Day and Christmas cards, as well as gifts such as glass. The shop was located in downtown Johannesburg. He worked from Mondays until Saturdays and earned only R150 (£13) per week. Reggie commented that the job provided him with the opportunity to meet new lovers. He seemed to have engaged in numerous sexual liaisons to recoup lost masculine status:

> I used to proposition each and every beautiful girl who came into the shop. The girls came to choose cards. It was really not too difficult to grab them. Many of them accepted. At lunch we would go [to have sex] to the flat of one of my friends in Plein Street and at night we would sleep at my own place. I really don't know how many women I had, but it was a lot. It happened every day. Some days I had two women: one in the day and one at night. It was more than eighty or a hundred. My

friends said that I was the principal of girls because I changed them so often. I tried to satisfy my painful heart. I did not prevent because I was looking for a child. Most of the time I ate flesh-to-flesh [had unprotected sex]. I only used condoms when the girls wanted it.

Reggie worked at Cardies only for a year and a half. In 1998 the shop became insolvent and closed down. He said that this was because black people do not really buy cards.

In 1998 Reggie befriended Clifford Mnisi, who was once President Mandela's bodyguard and knew a great deal about politics. A Portuguese man asked them to look after his home in southern Johannesburg, near the well-known George Gough migrant hostel, whilst he was abroad. But the homeowner never returned. There were rumours that he was a fugitive from the police, and also that Reggie had forged documents, showing that the Portuguese man had actually sold the home to him. Clifford assisted Reggie in finding a new position as a security guard at an ESKOM (Electricity Supply Commission) pay-point in a shopping mall. The position paid R1,500 (£125) per month, but was extremely dangerous. Masked men with assault rifles twice robbed shops in the mall. Again he had opportunities to meet lovers:

> It was the same in the shopping mall as at Cardies. The girls were still there. During the day I screwed them at the RDP [Reconstruction and Development Programme] homes at George Gough, and at night they slept at my home. I would go with one at lunch and take another one later. Then, tomorrow I would take more syrup [lovers]. All the time I did it flesh-to-flesh. I wanted to show that Zanele meant nothing to me. I used to screw all the nations: Shangaan, Pedi, Swazi, Venda, Ndebele, Zulu and Xhosa.

Reggie's friends who had visited him in Johannesburg confirmed that he had had many lovers, but they were of the opinion that that was because he could offer them accommodation near the George Gough hostel.

Experiencing Illness, 1996–2004

In Johannesburg Reggie periodically experienced illness, and his stomach cramps became progressively more severe. His health problems came to a head in 1996, when he developed a blistering fever. Reggie returned to Impalahoek to consult a Christian healer. She told him that his blood was polluted because he had broken a taboo – he had had sexual intercourse with a woman who had recently aborted and was therefore in a state of extreme heat (*fiša*). The healer cut a cross in his hair, rubbed soap on his head and melted it with a red-hot steel poker. This technique presumably made the heat escape.

However, Reggie suspected that there might well be deeper, more profound reasons for his distress. This is because his physical illness coincided with other forms of misfortune. In 2001, Reggie was again dismissed from work, and was also the victim of violence. On one occasion he and a friend became involved in a fist fight with Zulu men at a tavern. The Zulu men overpowered them and knocked out two of his friend's teeth that had gold fillings. On another occasion, Coloured men[4] robbed Reggie and threw him into a dam. Biomedical aetiologies of disease do not address the co-occurrence of sickness and other forms of distress, and Reggie again decided to consult a diviner and Christian prophet. The diviner instructed Reggie to sacrifice a goat, to thank his ancestors for having enabled him to survive these ordeals. The Christian healer revealed that misfortune (*bati*) contaminated Reggie's body. He asked Reggie to wash his body with water in which he had had to place an old brown cent, mutton fat and a chicken egg. The healer prayed for him, and instructed him to pour out the water in the form of a cross, hide the egg in tall grass and then walk away without looking back.

In 2003, only two years later, Reggie was once again struck down by excruciating stomach pains. He could not comprehend what was happening to his body. By this time there were many rumours about HIV and AIDS, but Reggie did not believe that these conditions applied to his situation:

> In Johannesburg people started talking about AIDS. They told us not to use the small street next to the Carlton hotel. This is because there were thugs. They had syringes and would put HIV on your buttocks, so that you would later get AIDS. They also stopped us from eating navel oranges because they said the farmers put AIDS in those oranges. Later they said a sore with a black spot is a sign of AIDS. My friends said that Basson [Dr Wouter Basson, head of the apartheid government's chemical weapons programme] came here with the disease. AIDS is like Ebola. It kills people. I wanted to know from other friends where AIDS comes from. They said it was in condoms.

Reggie's description of AIDS was informed by political discourse and by conspiracy theories, so common among South African men at the time (McNeill and Niehaus 2010: 25). These theories deflected attention from men's culpability for infecting themselves and others with HIV, and spoke about HIV/AIDS in a political rather than biomedical paradigm. Reggie believed that he was a victim of witchcraft, and in local belief witches are incapable of sending HIV/AIDS. In addition, he said that his sickness preceded the onset of the pandemic. Because he had been away from Impalahoek for more than sixteen years, Reggie believed he had been alienated from his kin and ancestors. His lack of protection had rendered him vulnerable to mystical attack. Reggie was now in a desperate situation. He was unemployed and extremely ill, and his friends were no longer prepared to support him.

The Quest for Therapy in Impalahoek, 2004–06

On 27 April 2004, Reggie's younger half-brother, Aaron, came to fetch him by car and took him back to Impalahoek. Reggie took up accommodation in his mother's home and in this way sought to heal fractured social relations. He told me that he constantly felt exceptionally tired, as if he had lifted heavy cement slabs. Reggie initially suspected that his maternal aunt might have bewitched him. She apparently swore at him because he had not visited her for more than fifteen years.

Reggie's brother Petrus had a wife, Afisi Khomane, who was a diviner, and she tried to nurse him back to health. But Afisi insisted that spirits from Mozambique afflicted Reggie and were calling him to become a diviner. These spirits strike the stomach. Afisi thus arranged for her mother, who was an instructor of diviners (*gobela*), to train Reggie. Reggie's mothers and siblings raised an amount of R3,500 (£292) for his apprenticeship, and also provided a ton of wood, an 80 kg bag of maize meal, a 12 kg bag of sugar, a blanket and a chicken for the rituals of the diviners. Reggie's training as a diviner helped him place his suffering in a meaningful symbolic framework. No fewer than five spirits manifested themselves whilst he was in trance. But Reggie's training did not reduce his physical discomfort and distress. In fact, his pains grew worse.

One morning, after Reggie had been to the toilet, his intestines protruded from his anus. His instructor was shaken, and felt compelled to ask Petrus to take him to Tintswalo hospital. In hospital Reggie was diagnosed with tuberculosis and confined to the tuberculosis ward for just over three weeks. He felt extremely disconcerted that the nurses and doctors disregarded his own accounts of his symptoms, but based their diagnosis on the statements of his instructor and on diagnostic tests. At this time there had been a great deal of propaganda and education about the HIV/AIDS pandemic, both within Impalahoek and also within the wider Bushbuckridge region, particularly by non-government organisations. Tintswalo formed part of a network of

three hospitals and six clinics that screened pregnant women for sero-
prevalence, provided voluntary counselling and testing, and treated
the symptoms of AIDS-related diseases. But only in 2003 did Masana
Hospital, about 30 km away, begin to make the antiretroviral drug
Nevirapine available.

Although nearly half of all tuberculosis patients at Tintswalo
hospital were co-infected with HIV (Pronyk 2001: 620), Reggie
claimed that medical personnel did not test him for HIV antibodies. It
is likely that they offered to test him and that he declined. Reggie was
confined to the tuberculosis ward – which he described as a polluted
space of death with little water and food, and with bleak prospects for
recovery:

> Each morning they woke us at six o'clock and gave me two tablets. Then
> we had to wash ourselves. But there was no water in the taps in our
> ward, and the nurses would bring water in buckets. You also had to buy
> your own soap, washing rag and Vaseline. I did not wash because the
> space for washing was too small and because I don't like standing na-
> ked with others. In the TB ward I wore cloth for the spirits. The nurses
> told me to take it off, but I refused. My mattress stank. It had the bad
> smell of urine.
>
> At tea time they usually gave us tea and bread. Sometimes it was
> different. Then we would get Jungle Oats [porridge]. This is number
> one. Visiting time was from ten o'clock to half past ten, and again from
> two o'clock till three. There was nothing in the evening. If you wanted
> to eat you had to bring your own food. Each day there was a preacher,
> who preached and told us the word of God.
>
> More than six people died in the ward when I was there. One of them
> died this side of my bed. The next one died that side of my bed. They
> brought other patients, but they also died. They put something like a
> tent at the place where someone had died, and removed the dead bodies
> with noisy trolleys. I was so scared. I feared that I might follow them.
> I shivered. After the deaths there is a bad aura [*seriti*] and I feared that
> the aura might come to me. I was afraid. In that ward you never knew
> who would die next.

Whilst in hospital, Reggie dreamt of large snake with seven heads.
It flew in a strong wind and settled in the trees above his head. The
snake, he said, instructed him not to take his medication, and prom-
ised to show him money. Reggie was not sure what to make of the
dream. In Bushbuckridge people see snakes as highly ambivalent
creatures. As animals from below the ground, where the deceased
are buried, they are viewed as messengers from the ancestors, but
they are also likely to be omens of death. In addition, snakes are also
associated with water and with precious metals, which are sources of
life, but also the cause of conflict and murder. Such revelatory dreams,

as we shall see, are highly significant in the context of health-seeking behaviour.

Reggie resumed his training as a diviner, after he was discharged from hospital. He anxiously defied the snake of his dreams and continued taking his tuberculosis medication. Although he still felt weak, he was compelled to display great endurance by waking up early each morning, invoking the spirits to greet visitors, and to dig roots and herbs in the forest. Reggie complained that his legs felt dry, and that he could no longer dance properly. Under these conditions, grave tensions emerged between Reggie and his instructor. He blamed her for making contradictory statements. After having said all along that spirits affected Reggie's legs, she now stated that he had trampled a potion called *sefolane* that witches laid in the path he used when walking to the shop to purchase cold drinks. Moreover, she constantly demanded more money, and reportedly said that if I did not pay her 'AIDS would attack me'. This, according to Reggie, amounted to a curse: 'I cried when I heard those painful words'.

Reggie, nonetheless, endured the pain, danced and graduated as a diviner on 31 May 2005. By now, he said, his family had paid his instructor nearly R15,000 (£1,250) for her services.

Taking ARVs in Impalahoek, 2005–10

At his mother's home, Reggie again became terribly ill:

> As I entered the yard of my mother's home everything turned upside down. I started to be sick again. I slept in a tent outside, vomited and coughed throughout the night. It was so painful in my chest. I also had diarrhoea and my nose bled. I thought that I was dying.

During this time his instructor's apprentices (*matwasane*) came to dance for him, and relatives gave him ointments for his legs. In June 2005, Reggie consulted a general practitioner, who, he said, did not test him for HIV antibodies, but merely prescribed tablets and told him to eat boiled, rather than fried, eggs.

Eventually Petrus took his ailing brother to the Rixile (Rising Sun) clinic at Tintswalo Hospital. Reggie told me that it was not his decision to consult the nurses at the clinic. 'I had heard of Rixile and did not want to go there, but Petrus wanted to know what was bugging me'. This compromise shows that decisions on therapeutic consultations are seldom those of individual sick persons themselves, as social surveys often presume. Instead, such decisions are the outcome of complex negotiations within therapy management groups – networks of carers, kin and affines – who mobilise around the sufferer to support them, decide on treatments, and collectively evaluate the outcome of therapy (Janzen 1978).

Fortunately, Reggie's encounters with the clinic provided a stark contrast to his earlier experiences in the dreaded tuberculosis ward. The clinic was within walking distance from his home and had begun to supply free HAART medication, as part of the government's national ARV 'roll out' programme, in October 2005. In addition, the clinic provided outpatient nursing, comprehensive treatment literacy programmes, and regularly monitored CD4 counts. By 2007 Rixile catered for 6,000 patients (MacPherson et al. 2008: 2). Reggie tested HIV-positive and was one of the first men to be placed on a course of HAART.

Reggie's detailed descriptions of procedures at the clinic shows that he rapidly acquired accurate biomedical knowledge about HIV/AIDS. When he arrived at Rixile, he said, nurses took blood from his finger, told him that he had tested HIV positive, and that he had measured a CD4 count of only 94, which was low enough to merit antiretroviral treatment. The nurses asked him to choose a time of day and henceforth take ARVs at twelve-hour intervals. They underlined the importance of therapeutic compliance, and instructed him always to use condoms during sexual intercourse, and always to use gloves when helping bleeding persons. The nurses did not raise any false hopes. Reggie explicitly told me: 'The tablets won't cure AIDS. They will only make the AIDS weaker'.

Reggie's perceptions were nonetheless far more complex, contradictory and ambivalent than the assumptions that social surveys about therapeutic literacy frequently make about those of health-seekers (Nachega et al. 2005). Despite being well informed of biomedical perspectives about HIV, AIDS and ARVs, and also about his own test results, Reggie could not bring himself to accept that he was really HIV-positive. He continued to suspect that his divination instructor had bewitched him, and had disguised the symptoms of his witchcraft-related sicknesses as AIDS.

> I don't know if they [the clinic nurses] are correct. This is because I do not know what AIDS pains are like. I did not believe the doctor. I thought that my instructor had bewitched me. This is because I started vomiting and bleeding through the nose at her home. She and her child put potions and stones in the corners of my room, and told me not to sweep. I did not give them permission to do so ...When someone prom-

ises you that you will get AIDS, you will remember it. I thought my
instructor was responsible. I thought she gave me AIDS.

Here, as in the case of Khabzela, acceptance of an HIV-positive
diagnosis would imply culpability, not merely for bringing about one's
own sickness, but also potentially for having infected numerous sexual partners.

> I don't think I have HIV. I do not believe it comes from unprotected sex.
> I'm not HIV-positive. The disease that I have is the very same stomach
> cramps that started in 1980. I do not know the name of this sickness.
> My disease does not come from sex. By 1980 I did not have a girlfriend.
> My girlfriends started in 1990. If it had been AIDS it would have killed
> me long ago. People with AIDS die in fifteen years: not in twenty-eight
> years. It is not sex. I never took dirty girls. I would only take good
> looking and clean ones. Ones who wash and wear clean clothes. AIDS
> might be there, but I selected my girlfriends.

Reggie, nonetheless, took the ARV tablets. His reasoning expresses a
fear of the power of words. In a similar manner as his instructor had
cursed him, he said, the nurses at Rixile told him that unless he took
ARVs he would die. Reggie feared that these words might well bring
about a tragic end to his life. 'I decided to drink the tablets', he said,
'because I'm afraid to die'. 'If I do not take these tablets people will lie.
They will say that AIDS killed me because I did not take the tablets or
follow the instructions'.

But Reggie also continued to take the tablets because he felt that his
health was improving and that he was consistently regaining strength.
Paradoxically, he had come to interpret the vivid and frightening
dreams as a side effect of antiretroviral medication,[5] and recognised
their immense therapeutic power.

> The tablets made me sweat and made me dream about dangerous
> things and about good things. Many times I dreamt about money. I once
> dreamt that I had R266 million [£19 million]. I dreamt that the whole
> plaza [shopping centre] and the sub-station [for electricity] was mine. I
> dreamt that the ancestors had given me these things. But it was not the
> ancestors – it was the tablets.
>
> Maybe there are drugs in those tablets. They reminded me about
> dead people and about forgotten things. Another time I dreamt that I
> saw seven-year-old kids. They had khaki uniforms and were holding
> cell [mobile] phones in their right hands. I did not know one of them,
> but I was meant to follow them. The kids were zombies.[6] They were not
> living human beings.
>
> The tablets also caused me to hear voices of people calling me and
> promising me money. Once I woke up at three o'clock in the morning
> and I heard voices. They called me to come to the dam. They asked me
> to bring my shit to them in a bucket and they promised to give me lots

of money. I walked to the dam, but I did not find the place [from where
the voices came]. I was full of mud and I was very tired. I heard music
coming from a door and I wanted to listen to the music. Then I entered
the yard, carrying a 5 litre bucket of shit. There was a woman with a
young boy and she gave me soft porridge. She begged me to eat. She
asked me what the shit meant and I told her that I came with the shit so
that people could give me money. She thought that witches were trying
to turn me into a zombie. I thought I was mad.

Reggie's visions articulated virtual encounters with money, a
prominent omen of death; encounters with zombies, who exist in the
realm located betwixt and between those of the living and the deceased; and also with the ancestors. The confrontation of such virtual
situations of danger is often interpreted as a form of battle-hardening
or immunisation against actual dangers, such as the risk of death
posed by sickness.

On 26 December 2006, Reggie received a vision from his ancestors telling him to go to the Zion Christian Church (ZCC) to which his
mother belonged. Here a prophet gave him holy water to drink and to
pour at his gate to protect the home against witchcraft. The prophet
instructed Reggie to drink Joko tea, FG coffee and salt each day:

> The prophet said that the witches will send snakes to my home and
> that I have to aill the snakes. So far I have killed about thirteen snakes
> in our yard. I found one in the shack and one underneath the drum of
> water in the kitchen. There was one on the kitchen door and another
> in between the bricks ... These are not snakes from the ancestors [*noga
> ya badimo*] who bring luck to the family. They are snakes from the bush
> who bring bad luck. They have the devil in them.

Since then, Reggie has attended church each Sunday, and drank Zion-
ist coffee and tea each day. This, he said, facilitated his recovery.

When I met Reggie in July 2007, I was surprised when he greeted
me at the gate of his mother's home. He appeared to be in perfect
health and was cultivating a new patch of vegetables. Reggie himself
commented about his renewed life:

> When I was sick my mother did everything for me. At first I could not
> wash my own clothes. I was too weak. I could not jump and I could not
> walk to the plaza [shopping centre] or to church. I moved very slowly. I
> only became better after I went to church and took their prescriptions.
> Now I can walk and I can run. I can also carry three 25 litre barrels of
> water, and I can plough maize in the garden. They [the ZCC] fixed my
> leg and the pain is better.

Reggie's most serious concern was that he had not yet received a
disability pension. The nurses at the HIV clinic asked him to consult

the social workers and to obtain an affidavit from the police station before forwarding his application. He desperately needed a regular income to purchase the proteins and vegetables that nurses had recommended he should eat.

Before parting company, we discussed the upcoming election for ANC president, to be held in Polokwane in 2009. Reggie described himself as a firm supporter of Thabo Mbeki, whom he hoped would defeat Jacob Zuma. His preference was not influenced by their respective policies on the distribution of ARVs, but rather by ethnic stereotypes formed during his sojourn in Johannesburg. Reggie said that he did not wish to see any Zulu person as South African President, because Zulus have a reputation for tribal chauvinism and for violence. With respect to the use of ARVs, his own experiences clearly stood apart from discussions in the political domain.

Conclusion

Biographical approaches do provide unique insights. In this case they advance our understanding of the extremely complex constellation of factors that facilitate and inhibit the use of antiretroviral drugs in South Africa. The life stories of ordinary South Africans are significant in that they enable researchers to gain rare glimpses into domestic realms and 'deep knowledge' (Apter 2007), so frequently concealed beneath public political discourses or else guarded by a veil of silence (Stadler 2003). They also enable us to transcend rigid dichotomies between (scientific, biomedical) knowledge and (folk) belief that so obstruct an understanding of local experiences of sickness and of therapeutic practices (Good 1994).

As in the more well-known case of Khabzela (MacGregor 2005), the experiences of Reggie Ngobeni show that in situations of medical pluralism, knowledge does not imply unswerving commitment to one set of beliefs – witchcraft, pollution, spirit possession or viral infection – and to a single elusive truth. Reggie encountered an overabundance of indeterminate meanings that had not crystallised into a single dominant explanatory model (Geschiere 1998). He constantly tried out new concepts and beliefs, and his practical considerations often outweighed explanatory consistency. For Reggie, different specialised authorities – diviners, Christian healers, politicians, general practitioners and HIV clinics – may act as guarantors for the status of fact.

Both biomedicine and folk healing comprise multiple, coexisting and competing paradigms. Popular notions about the sexual transmission of HIV and fears of witchcraft and spirit possession may well obstruct therapeutic efficacy. Yet it is important to note that Reggie's consultations with biomedical practitioners and his experiences in an over-crowded tuberculosis ward did not lead him to being tested for HIV antibodies. In fact, it was an instructor of diviners, not a general practitioner, who referred Reggie to hospital. Moreover, the therapeutic milieu that Reggie encountered at the Zion Christian Church complemented the effects of ARVs. The church provided him with much needed social support, and a powerful religious rationale for health maintenance. Adherence to rules of the church also enabled him to refrain from smoking and drinking alcohol, often inimical to more secular models of masculinity. The case also demonstrates that health-seeking behaviour, far from being an initiative of individual sufferers, is an outcome of continuous negotiations within broader therapy management groups.

In the end, practical considerations such as continued pain held sway, leading to Reggie Ngobeni's decision to use ARVs. Yet he did not abandon his perception of himself as a victim of witchcraft rather than HIV. His adherence to HAART was based upon its innate efficacy, and upon his desire to avert death, rather than any specific meanings that these drugs encoded. There are complex cognitive and emotional advantages to being a victim of witchcraft rather than AIDS. The pain, misfortune and interpersonal tensions that Reggie associated with witchcraft had a long history, preceding his 'HIV-positive' diagnosis. Witchcraft was less stigmatising, and was not communicable to others. Accepting an HIV-positive diagnosis would imply that he, himself, was to blame for his own sickness. Moreover, it would raise the unbearable possibility that he might well have infected numerous sexual partners with an incurable illness.

In sum, the capacity of life stories to capture the unfolding of shifting, indeterminate and contradictory meanings in individual lives make them an extremely valuable addition to more synchronic methods. In the case of the HIV/AIDS pandemic, an empathetic understanding of these factors may be of vital importance to making therapeutic interventions more effective.

Notes

1. Only in 2008, after President Mbeki's presidency had ended, did national practice fully confirm to international guidelines. By 2012, 1.9 million HIV-positive citizens were using HAART (Smith 2012).
2. I have used pseudonyms to protect the identity of my informants. All local expressions are in Northern Sotho.
3. Agricultural betterment schemes were implemented throughout the South African Bantustans during the 1960s. These schemes involved the division of land into residential, arable and grazing areas. Very few households in Impalahoek could retain access to the land they previously cultivated.
4. In the South African social landscape, Coloured people are considered to be the descendants of the indigenous Khoisan population, as well as people descended from mixed-race couples.
5. Biochemically, Efavirenz, which is an important component of antiretroviral treatment in South Africa, affects the central nervous system. Signs of this affect include dizziness, insomnia, impaired concentration, mania, and extremely vivid dreams and nightmares. The symptoms occur within the first few days or weeks, and usually resolve spontaneously (Carr and Cooper 2000: 1423–30).
6. Witches allegedly changed their victims into zombies (*ditlotlwane*). They first captured the victim's aura or shadow (*seriti*) and then progressively took hold of different parts of his or her body, until they possessed the entire person. But witches would deceive his or her kin by leaving an image of the victim behind.

References

Apter, A. 2007. 'Griaule's Legacy', in *Beyond Words: Discourse and Critical Agency in Africa*. Chicago: University of Chicago Press, pp. 97–129.

Ashforth, A. 2002. 'An Epidemic of Witchcraft? Implications of AIDS for the Post-Apartheid State'. *African Studies* 61(1): 121–44.

Bertaux, D. (ed.). 1981. *Biography and Society: The Life History Approach in the Social Sciences*. Berkeley: Sage, pp. 1–5.

Biehl, J. 2007. *Will to Live: AIDS Therapies and the Politics of Survival*. Princeton and Oxford: Princeton University Press.

Brown, K. 2001. *Mama Lola: A Vodou Priestess in Brooklyn*. Berkeley: University of California Press.

Carr, A. and D. Cooper. 2000. 'Adverse Effects of Antiretroviral Therapy'. *Lancet* 356: 1423–30.

Casagrande, J. (ed.). 1960. *In the Company of Man: Twenty Portraits of Anthropological Informants*. New York: Harper.

Chernoff, J. 2003. *Hustling is Not Stealing: Stories of an African Bar Girl*. Chicago: University of Chicago Press.

Crapanzano, V. 1980. *Thuhami: Portrait of a Moroccan*. Chicago: University of Chicago Press.

Dahab, M., et al. 2011. 'Contrasting Reasons for Discontinuation of Antiretroviral Therapy in Workplace and Public-sector HIV Programs in South Africa', *AIDS Patient Care and STDS* 25(1): 53–59.

DiGiacomo, S. 1987. 'Biomedicine as a Cultural System: An Anthropologist in the Kingdom of the Sick', in H. Baer (ed.), *Encounters with Biomedicine: Case Studies in Medical Anthropology*. New York: Gordon and Breach, pp. 315–46.

Fassin, D, F. Le Marcis and T. Lethata. 2008. 'Life & Times of Magda A: Telling a Story of Violence in South Africa', *Current Anthropology* 49(2): 225–46.

George, G. 2006. 'Workplace ART Programmes: Why Do Companies Invest in Them and Are They Working?' *African Journal of AIDS Research* 5(2): 179–88.

Geschiere, P. 1998. 'Globalization and the Power of Indeterminate Meaning: Witchcraft and Spirit Cults in Africa and East Asia', *Development and Change* 29(4): 811–37.

Good, B. 1994. *Medicine, Rationality and Experience: An Anthropological Perspective*. Cambridge: Cambridge University Press.

Government of South Africa. 2010. 'The National Communications Survey of HIV/AIDS, 2009'. Retrieved 25 June 2010 from www.info.gov.za/issues/hiv/survey 2009.htm#implications

Helman, C. 1984. 'Disease and Pseudo-Disease: A Case History of Pseudo-Angina', in R. Hahn and A. Gaines (eds), *Physicians of Western Medicine: Anthropological Perspectives on Theory and Practice*. Dordrecht: D. Reidel, pp. 293–331.

Holy, L. and M. Stuchlik. 1983. *Actions, Norms and Representations: Foundations of Anthropological Inquiry*. Cambridge: Cambridge University Press.

Illife, J. 2006. *The African AIDS Epidemic: A History*. Athens, OH: Ohio University Press.

Janzen, J. 1978. *The Quest for Therapy in Lower Zaire*. Berkeley: University of California Press.

Leclerc-Madlala, S. 2006. '"We Will Eat When I Get the Grant": Negotiating AIDS, Poverty and Antiretroviral Treatment in South Africa', *African Journal of AIDS Research* 5(3): 249–56.

MacGregor, L. 2005. *Khabzela: The Life and Times of a South African*. Johannesburg: Jacana.

MacPherson, P., M. Moshabela, N. Martinson and P. Pronyk. 2008. 'Mortality and Loss to Follow-Up among HAART Initiators in Rural South Africa', *Transactions of the Royal Society of Tropical Medicine and Hygiene* 103(6): 588–93.

McNeill, F. and I. Niehaus. 2010. *Magic: AIDS Review 2009*. Pretoria: Centre for the Study of AIDS, University of Pretoria.

Mfecane, S. 2010. 'Exploring Masculinities in the Context of ARV Use: A Study of Men Living with HIV in a South African Village', Ph.D. thesis. Johannesburg: WISER, University of the Witwatersrand.

Mintz, S. 1974 [1960]. *Worker in the Cane: A Puerto Rican Life History.* New York: Norton and Company.

Nachega, J., et al. 2005. 'HIV/AIDS and Antiretroviral Treatment Knowledge, Attitudes, Beliefs and Practices in HIV-Infected Adults in Soweto, South Africa', *Journal of Immune Deficiency Syndrome* 38(2): 196–201.

Nattrass, N. 2007. *Mortal Combat: AIDS Denialism and the Struggle for Antiretrovirals in South Africa.* Durban: University of Kwaulu-Natal Press.

Niehaus, I. 2006. 'Biographical Lessons: Life Stories, Sex and Culture in Bushbuckridge, South Africa', *Cahiers d' Etudes Africaines* 46(1): 51–73.

———. 2007. 'Death Before Dying: Understanding AIDS Stigma in the South African Lowveld', *Journal of Southern African Studies* 33(4): 845–60.

———. 2013. *Witchcraft and a Life in the New South Africa.* New York: Cambridge University Press.

Posel, D. 2005. 'Sex, Death and the Fate of the Nation: Reflections on the Politicization of Sexuality in Post-Apartheid South Africa', *Africa* 75(2): 125–53.

Pronyk, P. 2001. 'Assessing Health Seeking Behaviour Among Tuberculosis Patients in Rural South Africa', *International Journal of Tuberculosis and Lung Disease* 5(7): 619–27.

Skhosana, N., H. Stuthers, G. Grey and J. McIntyre. 2005. 'HIV Disclosure and other Factors that Impact on Adherence to Antiretroviral Therapy: The Case of Soweto, South Africa', *African Journal of AIDS Research* 5(1): 17–26.

Smith, D. 2012. 'HIV Drugs Increase South African Life Expectancy by Five Years', *The Guardian* 3 December. Retrieved 1 March 2013 from http://www.theguardian.com/world/2012/dec/03/aids-drugs-south-african-life

Stadler, J. 2003. 'Rumor, Gossip and Blame: Implications for HIV/AIDS Prevention in the South African Lowveld', *AIDS Education and Prevention* 15(3): 357–68.

Steven, M., A. Cockroft, G. Lamothe, and N. Andersson. 2010. 'Equity in HIV Testing: Evidence from a Cross-Sectional Study in Ten South African Countries', *International Health and Human Rights* 10(23): 21–33.

UNAIDS. 2010. 'UNAIDS Report on the Global AIDS Epidemic 2010'. Retrieved 15 June 2012 from http://bit.ly/hg5pcw

Werbner, R. 1991. *Tears for the Dead: The Social Biography of an African Family.* Edinburgh: Edinburgh University Press.

Chapter 3

AN 'UP AND DOWN LIFE'

UNDERSTANDING LEPROSY
THROUGH BIOGRAPHY

James Staples

In common with other biographies of people in India (cf. Parry 2004: 286), synoptic life-history accounts of people with leprosy tend to follow conventionalised narrative forms, with the onset of leprosy causing a violent rupture in otherwise positively construed life courses. Many of my informants in Anandapuram[1] colony, on India's southeast coast, as well as in leprosy colonies in Hyderabad and, further north, in Haryana, were well practised in telling their stories to the representatives of donor agencies and other potential patrons. As a consequence, they were also much more aware than those I worked with from non-leprosy backgrounds of the power of such narratives to obtain access to funding and other resources. These stories are in themselves informative about the politics of representation, and might even be seen as part of a project of identity formation (Rosenwald and Ochberg 1992; Frank 1995). In terms of capturing the lived experiences of people affected by leprosy, however, they often obscure more than they reveal.

In this chapter, I explore how more nuanced accounts might be achieved through more intensive biographical interviews carried out over longer time periods and in different locations, set against a backdrop of more conventional, detailed ethnographic fieldwork. In particular, I focus on a series of interviews I conducted with one person, whom I shall call Das; a leprosy-affected man I have known and worked with for over twenty-five years, and whose stories not only illuminate the experience of leprosy, but shed light on a wide range of issues pertinent to life more generally in post-independence India. Indeed, the biological fact of leprosy – because it is what distinguished patients from others in the general population – tends to be overemphasised in conventional accounts of those with the disease, and it is important to recognise that leprosy is only one of many factors affecting the lives of those with the disease. Although the growing popularity of life-history accounts has sometimes been linked to the wider disciplinary shifts in anthropology from 'structure' to 'agency' and from 'culture' to 'voice' (Parry 2004: 283), such stories can also serve to bridge the gaps between these polarities, documenting not simply the capacity of individuals to act, but the converging contexts in which those actions are shaped. As Arnold and Blackburn put it:

> [L]ife histories should not be seen as ... a narrowing down or even a disavowal of grand themes ... Rather, life histories enable us to render more intelligible precisely the complex of forces at work in modern societies and to reflect further, and from more solid foundations, on many of the major themes that dominate the subcontinent – gender, modernity, colonialism and nationalism, religion, social changes, family and kinship, and interrelationship between self and society. (2004: 5–6)

I also explore here the distinctiveness of such a research methodology – which, although far from new, arguably remains underused in South Asian ethnography[2] – and I consider its fit with conventional forms of participant observation.

I begin, then, by returning to some earlier recordings of Das's life story, both to illustrate some of the shortcomings of standardised life-story accounts, and to offer comparative data against which subsequent renderings of the same man's life might also be read.

Representing Das

Although Das had a High School education and good job prospects, after contracting leprosy he spent the next 20 years hiding from the shame it brought him by working for tips as a porter on Madras Central railway station. Reunited with his father, who also had the disease, he came to Anandapuram where his schooling was finally made good use of in the community's central office. Now, with 10-years' office experience, he's been put in charge of the day-to-day running of all Anandapuram's development programmes. The £50 a month [this charity] provides for Das's salary helps to ensure that your donations are well used – and that a leprosy patient's skills aren't wasted.

Das's conventionalised life story, as captured in both the fundraising pamphlet quoted from above, which I produced in 1995 for a UK charity that supports Anandapuram, and a longer newsletter feature that told the same account in more dramatic detail, were – like many stories about people affected by leprosy – written as exemplars of the leprosy life trajectory. They begin by recounting the rejection, suffering and shame that is assumed to result from negative social reactions towards leprosy – because leprosy is often seen as a punishment for previous wrong-doing (see Staples 2007). This is followed, in turn, by reintegration into the leprosy colony – often accompanied, at least in missionary accounts, by conversion to Christianity. They are then rounded off with a 'happily ever after' ending. Such an ending, as in this case, is often presented as contingent on continued funding. Because such stories follow a familiar structure, they reinforce one another and the genre, making it a difficult form to break out of, either by the tellers or recorders of these narratives. As a consequence, when I interviewed people in Anandapuram and other leprosy colonies elsewhere in India about their lives, these were the kinds of stories they generally told me. They recounted past abuse from relatives who no longer wanted to drink or eat from the same cups and plates as their leprosy-affected spouses or siblings; cruel jibes from neighbours; the impossibility of finding employment; and their difficulties in finding marriage partners. Separation – induced by the stigma – always followed, and although the leprosy stigma continued to plague their lives, positive developments had also very often taken place, proving, in line with messages promoted by all the major leprosy aid agencies, that leprosy was curable, only mildly contagious and no logical block to getting married and having children.

For the purposes for which they were written, these stories clearly have some value. Presented in the right outlets or told to the right people – foreigners or other potential donors – they encourage empathy and, as a consequence, sometimes funding. Indeed, the story from the pamphlet cited above was published, along with two other similar life stories, under the heading 'Three very good reasons for supporting [the charity]'. They were used as examples of what can be achieved by leprosy-affected people if they are given support. The stories also enabled both the storytellers and those who read them to feel positive about what has happened: that life is now better than it once was in spite of – or perhaps even because of – leprosy. A common trope in other life-story accounts I collected from leprosy patients, particularly those of older women, was the expression of gratitude that they had contracted leprosy, because through the disease they had got to know 'the true God'.[3]

When stories of this kind are taken literally as representations of the whole truth, however – as objective representations of reality rather than as stories told to effect change – and are used unproblematically as the basis for developing policy, difficulties arise. Donors end up bemused at the disjuncture between the intent of their programmes, developed to help people with leprosy, and the results. Why, when people interviewed say all they want is the opportunity to work and to stand on their own feet, for example, do such programmes so often fail in terms of the donors' objectives? One reason is because such case studies convey only a formulaic, highly stylised version of reality. The dominant narratives about leprosy on which they are based are internalised, very often, by those who go on to tell them as though they were memories of personal experience, in much the same way that many of our perceived memories of events in early childhood are more likely memories of others' accounts of those events (Bloch 1998). Indeed, it was not uncommon, more than ten years after I had written them, for people to quote back to me almost verbatim things I had written in community publicity materials about their lives, their memories shaped not only by the events themselves but by my recording of them in a particular way. Such stories also, as Niehaus notes, conflate 'representational models, normative notions which ascribe meanings to actions, and the specific acts performed by individuals' (2006: 15; also see Holy and Stuchlik 1983).

What I want to posit here as an alternative are more detailed life-history accounts, conducted over a longer period, and which re-interrogate respondents over time and in different places. In combining these accounts with ethnographic observations, they come closer to what Frank describes as 'cultural biography' (2000: 2) than either simply 'life-focused' or 'story-focused' accounts (Peacock and Holland 1993: 369–70). As such, because they are written up less to illustrate a particular point or have a particular effect and more to provide a rich, fine-grained account of someone's life from which insights might subsequently be extracted, they are also less constrained by the form through which they are mediated than, say, the fundraising pamphlet vignette or the illustrative case study in a more wide-ranging academic article. This is not, of course, to suggest that any account can appear unmediated, nor is it to suggest that they are any truer, in an absolute sense, than those presented through other genres. Indeed,

self-reflection on the presentation of these accounts as well their content is a vital component of understanding them. Because they are
richer and less essentialised, however, they at least have the potential
to capture more of the diversity of someone's life experience, without
the requirement to impose an overall coherence upon it.[4]

In the next section I set out the background to the interviews I
undertook with Das for the project in 2009 and 2011 (Staples 2014),
and draw out what is particular about the kind of interviews that
were undertaken. The subsequent section offers a highly truncated
rendering of Das's account – an account which, in its own way, is as
edited as the case study accounts I critique above. Necessarily selective
though it is, I have tried to include elements that go against the grain
of what Das presents as the overarching narrative thrust of his story,
and which hint at a more nuanced – and consequently more telling
– picture (cf. Arnold and Blackburn 2004: 13). The final section attempts to analyse the material I have presented, to compare it with
other forms of life story, and to argue why such an approach has a
more general applicability in contemporary anthropology.

Interviewing Das

I first met Das in early 1985, when he came with his father to Anandapuram leprosy colony's central office looking for work. Such visits
were quite common, since the office administered a range of social
development and welfare programmes. I was there in my final days
as a school-leaver volunteer, having spent six months helping with
correspondence, giving English classes and setting up – not very
successfully – a small printing press for producing the very kinds of
newsletters and publicity materials that propagated the kind of life
trajectories described above. Following this brief encounter, I met him
again in August 1986, when I returned to the village for a second stint
as a volunteer, and when Das – now married and working in the office
as a bookkeeper – was dispatched to meet me at Bombay airport and
accompany me on the 700 mile journey back to Anandapuram. We
worked together over the next six months as colleagues; he helped me
when I returned again to do my first, fledgling undergraduate field research in 1989; and we worked alongside one another again in 1996,
by which time he had taken charge of administering the colony's social development and welfare programmes. By the time I returned as
a full-time anthropologist for a year between 1999 and 2000, he had
resigned that post – taken over by a succession of local outsiders – to

return to his previous role as financial controller. He came to greet me at the railway station and gave his account of what had been going on in the village during our three-hour car journey back (see Staples 2007, Chapter 8, for a detailed account). He worked for me, sporadically, as a research assistant during that period, as well as serving as a major informant. He also remained a friend.

In 2005, when I began work in a new field site in Hyderabad, he was no longer working in Anandapuram, and left a temporary job with an NGO (non-government organisation) in Chennai (previously Madras) to stay with me and my family and work as my research assistant full-time. On my subsequent trips to Anandapuram – in the summers of 2007 and 2009, to carry out research on suicide in the community – he continued working with me in this capacity. The latter visit also included around thirty hours of taped interviews about his own life, which I continued to discuss with him on a four week visit in 2011.

My current project, then, draws both on my own, first-hand knowledge of Das's life as I have seen it unfold over the past twenty-five years; my records of fragments of it, strewn throughout my field notes; and the more recent and ongoing series of interviews and conversations, most of them taped, during my 2009 and 2011 visits. As English was Das's second language – after Tamil but ahead of Telugu or Hindi – all our formal interviews and nearly all of our conversations were also in English, and my reproduction of Das's words in the following are verbatim quotes. I also interviewed and talked to some of those close to him, in both English and Telugu, amassing both formal, taped interviews and notes that draw on casual conversations and passing comments. While the former were prearranged meetings, when I sat down with people and intentionally asked them to recount various stories about Das in a semi-structured way, the latter were based on chance encounters; when, for example, I was chatting to someone I had run into in the street or the tea shop, and a story concerning Das emerged, unplanned, amid the flow of our conversation. Although at the time I had only considered the prearranged meetings as 'interviews', in retrospect – and in thinking through my material for this chapter – it occurs to me that my other conversations might also be classified as such. However unexpected on my part the invoking of Das might have been in such contexts, the fact that I would then continue those conversations in pursuit of data – which I would recall and note down later – suggests that they too were transformed into some kind of interview.

In 2000, along with others in the village, Das also kept, at my request, an 'informant diary' – in which he was asked to record his day-to-day activities as well as events going on around him in the village – and, when we were in Hyderabad, I asked him to keep a separate set of field notes so that I could compare our perspectives on events. So while a series of intensive interviews are at the centre of my current project, my reading of them is closely informed by these other sources, including references to my own copious field notes and diaries.

In terms of our most recent interviews, we usually spoke – in sessions lasting between thirty minutes to around three hours, but usually about an hour long – in the early mornings, either side of breakfast, or in the evenings, after dinner, on the verandah of the Mahila Mandal[5] building, part of which also served as a kitchen for guests to the community. It was a relatively neutral, shaded place on the outskirts of the village, and while we were disturbed often, we attracted less attention than if we had spoken at, say, Das's own house, where neighbours would have congregated together very quickly.

We also spent around a week travelling back to some of the places that featured in Das's earlier narratives: to his ancestral home in Tamil Nadu, where I saw the place where he was born, and where the village headman entertained us with coffee; to Kumbakonam and Chennai and the various locations where he and his family had lived and where his father had opened up canteens and fast-food stands; and to the station platform where he spent more than a decade (1974–85) working as an unofficial porter, hotel tout and sometime tourist guide. In several of these locations, and especially the last, we ran into people who had known and lived with Das and who had featured in the accounts he had given during our taped interviews: together they re-pieced together the narrative, subtly enriching and/or shifting the earlier accounts and, sometimes, giving them new meaning. In 2011 I also travelled with Das to where he lived, in what is now Mumbai, and to visit the factory where, for a short time, he worked, as well as the railway stations he operated in as a porter and the racecourses and other locations where he won and lost his money.

It was this literal reconstruction of Das's movements through space – albeit on fast forward – by going back to the places where he had spent formative time and which he considered important in his life trajectory that was innovative about this particular approach to recording life stories. These journeys also gave shape and colour to his narratives: I could literally visualise where the events he described had taken place and, sometimes, the people who they had happened to in ways that his words alone did not make possible, and on many occasions this changed my understanding of Das's recollections of particular events. For Das himself, going back also transformed the ways in which he recalled – or reconstructed – the memories he had been drawing upon. Elements of the story that appeared missing from earlier accounts were forthcoming on location, as were anecdotes about people not previously mentioned.

This is not, of course, to say that the newer versions of his stories were necessarily more accurate. He was still, to be sure, involved in editing and representing his life in certain ways and to particular effect, often self-consciously framing his life as being, in his words, 'just like a cinema film'. For example, having read *Q & A* (2005) – the novel by Vikas Swarup on which the more recent film *Slumdog Millionaire* was based – when he lived with us in Hyderabad in 2006, Das often compared his life self-consciously to that of Ram Mohammad Thomas, the novel's protagonist. In 2009, on train journeys between the places where he had lived, he also read parts of my copy of Gelya Frank's *Venus on Wheels* (2000), an anthropologist's biographical account of Diane DeVries, an American woman born without arms or legs. 'Her life reads just like mine!' he said. When I expressed surprise that he, as an Indian Brahmin man who had been affected by leprosy, should find much in common with a white, working-class suburban American woman born without limbs, he explained that DeVries, too, had had an 'up and down sort of life', in which things did not just get progressively better or worse in a linear trajectory, but shifted back and forth in a much messier, less narratively convenient fashion across time. Such exposure to these and other[6] genres of storytelling clearly shaped the form that Das's stories took, offering him a rough template through which to construct his own account. It was certainly a different kind of narrative to those I collected from less literate informants, or from those less accustomed to my particular ways of working. Das was relatively unusual among his generation in the village, for example, in knowing his precise date of birth. Nevertheless, our most recent interviews were certainly richer than earlier accounts and, because they were stretched out over much more than a single telling and were not necessarily told in chronological order, they were no longer obliged to conform to the overarching narrative structure that Das gave to the overall story of his life. This made them much more generally informative.

In terms of interview technique, my approach, from the outset, was simply to ask Das to tell me about his life and to go wherever it took us. First, he followed the format that he had used in the past: he summarised the entire story, from his childhood to his present po-

sition, compressed into about an hour. It was a tale of a positive beginning wrecked by the onset of leprosy, followed by his remarkable
ascent from vagrant station porter to chief functionary of an NGO.
This was useful in telling me what was important to him – or at least
what he thought was important that I should know about – but it
clearly skipped over key events in order to focus on central themes,
many of them already familiar from the earlier profiles I referred to
above for newsletters and fundraising pamphlets. His synoptic account also ended around 1995, before things went awry again and
the positive ending, which rounded off the story so well, was spoiled.
My subsequent approach, then, was to go back to points in the narrative on which he had not provided much detail or on which I was
unclear (either on what had happened, what the motivation was, or
what Das had made of particular events) and to get him to elaborate.
I would begin by saying something along the lines of: 'I want to ask
you a bit more about life in your mother's village...' and then let him
take the story in any direction he wanted, inserting prompts that in
turn elicited more responses. I see from my transcriptions of our interviews that usually these interjections were just single words denoting
themes, such as 'Food?' 'School?' 'Friends?' or simple questions along
the lines of 'When?' 'And?' or 'So?' After each interview I would tran-
scribe the recordings and read them through, drawing out further,
more probing questions each time, and returning to points that I had
not understood or if I was confused about chronology. Often I would
begin simply by trying to set the scene: for instance, 'So I want to
take you back to the Ultra Marine Blue Company in 1967 ...' and this
would be sufficient to start him talking.

In this way the interviews became more and more detailed and covered shorter and shorter periods of history. We progressed in a broadly
chronological direction, backtracking at each stage to confirm and
elaborate on the story, until we reached the present.

Das's Story

The longer-term project from this research is a book length biography about Das. By focusing on the relationship between us, the book
also has something to say about the relationship between research
assistant and anthropologist that is so central to the production of
ethnographic knowledge, but often sidelined in our written accounts
(Staples 2014). For now, however, a necessarily brief synopsis of what

Das told me will suffice to draw out the differences between this kind
of biography and the shorter case studies I critiqued above.

Das was born into a high-status Brahmin family (a fact anyone who
speaks to him will learn very quickly[7]) in a small village in Tamil Nadu
in 1950. His parents were distantly related, their marriage providing
a solution to problems faced by both partners' families. His mother's
father had died before she was born, and her mother had no money for
a dowry, just an acre of land in her village. His father's family, meanwhile, were keen to have him married so as to stop him 'going here
and there'. 'He'd been a wanderer', as Das put it, 'he never went much
to school'. This was in contrast to his younger brothers, two of whom
became school teachers and the third a priest. Marriage, it was hoped,
would force him to settle down. As Das's mother was an only child, her
husband went to live with her and her mother in her village.[8] Already,
I might interject here, the story is rather less auspicious than the start
described in more synoptic narratives, in which Das's background
is presented in grander fashion, with Das born high caste and with
a bright future stretching out ahead of him. Such scene-setting was
most likely a device to emphasise the fall that comes later.

In earlier versions of Das's story, his father absconded on the discovery that he himself had leprosy, a seminal event implying the
shame was too great and that he wanted to spare his family the stigma
of leprosy. There are, no doubt, elements of truth in this but, as it
emerged during our ongoing interviews, this was not the first time his
father had absconded. In addition to his youthful wanderings, after
marriage he had first left home when Das was six. He had gone to the
relatively close-by temple town of Kumbakonam, only summonsing
the family there when he was admitted to hospital with cholera. He
had disappeared again soon after he was discharged, and was away
when Das's only sister and his maternal grandmother both died of
small pox, contacting them a year or two later to say he had set up a
business in Kukur, and that they should join him there. The business
was not a success, however, and they all returned to Kumbakonam –
which is where Das's brother, ten years his junior – was born. Most
of Das's schooling was also in Kumbakonam, up to tenth standard,
although he missed the final exams – 'I think I didn't bother to turn
up for them', he recalls, vaguely – and had to retake them later in
Madras. Their father left Kumbakonam again after his new snacks
business ran up debts that he could not pay off. This time he returned
after a year or two to shift the family to Madras, where he had rented
a house and set up a handcart business selling sweets and savouries.
A year later, with finance from Das's mother's maternal aunt and her

husband, who was a senior tax inspector, he established a meals mess for students. Like all the other businesses, bar the handcart, it made a loss and, after holding out for about a year, Das's father decamped again in the late 1960s, this time for good. This made for four major documented departures, none of them specifically related to leprosy, although Das thinks that his father knew he had the disease when he left for the last time, and that this might also have shaped his decision.

Das's own departures were not as strictly leprosy-related as earlier accounts suggested either. He stayed at his first job, acquired with the recommendation of the uncle who had financed his father's past businesses, only a month. 'I suppose', he explained, 'it was because I was young, about seventeen, and this wasn't really the time for working, it was the time for wandering and that. One day I was late, missed the train, so I stayed away, hung around with friends and played cards. I didn't go again the next day, just left the house at the usual time and came back at the right time in the evening, but then my mother found out I hadn't been going, and shouted about how I would spoil my uncle's reputation. So I walked away. I took money to go to the cinema, but ended up on a train to Calcutta'. Even before this, as it finally emerged as Das pointed out places he had spent time in on our seven-hour bus journey back from Kumbakonam to Chennai, he had been prone to leave home every now and then, staying away for a few days at a time and sustaining himself by helping out on tea stalls, where he would offer to wash glasses for a few paise or a meal.

After some escapades in Calcutta, he ended up back in Madras Central Station, where he stayed for a while – helping out on a woman's fruit stall outside the station. A relative came across him there a few months later, returned him home and, soon after, his maternal uncle again fixed him up with a job, this time in a knitwear machinery factory in Bombay, where he went to work as a storekeeper. He had been there for seven months, sleeping in the storeroom itself, when the watchman told him he should get his thickened earlobe checked out by a doctor. He did, and was diagnosed with leprosy. He did not even return to the factory to take his suitcase, he said, but went from the hospital 'to the station and started that kind of life again'. Neither did he return to the hospital to take the prescribed treatment. 'What was the point? My life was over!' he said, alluding to the fact that leprosy, as a highly stigmatised disease, meant social death. A year or so later, however, his condition worsened, and one of his platform friends, a successful ticket tout who eventually established an equally successful travel agency, got him checked in to a leprosy hospital in Gujarat, sending him spending money throughout his stay there. Das had helped this man, a fellow Tamilian, when he first came to the station; this was his way of repaying Das's earlier kindness. However, Das grew bored of the hospital routines after about six months; boredom, followed by flight, emerging as a significant motif in Das's life story. On a whim one day he walked out and came straight back to Dadar station. In addition to unofficial portering – carrying people's bags and finding them seats on busy trains – he also ran a card school for a couple of years, and made additional income as a hotel tout, taking tourists, especially foreigners, to cheap nearby lodges. The hotel owners paid him commission, and the tourists gave him tips, so it was, he told me, a good and interesting way of making money and improving his English.

Das presents a rather rosy picture overall of life on the station: 'It's like, when I was on the station I felt free. I had nothing at all, but also no burdens. So maybe it's better not to have anything'. Das was, however, now speaking as a man now burdened with debts and the needs of a wife and two children, and I suspect this shaped his recollection. It was clear that platform life was also hard. After four or five years on Dadar station, he was again ready for a change, and, as he missed his native state, in 1974 he decided to work on Madras Central Station. His time there coincided with the 21-month state of emergency declared by then Prime Minister Indira Gandhi in 1975, and – although he made little direct reference to this wider context – it was during this period that he was arrested several times without charge and spent time in prisons before being released. Along with his friends he also underwent a vasectomy when it was encouraged by the state's family planning programme. Such events were recalled without rancour: they were, as he put it, just the way things were for people like him.

It was also during his time at Central Station that, sometime later, he was reunited with his younger brother, also leprosy-affected and working there as an unofficial porter. This was a pivotal event in all tellings of Das's story, and when we visited he showed me the two peepal trees under which the two men, who had been estranged for many years and had not recognised one another, finally made the discovery that they were siblings. It is a story his brother is also fond of telling. There were several more twists and turns: his stories include colourful sexual exploits, incidences of violence, and visits to places he had never been to before as a tour guide for foreign tourists he met off trains ('I could read the Tamil signs on things and they couldn't, so I could pretend I knew all about the ancient wall carvings!'). But the next pivotal moment in his account was when the two brothers were finally reunited with their father in 1980, after Das spotted him on the platform.

Their father had spent the first three years after his departure from the family home in two leprosy hospitals, and had met and married his second wife – also a Brahmin leprosy patient – in the second one. Together they had moved to a leprosy colony run by the Roman Catholic Church, where they converted and spent the next few years, before shifting to Anandapuram, which was much closer to the hospital where, by then, they were receiving treatment. The regime in Anandapuram was also more liberal: as a self-run colony, they could come and go as they pleased, and begging was not prohibited. They were living in Anandapuram in a mud and thatch house they had constructed and were making a living from begging when Das met him on the station, and he persuaded both his sons to become members of the colony and to visit him there periodically. The brothers had also contacted their mother at around the same time: she had gone to live with the maternal aunt and her husband, by then relocated for a few years to Bombay, helping them to rear their children and run the household. Das and his brother visited her every so often over the years that followed, although she was never told that her husband had remarried.

Unlike his brother, who married and settled in the village fairly soon after they had met in the station, Das found it difficult to stay there for any length of time, only moving there permanently in 1985, when his father and stepmother arranged his marriage to a young, Madiga caste girl. The Madiga, or cobbler, caste was one of the caste groups previously classified as 'Untouchable' and – had leprosy not been a factor in their lives – marriage between a Brahmin, the highest caste ranking, and a Madiga would have usually been unthinkable. Das told me that his father had thought – rather ironically, given his own former propensity to abscond – that if he were married he would stay there with the family. Das, by now thirty-five, was also starting to feel too old for what he called 'the platform life'. The wedding followed Das's baptism at local prayer meetings, during which he was officially converted to Christianity. His new wife had already had a difficult life at home: after her father's premature death she had been left to care for her younger siblings while her mother went begging with her new husband. However, she was not keen to marry a man so many years her senior, even if he was of higher social status (she was around fourteen, and only started menstruating a year later). The payment to her stepfather – which Das says he only learned about after the event, and was unhappy about – helped ensure the union took place. 'She was very shy, very timid', he remembers of his wife, 'and because she came from that group, that caste, she didn't know how to do lots of things around the house properly'. She did not, for example, know how to prepare the vegetarian curries that were commonplace in a Tamil Brahmin household. It was more than a year later before the marriage was consummated, and a vasectomy reversal operation and ten years before the births, first, of a son, and three years later, of a daughter. His father also helped him get a temporary job in the office, which became permanent when he taught his more senior colleagues a better way to balance the books. Working alongside the British nurse who served as the colony's administrator until 1995, he became her right-hand man, and was a well-respected figure in the community.

Meanwhile, however, towards the end of that period, he also started making regular trips – some of which were facilitated by the travel required of his job – to see his old friends in what was now called Chennai and to go with some of them back to the horse races. Although Das maintains that he made more money than he ever lost at the races or in card games, he ran up large debts during that time, which he struggled to pay off, particularly as local interest rates were very high.

When the nurse left in 1995, Das was appointed Administrative Officer. This was the top job in the Colony, answerable to an absent management committee and the community's elected village elders. His story from this point details the many difficulties in managing the role at a time when a new consciousness of outside authority and legal rights was developing in the village: when people would go to the police rather than the elders with their problems; when workers on rehabilitation programmes set up a trade union to campaign against low wages; and when one man – unfairly dismissed by the elders – took his case to court. Much of the next few years were taken up attending court cases and being pressed by the elders, as he recounted it, for money, alcoholic drinks and biryani dinners. He felt increasingly crushed by the pressures that were mounting upon him. His personal debts were spiralling out of control and he was drinking more heavily. A love affair with a village woman closer to his own age – conducted mainly in hotel rooms, which she paid for – offered some respite, but it was clear he found himself in an increasingly impossible situation.

He resigned from his post in 1999 – only to be reinstated by the elders in 2001 and removed from the post again a couple of years later – and there have been six incumbents of the post in the intervening decade. Das took a job for a while with another NGO back in Chennai, but complained that it did not pay enough to cover the expenses of living there, and was keen to take up my offer of coming to work with me again between 2005 and 2006, when he lived with us and worked as my research assistant in Hyderabad. His father, who was begging in Mumbai, died during this period: we were back in Anandapuram for a few days when the news came through from a Mumbai returnee. Unable to bring his body back from the other side of the country, his fellow beggars from the colony had left him at the roadside to be cleared away by the municipality.

Das returned for a while to work for the same NGO in Chennai in early 2007, this time surveying the beneficiaries of post-tsunami funding in fishing communities along the Coromandal coast. He enjoyed this work, but became bored again when it was over and he was returned to the office. He had to rent a room and buy his own food, which took up most of his salary, and it was, he said, a 'machine routine'. The death of his mother a couple of months later, when she was hit by a mineral water delivery van as she crossed the road to go to temple, was the catalyst that sent him back to the village once again. His mother had been looked after financially by the Madras uncle's sons, and she left him a small inheritance that enabled him to pay off some of his debts, and also buy some furniture and some gold for his wife. He was not working when I returned to Anandapuram in the summer of 2007, but the inheritance appeared to have given him some reprieve and lifted the spirits of both Das and his wife. However, both the money and the gold was gone by the time I returned to the village two years later in 2009, and he was working for daily wages as a quality checker in the community's weaving unit (and sometimes as a research assistant to a visiting anthropologist). By 2011, my most recent visit, his once black hair had turned entirely white and he had accepted, he told me, that he was 'an old man'. He continued to survive on daily wages and on help from his younger brother, who had invested his share of their mother's inheritance in an autorickshaw business.

Discussion

Although I have only begun to scratch the surface of Das's life stories in the summary above, there is already sufficient detail to highlight important deviations from earlier accounts, and to illustrate some of the advantages of the research method proposed.

Firstly, in terms of throwing light on the broader subject matter – on the lived experience of leprosy – Das's story shows very clearly that while the onset of leprosy has very important implications for those affected by it, a specific focus on the disease, as is common in case-history accounts, downplays its interconnections with other factors, relationships and social institutions. Das's father's final departure from his family and Das's sudden move from the knitwear factory were certainly triggered by the discoveries that they had leprosy, but it was their existing propensity to abscond from difficult situations that made it a possibility of action in the first place, while other factors beyond a reaction to 'social stigma' – the pull of freedom and the known excitement of station life, in Das's case – made flight more of a probability.[9] Had they been women, for example, or had they been financially better off or, in his father's case, at least solvent, leprosy may not have led to their respective departures. Wider factors impact on how leprosy is experienced and managed at the level of the individual, then, and leprosy – in all its social and biological manifestations – is only one of the many prisms through which the lives of those affected by it are filtered.

The multilayered biographical accounts from leprosy-affected people that are so vital for telling us anything beyond the obvious about the experience of leprosy are also, necessarily, informative of much wider social experiences. Das's story also has something to tell us about how the categories of caste, class, gender and so on are experienced and reproduced through individual lives, and, importantly, about the intersections of these categories in individual people. In common with the essays in Arnold and Blackburn's (2004) collection on life histories in India, it shows that there is no mutually exclusive dichotomy between collectivity – the paradigm often associated with South Asian social life (cf. Marriott 1976) – and individuality, but a continuous interaction between the two poles (Arnold and Blackburn 2004: 5). As Watson puts it, apropos of South East Asia: 'Debate on categories of self in other societies turns not on denial that a sense of self exists, but on the recognition of the different perceptions that obtain among different cultures concerning the relations – psychological, moral, spiritual – between self and others within society' (2000: 134–35).

In terms of caste, for example, we learn that leprosy has changed how Das's relationships are constructed in relation to it: he married someone of lower caste status than in other circumstances would have been permitted by his family, let alone encouraged in the way it was. Das's frequent references to his Brahmin (and Tamil) heritage, however, offer strong evidence that caste remains important to him as a marker of identity and social status. Brahmin-ness, for him, manifests itself through the kinds of food he prefers to eat – vegetarian and without too many spices; meals, and even snacks, including particular varieties of food eaten in a particular order; the way he likes to drink coffee (from a small steel cup contained within a matching steel bowl); and in the ways he drew comparisons between himself and others. Expressing horror at his half-Madiga son's skill with a catapult, for example, he told me: 'Really, I am shocked about that. I never did anything like that: hunting, fishing, eating fish or mutton. But he does all these things. He'll catch fish by hand when they clear the fish pond, put them in his pocket and bring them home to his mother. And with the catapult he hits birds and other creatures, like a hunter! But then, his mother didn't know Brahmin ways ...'.

His caste identity was not just something he internalised, however, he felt it also made a difference in how people responded to him, and how, as a consequence, his life took shape. The fruit seller who helped him at the station, for example, trusted him, he said, because he 'spoke and looked like a nice Brahmin boy. I had a fair complexion – not like now – and good manners, so people were respectful'. In short, as it emerges in Das's story, caste is not just about relative ritual pollution and purity negated by leprosy – as a collectivist-type account might have it – but much more about personal identity and, in his relationships with other poor people, relative status.

Socio-economic class and, more specifically, poverty and social exclusion also overshadow much of Das's story, however, further detailing the wider context against which his leprosy is experienced. His family, despite his father's repeated attempts to run profitable businesses, was poor from the outset: virtually landless, victim to disease and premature death, and dependent on more economically secure relatives to bail them out. They existed on the peripheries of their community and wider kin group even before leprosy became a factor. Das, despite his caste consciousness, was very aware that he was not part of a ruling elite and that his immediate family were the 'poor relations' within his wider kinship group. He saw nothing odd or particularly unjust, for example, about his arrests without charge, or – even when he fought back one day and cracked open a police officer's head with an iron bar – about the everyday violence to which he and those living alongside him on the station platform were subjected. His leprosy status might have fed into his social exclusion and his acceptance of it, then, but it was also formed – as it was for most people I knew with leprosy – by a more general exclusion from power and economic resources. Poor people expected to be ill-treated by those in authority, and, for the most part, their strategies were about avoiding or managing that ill-treatment rather than confronting it head on.[10]

At the same time, Das's story also has much to say about what it was to come of age in urban India in the late 1960s and to be a man in a particular patriarchal society in the intervening years; about personhood and agency; and, related to this, a tendency towards passive acceptance. In relation to the latter, it was striking in Das's accounts how much he spoke of things happening or being done to him rather than by him as an agent of change. In part, this might have had something to do with linguistic categories. In Tamil, Das's mother tongue, emotions are often expressed intransitively, so rather than saying 'I am afraid', for example, the Tamil *ennakku payam* literally translates as 'to me there is fear'.[11] Dravidian modes of expression might also account for the somewhat stylised ways in which he recounted emotional experiences (cf. Appadurai 1990; Ramanujan 1974; Kakar 1997). Sadness, for example, was nearly always reified with the phrase '... and I cried for sometime'. The extent to which language literally shaped Das's experience of the world I do not know, but it was certainly the case that he did not attribute responsibility to himself for events in the way I might have interpreted them. His rising debts to the office during his tenure there, for example, were presented variously as the fault of the community's elders – who had pressurised him to buy them food and alcoholic drinks, which he could not put through the accounts; his wife's occasional purchase of jasmine for her hair from passing flower sellers; and, especially, the birth of his daughter. 'After she was born I had a lot of problems: that's when the drinking and everything happened', as he explained it. At times Das also invoked karma – the current consequences of events in previous lives – to account for events that were inexplicable without reference to his own actions. Although at other times Das also claimed not to believe in karma, it was, I would argue, embodied as a plausible, reflex response to the otherwise implausible.

What my work with Das has also made clear is the kind of historical perspective that accounts based only on participant observation in the present cannot provide. In this case, an individual's stories tell us not only about life for relatively poor, ordinary people in India since Independence in the second half of the twentieth century – stories otherwise mostly untold – but also show how well-reported, apparently critical events, like the state of emergency in the 1970s, or the tsunami in December 2004 are experienced and remembered by people on the ground. For most people, unless they are very directly involved in such occurrences, the events that make international press headlines remain relatively peripheral.[12] Das knew about the emergency, for example, but only mentioned it by name when pressed, and only loosely connected his incarcerations and his vasectomy operation with it. For him, casual police brutality and arrests were considered part and parcel of station life, and, as illustrated by the subsequent policy of rounding up those caught begging and putting them in residential homes that was going on in Hyderabad during our 2005–06 fieldwork, something that continued to affect marginalised people in the present. 'We weren't bothered about the government and politics and things like that', he told me, when I asked how the emergency had affected him. 'Maybe that's why things happened to us, but we didn't know much about what was going on outside, and why should we care?' The tsunami, too, and the international response to it became, in Das's accounts, a brief employment opportunity: 'This was a nice job for me', he said, 'I wasn't tied to one place, I got to travel around, take food outside, and meet new people. It was very interesting work'.

None of this, of course, is to posit a turn towards biographical interview at the expense of researchers actively immersing themselves in the lives of the wider communities of which their informants are a part – the 'hanging out' over time that is usually glossed as 'participant observation'. Indeed, my analysis of Das's biography is made possible only against the backdrop of prolonged ethnographic research in the village where he has spent most of his time over the past twenty-five years. Nevertheless, probing biographical interviews – which probe not through the aggressive questioning but through gentle persistence, and through creating contexts in which informants are less constrained by expectations of the time it should take to summarise their lives – offer unique lenses through which the interplay of social categories might be observed and better understood.

Das is not representative of every leprosy-affected man in India, still less of men more generally, but, as Margaret Mead argued long ago, all kinds of people – including those with physical impairments like Das – can still serve as perfect examples of life in their nations, 'provided that their individual position and individual characteristics are taken fully into account' (1953: 648; Frank 2000: 61).

Conclusion

Biographies are particularly useful for gathering and presenting ethnographic data, because they render otherwise dry material accessible to a wider audience than is otherwise likely. Life stories, because of the empathetic engagement they induce in their readers, can get across a sense of what it is or was like to live in a particular place at a particular time, in ways that are sometimes obscured in other genres. In short, the nitty-gritty of other people's lives can make compelling reading.

This is not, however, just a matter of style: a commitment to nuanced biographical accounts also has political implications. A focus on leprosy as the central element of the life stories of those I worked with – the focus that emerges through synoptic accounts – averts our gaze from the broader sociopolitical and economic contexts within which leprosy is experienced. Life before and after the disease in such accounts is presented almost uniformly as good, allowing those charged with the management of leprosy to frame solutions without reference to the wider conditions of people's existence in which the disease became a problem in the first place. The status quo is presented unproblematically as the positive state to which one might want to and should return. This might necessarily be the case for small NGOs, which do not have the resources to tackle what Farmer (1995) and others have called the 'structural violence' that shapes the lives of poor people, but as anthropologists we are required to explore further and deeper. Detailed life-story accounts – which capture, as Pat Caplan (this volume) puts it, both a life and a time – are particularly good at providing that wider context. In Das's case, as I hope to have shown, they illustrate how the onset of leprosy, as one of a range of factors that have shaped his life, was experienced and responded to against a backdrop of pre-existing poverty and social exclusion, as well as in relation to the dominant social categories of caste and gender.

Acknowledgement

An earlier version of this chapter appeared as 'Nuancing "Leprosy Stigma" through Ethnographic Biography in South India', *Leprosy Review* 82(2): 109–23.

Notes

1. A pseudonym. Other names have also been changed in this chapter to protect the identities of those referred to.
2. Classic exceptions to the lacuna include Freeman (1979), Moon (2001) and Desjarlais (2003).

3. 'Conversion narratives' of this kind are also part of a wider genre of South Asian storytelling, including the stories of Bhakti saints (Arnold and Blackburn 2004: 14), in nationalist discourse (Krishnadas 1951) and in the telling of ordinary lives (Desjarlais 2003: 118).

4. Linde (1993) argues that in creating our life stories we also create a narrative coherence, which does not exist in reality, but which is necessary in order to develop a coherent sense of ourselves. By taking informants' stories in parts, however – spread out over time – discrepant versions of the same person's life can also be allowed to coexist.

5. The Mahila Mandal is the community's women's society, and their building is used for their occasional meetings and for various small-scale income generation projects, such as the stitching of cosmetics bags for an export order.

6. Das was also a keen viewer of Tamil and Telugu popular cinema, as well as an avid reader – at least on train journeys – of Tamil detective novellas.

7. Tamil Brahmins I met were often very proud of their caste identities. As one professor of Indian anthropology recently told me: 'You'll always know when someone's a Tamil Brahmin within ten minutes of meeting them: they'll find a way of telling you!'

8. Although marriage is ideally virilocal, there were many instances in my field notes of marriages that did not, for a variety of reasons, conform to this norm.

9. See also Hacking's (1998) notion of an 'ecological niche', when the convergence of particular factors at particular points in history makes possible or likely certain social phenomena that might disappear at other junctures in history.

10. This is not to suggest, as Moffatt (1979) argued (supported by the analyses of, among others, Hocart (1950) and Dumont (1980)) that the disenfranchised in India are necessarily in consensus with the system. However, except for in cases where they have organised themselves collectively – as in Dalit protest movements or in leprosy colonies – they were realistic about their capacity to bring about change and 'adjusted' – to use a popular phrase among my informants – to their situations accordingly.

11. I am grateful for David Mosse (personal communication, 1999) for pointing this out during discussions about my original 1999–2000 fieldwork.

12. See, for example, Edward Simpson's (2009) work on how events that appear to the world as extraordinary – such as the Gujarat earthquake in 2001 – are often experienced in very ordinary ways for those who live through them.

References

Appadurai, A. 1990. 'Topographies of the Self: Praise and Emotion in Hindu India', in A C. Lutz and L. Abu-Lughod (eds), *Language and the Politics of Emotion*. Cambridge: Cambridge University Press, pp. 92–112.

Arnold, D. and S. Blackburn. 2004. 'Introduction: Life Histories in India', in D. Arnold and S. Blackburn (eds), *Telling Lives in India: Biography, Autobiography and Life History*. Bloomington: Indiana University Press, pp. 1–28.

Bloch, M. 1998. 'Autobiographical Memory and the Historical Memory of the More Distant Past', in *How We Think They Think: Anthropological Approaches to Cognition, Memory and Literacy*. Oxford: Westview Press, pp. 114–27.

Desjarlais, R. 2003. *Sensory Biographies: Lives and Deaths among Nepal's Yolmo Buddhists*. Berkeley: University of California Press.

Dumont, L. 1980. *Homo Hierarchicus: The Caste System and its Implications*. Chicago and London: The University of Chicago Press.

Farmer, P. 2005. *Pathologies of Power: Health, Human Rights, and the New War on the Poor*. Berkeley: University of California Press.

Frank, G. 1995. 'Anthropology and Individual Lives: The Story of the Life History and the Life History of the Story', *American Anthropologist* 97: 145–48.

———. 2000. *Venus on Wheels: Two Decades of Dialogue on Disability, Biography and Being Female in America*. Berkeley: University of California Press.

Freeman, J.M. 1979. *Untouchable: An Indian Life History*. London: Allen and Unwin.

Hacking, I. 1998. *Mad Travelers: Reflections on the Reality of Transient Mental Illnesses*. Cambridge, MA: Harvard University Press.

Hocart, A.M. 1950. *Caste: A Comparative Study*. London: Methuen.

Holy, L. and M. Stuchlik. 1983. *Actions, Norms and Representations: Foundations of Anthropological Inquiry*. Cambridge: Cambridge University Press.

Kakar, S. 1997. *Culture and Psyche: Selected Essays*. Delhi: Oxford University Press.

Krishnadas. 1951. *Seven Months with Mahatma Gandhi*. Ahmedabad: Navajivan Press.

Linde, C. 1993. *Life Stories: The Creation of Coherence*. New York: Oxford University Press.

Marriott, M. 1976. 'Hindu Transactions: Diversity without Dualism', in B. Kapferer (ed.), *Transaction and Meaning: Directions in the Anthropology of Exchange and Symbolic Behaviour*. Philadelphia: Institute for the Study of Human Issues, pp. 109–42.

Mead, M. 1953. 'National Character', in A.L. Kroeber (ed.), *Anthropology Today*. Chicago: Chicago University Press, pp. 642–67.

Moffatt, M. 1979. *An Untouchable Community in South India*. Princeton: University Press.

Moon, V. 2001. *Growing Up Untouchable in India: A Dalit Autobiography*. Lanham, MD: Rowan and Littlefield.

Niehaus, I. 2006. 'Biographical Lessons: Life Stories, Sex and Culture in Bushbuckridge, South Africa', *Cahiers d'Etudes Africaines* 1(181): 51–73.

Parry, J. 2004. 'The Marital History of "A Thumb-Impression Man"', in D. Arnold and S. Blackburn (eds), *Telling Lives in India: Biography, Autobiography and Life History*. Bloomington: Indiana University Press, pp. 281–318.

Peacock, J.L. and D.C. Holland. 1993. 'The Narrated Self: Life Stories in Process', *Ethos* 21(4): 367–83.

Ramanujan, A.K. 1974. 'Indian Poetics: An Overview', in E. Dimock (ed.), *The Literatures of India: An Introduction*. Chicago: University of Chicago Press, pp. 115–18.

Rosenwald, G.C. and R.L. Ochberg. 1992. *Storied Lives: The Cultural Politics of Self-Understanding*. New Haven: Yale University Press.

Simpson, E. 2009. 'The Anthropology of Catastrophe', *Brunel Anthropology Research Seminar*, 3 December 2009.

Staples, J. 2007. *Peculiar People, Amazing Lives*. Delhi: Orient Longman.

———. 2014. *Leprosy and a Life in South India: Journeys with a Tamil Brahmin*. Lanham, MD: Lexington Books.

Swarup, V. 2005. *Q & A*. New York: Scribner.

Watson, C. W. 2000. *Of Self and Nation: Autobiography and the Representation of Modern Indonesia*. Honolulu: University of Hawaii Press.

Chapter 4

FINDING MY WIT

EXPLAINING BANTER AND MAKING THE EFFORTLESS APPEAR IN THE UNSTRUCTURED INTERVIEW

Katherine Smith

The ways in which joking relationships are forged and maintained are still relatively understudied aspects of social life. Joking relationships and the kinds of humour that may be involved in them are not always easy to capture or identify unless they are explained, which tends to demystify their purpose. It is not uncommon to hear the claim that the more one attempts to explain a joke, the less amusing that joke becomes. When the mechanics and mystification of a joke or joking behaviour become exposed through explanation, the intended message and responses take on a different form, and the situation in which the joke was told and the content of the joke are, usually, not humorous anymore. This chapter explores the ways in which the unexplained, quick-witted banter between members of Starlings social club in an area of north Manchester that I have called elsewhere 'Halleigh' (Smith 2012a) was explained in unstructured interviews. It explores both the ways in which an interview context was created in order to provide a space in which to demystify practices that usually evade common practices of literalisation, and to clarify ways in which an outsider may relate and forge a meaningful relationship with the regulars at Starlings through engaging in derogatory banter.

The forging of close relationships in Starlings, the sense of familiarity between individuals and (re)constructions of belonging and 'otherness' were continuously maintained through what individuals in Starlings would refer to as 'having a barter' (as opposed to 'banter'). Similar in many ways to the earlier works of A.R. Radcliffe-Brown (1940) and Max Gluckman (1960) on joking relations in Africa, having a barter involves the exchange of insults in conversation, sometimes very derogatory, but quick-witted insults that must be 'taken in the spirit that they are intended'. Ideally, insults are exchanged in the spirit of not taking offence, but also as a means of affirming the initial speaker's knowledge of the intentions of others. The intentions of others are assumed to be 'harmless' even though they appear as derogatory insults. The more or less derogatory and potentially offensive the comment demonstrates degrees of familiarity between people. In the context of a social club this is a way of relating and maintaining social bonds that was reflexively described by people in Starlings as 'politically incorrect' and thus silenced in wider social contexts.

This chapter is intended to go some way into explaining the inexplicable through exploring how having a barter serves a social and individual purpose in the establishing and maintaining of the 'life projects' (Rapport 2003, 2006) of individual members of Starlings, as well as about how I became privy to a particular 'insider' understanding of the mechanics and language of having a barter through the ethnographic interview. It goes on to demonstrate that the ethnographic, unstructured interview in Starlings was more than a privileged space in which I, as a researcher, could gain access to explanations that would otherwise and necessarily go 'unsaid'. The interview context, set apart from the other activity happening in Starlings, became, then, a space within which social problems were discussed, and people could situate themselves and others along boundaries of who to have a barter with and who not to, in the first place. The distinctiveness of the ethnographic interview, and its demarcation as something 'else' and different happening in Starlings allowed for the demystification of having a barter to happen. I was then able to put my newly acquired knowledge of having a barter into practice in Starlings.

Having a barter provides a sort of 'privileged zone' (Boon 1972; see also Chock 1987) within which ideas of belonging and otherness operate and are maintained through important exchanges of feigned anger or animosity expressed through socially evocative tropes, inexplicit intentions and structured relations. If a person is perceived potentially to take offence, they were not given the opportunity to enter into this kind of conversational exchange. Quite simply, one would not have a barter with an unfamiliar person. Responses to having a barter were, then, imaginatively transposed onto regional and even national levels.[1] The implications of carrying out unstructured interviews involve a new kind of understanding about how processes of differentiation are facilitated through having a barter, and why unfamiliar people, and people who may be locally perceived not to take the language in the spirit in which it is intended, are not socially 'integrated' as they are not included in this form of relating. The questions I asked in interviews in Starlings were performative marks on a line past which everyday conversation does not normally tread. But in so doing, worlds of practice on national, regional, local and personal levels were opened up.

Interviews in Starlings

Halleigh is an area of north Manchester that is commonly referred to as a 'working class' area situated four miles north of Manchester city centre in the north of England. It comprises a series of social housing estates, and at the time of my fieldwork (June 2006–June 2007) was a predominately 'white', 'English' area (ca. 11,000 residents). Starlings, an ex-working men's club, still required regular customers to become members by paying an annual subscription of £4.00, and the members would then 'own' the social club cooperatively. Inside Starlings, the snooker room, which included two snooker tables, and the main room, which included the bar, a dance floor and a stage, were filled with cigarette smoke, laughter and loud voices during opening hours. I worked behind the bar at Starlings and came to know a group of regulars, particularly members of the Starlings ladies' darts team. This group of nine women were all 'born and bred' in Halleigh and had known each other for most of, if not all of, their lives. They were also the ones I would go to in order to ask the questions that I felt to be awkward and needed more explanation than I could tease out of a particular moment. As the 'American', 'anthro-something researcher' or 'doe-eyed Yank', as I was often referred to in Starlings, I was permitted to ask questions that I would quickly learn were perceived by the regulars to be humorously naive. Most of the women in the ladies' darts team were mothers and wives and aged between thirty and forty years old. When I worked behind the bar in the evenings at Starlings, it would always be alongside one of the members of the ladies' darts team. The casual work over time allowed a way for me to come to know and forge relationships with the women, who are still very good friends. It also meant that I had both roles as researcher and as bartender (or 'barmaid') and the members of the ladies' darts team were often keen to facilitate my movement between these two roles. I would go to them to ask about and discuss my methodological choices and things that happened or that I had noticed but could not recognise or contextualise. They would often intervene in my research and tell me who to interview, what kind of questions to ask and how to behave in a certain situation that they anticipated I might not fully understand.

When I followed the advice and direction of the ladies' darts team, most of the interviews that I carried out in Starlings were unstructured. In the day-to-day life of Starlings, the unstructured interview was a way to be opportunistic, as it provided a space to respond to the 'twists and turns of a conversation' (Skinner 2010: 115), and to respond on the spur of the moment. They would often set up interviews for me, and talk about the interview to other regulars, as if there was a mutual benefit that could come from it: someone would be able to speak about something openly, freely, without perceived judgement and there was a consciousness raised in Starlings about how the potential outcome of this research could also play a part in challenging wider social preconceptions about the lives and relationships of the people in Halleigh. Negative stereotypical connotations attached to the idea of being a 'white', 'working class' 'English' person were a preoccupation and shared concern for many people throughout Halleigh. There was a common fear that the term 'working class' can be used to call someone 'scum' and that being a 'white', 'working class' English person from an area like Halleigh would fix its residents in misleading and unfair representations of them as a 'type' of person to expect from such an area (see Smith 2012a). Starlings was a space within which these concerns could be raised, challenged and subverted through having a barter.

When I took notes in my notebook it was often because I noticed something said or something someone had done that I did not understand or could not recognise. My note-taking was intermittent. I would keep my notebook behind the bar and grab it to write down some notes to remember. The unstructured interview, then, was also an opportunity for me to unpack and ask questions about the jotted notes I would take throughout the night.

During a ladies' darts team tournament in Starlings one evening, around Christmas time in 2006, I noticed two members of opposing teams, Maria and Lois, shouting at one another. Maria and Lois were competing against one another in the tournament. Lois was wearing a festive, white top hat, on the top of which stood two small green Christmas trees and a snowman. Their conversation was about Lois' top hat. Maria wanted to know where Lois had purchased it. As they spoke to and shouted at one another, I frantically scribbled parts of their conversation in my notebook.

Maria	Where'd you get your hat from, trollop?
Lois	I'm not telling you. You'll go out and fucking get one!
Maria	Oh, stick it up your arse!
Lois	I can't. It has prickly trees on top.
Maria	You're used to sticking prickly things in your arse!
Lois	Don't start picking on me because I can't defend myself!
Maria	Where'd you get your fucking hat from, trollop?! (Maria's voice became louder)
Lois	Harpurhey! Now, fuck off! (Harpurhey is a town, not a shop, which is what Maria wanted to know in the first place.)
Maria	Oh, fuck off!
Lois	B&M! (The shop in Harpurhey) Now, kiss my left-wing arse!

Maria and Lois' rapid responses to one another sounded effortless and there was visibly a pleasure derived both in the effortlessness as well as the exchange and laughter from the rest of the ladies' darts team. Because of the speed at which their insults were delivered and the wit required, it appeared, on the surface, as though it was a sort of second nature, delivered socially, as if the thoughts expressed in their verbal exchange of insults were there to be accessed easily and effortlessly. While Maria and Lois did not laugh, the laughter of others propelled their exchange. It continued with little bursts between Maria and Lois throughout the evening, followed by fits of laughter from other team members. Significantly, after this conversation, I learned from Bernice, another member of the ladies' darts team, that Maria and Lois had known each other since childhood and were the best of friends.

This form of verbal engagement was not an isolated incident or exchange (cf. Leveen 1996: 30) but very much part of everyday conversation occurring in Starlings and in other contexts throughout Halleigh. Maria and Lois' exchanges were more than a kind of testing of the boundaries of their friendship. This exchange was at once particular to them because of their lifelong friendship, as well as a performance to show the others that bond, giving an opportunity to identify and show an understanding of having a barter by responding with laughter and not taking offence.

This kind of banter, when explained out of context, appears familiar. Indeed, when I lecture on this topic in the classroom now, I hear knee-jerk responses from students who feel they are quite familiar with this kind of banter and derogatory exchange between friends. It is not uncommon to hear of friends establishing, pushing and testing the boundaries of friendships through the exchange of insults. An interesting comparative example of joking relationships can be found in the work of Les Back (1996), who illustrates how young men in a London estate, which he called 'Riverview', negotiated the alterations of the meanings of insults or 'wind-ups' through what he called 'duelling play' in Riverview's youth clubs (Back 1996: 74). Back explained that this negotiated alteration dislocates practice from what it 'stands for' in wider usage, and polices the sensitive lines of significance in relationships. Through this process of creating 'sham conflicts' the boundaries of friends and extra-kin associations are negotiated (1996: 74). Back used transcribed interviews of the 'exchanges' and showed how the boundaries of tolerance within dyadic friendships are intended to also demarcate those who are included and excluded in a group in a 'play context' (1996: 75). This is not unlike what I had noticed in Starlings and, here, between Maria and Lois. However, the process through which I came to an understanding of this dynamic, through the unstructured interview, and the particularities of this kind of exchange in Starlings, provided an inroad for an understanding of this kind of banter, how I might participate in it and a significant way to 'belong'.

When I first began working in Starlings, I noticed that the language the regulars would use with each other differed from the ways in which they would speak to me. Their language was more polite, more formalised, when I first began to work behind the bar. This was not surprising, and is something that other anthropologists have encountered in their research (see for example, Hendry 1992: 166–67). But the significance of this difference was in both the ways in which I came to be included in the same kind of conversation through the unstructured interview and what this difference might tell us about wider social relations and the exclusion of unfamiliar individuals and groups of people. The quick-witted slinging of insults back and forth in everyday conversations in Starlings was not only less formal than the way they would speak to me at the beginning of my fieldwork, but also they simultaneously demonstrated a profound knowledge of the personalities and everyday lives of each other through knowing who to pick on, what to insult and how derogatory they can be. In order to participate in having a barter and practise a particular knowledge about how to 'belong', I wanted to ask questions about what had happened between Maria and Lois.

I first asked Bernice and Janet, two members of the ladies' darts team, about what had happened between Maria and Lois. Bernice, Janet and I got our drinks, and we sat down together at a table. Importantly, they knew I was going to ask questions about the 'type of humour', as I referred to it at the time, that I noticed in Starlings. And so they chose a table at the far end of Starlings, away from the majority of people. This was going to be 'an interview'. 'Katie's going to ask us some questions for her work. She wants to know about how we take the piss', Bernice announced to the others around the bar. This comment was met with jocular remarks from others: 'Bloody hell! Bernice, tell her fuck off. That'll teach her!'

As we sat down in our separated space out of earshot of the others in Starlings, Bernice and Janet began by asking each other how to explain it to me.

Bernice	Well, it basically means just having a barter, doesn't it?
Janet	Yeah, it's just the way we are. We take the piss.
Bernice	It isn't really insults. Well, it is, but we just like to have a laugh. We just wind each other up. No one gets offended or anything. We just all sort of know that it's just a laugh, you know?
Katie	Did you say having a barter or having a banter?
Janet	No, no.
Bernice	No, having a barter. That's just what we call it. I don't know where it came from, really. But it's just like when, you know, someone says they were having a nice day before seeing you. You know? You laugh because you take it in the spirit it's intended. That's all it's about, really.
Janet	Yeah, you can't get offended by it. It's just someone trying to wind you up. I guess when other people hear it, it must shock them, really. I guess it's something that we just do because we've known each other for so long. We know we can do it and we just get on with it, you know? There's no harm behind it.
Bernice	No, you have to take it in the spirit it's intended. Otherwise, we'll become bullies! People would hate us, and then we'd probably hate them because they took it the wrong way. So, you know, sometimes we just don't do it because it's not meant to offend anyone, but I'm sure that if someone didn't know us, it would do. I mean, I don't know, maybe they wouldn't. You just don't want to offend anyone, especially nowadays when it could be taken as something really bad.

Bernice is raising a common local concern with the sense of unfairness in how people in Halleigh, as a collective, are portrayed and represented in the media and by government, as 'white', 'working class', 'scum' (see, Smith 2012a, 2012b) and the fear that this particular way of relating and establishing relationships reaffirms particular social understandings of the white working classes in Britain, as opposed to the viability and morality of the person. As individuals, people in Halleigh felt defined by others in terms of their location – the kind of place in which they lived – and that they were situated within the rigid, undermining and negative framework of the 'white working classes'. Categories, or, as many people in Halleigh referred to them, 'labels' imposed from the outside, simplified and solidified the realities of everyday subjectivities, positionings and locations of individuals (Smith 2012b). The irony of stereotypes is that they gain significance through performance (Chock 1987). The feigned aggression as a performative aspect of having a barter was reflexively referred to as politically incorrect and thus potentially problematic in wider social settings. Tendencies towards racism, violence and segregation are locally perceived to be what is expected of residents of areas such as Halleigh – an expectation they know to be profoundly unfair. The conversation continued:

Janet	You don't want to end up in jail or in a riot! No, you just know when you can just sit back and have a good old natter and have a barter with someone and when you probably should just watch what you say. Like, I don't have a barter with anyone at my work.
Bernice	No, but you have different situations, don't you?
Janet	Well, yeah. You could lose your job. You could get a complaint put in about you. You just don't know. But there are a couple of people in work who I can joke like that with, but we don't do it often and no one really hears it. It's mostly just at home or in Starlings or somewhere like that.
Bernice	But in Starlings, you know we work here too. But it's different.
Katie	Why is it different?
Bernice	Because we know everyone here. We've known everyone here for donkey's years. You just know because they say things to you and you have a laugh. You say things to them, they have a laugh. You have to laugh at yourself! You have to; it's just what we do. And it can be anything!
Janet	Yeah, did you hear Tiffany and Maria the other day? Imagine that at work!
	[Laughter]
Bernice	Well, yeah, but those two are at each other's throats like a couple of fucking terriers anyway! No, they are, but then you know that they would do anything for each other. You know Maria would kill anyone picking on Tiffany.
Janet	Yeah, only we can pick on Tiffany!

This impromptu unstructured interview provided a space within which a largely taken-for-granted assumption could then be explained, a space within which I was given a knowledge and understanding of ways of relating that go without everyday explanation. Bernice and Janet's questioning of each other and their explanations of examples of when one should and should not have a barter necessarily created a transformational space within which I was privy to a conversation, and I crossed over from an outsider to an insider. When a person begins to have a barter with someone, several things are being pointed to, practised and performed at once: they are testing and maintaining the boundaries of their relationship, engaging in a specific and locally known act, (re)establishing and enacting a way of belonging in Starlings and they are expressing the understanding that the other person will take the insults in the spirit in which they are intended, that there is a shared aesthetics of humour and that the relationship is already strong enough to be tested.

My attempts at participating in having a barter in Starlings were, at first, slow and proved to be humorous in and of themselves because of my feeble retorts. I was slow to think of an insult to respond with. It required much effort on my part to think of something to say quickly, and that effort slowed me down. As I was getting to know people, I lacked the depth of knowledge about others that they had among themselves, so I was stuck with drawing on common, usual insults that lacked the punch of those I would receive. However, through using this form of humour over time, I noticed subtle changes in the way people would speak to me. Despite the fact that I found having a barter and the returning of insults quite difficult to begin with, when I found myself in situations where someone would yell something to the effect of, 'Yank, get me a pint, you lazy so-and-so', as long as I responded with any insult, however pale in comparison, people would laugh and continue to insult me, which I readily welcomed as complimentary. Through routine practice, and the ways in which people began to speak to me, I became aware that my familiarity with others and vice versa had become noticeable to others. Through demonstrating a commitment to their dialogue and paying attention to the stories and experiences of others so that I had knowledge of what I can pick on, I was also taking the local sense of humour in the 'spirit in which it is intended' (cf. Gottlieb and La Belle 1990). Once this became socially recognised, my status as an active member in their group changed.

Personalism and the Re-purposing of Language

Starlings is open to the public, but members must sign non-members in as guests and the guest should pay £1.50 on entry to the social club. It was not uncommon to see the occasional guest being signed in with a member, but most of the time 'regular guests' did not formally sign in. The degree of familiarity members of the social club had with visitors was often expressed through whether or not they were asked to sign in.

When an unfamiliar guest did once come into Starlings and was not accompanied by a member, he was not asked to sign in or for an entry fee; he entered to be greeted with a brief moment of silence. He was a thirty-something black man with a Manchester accent. He was on his own. It would turn out later that he was waiting for two of his friends, also unfamiliar guests, to join him for a pint. His entrance and presence at the bar changed the conversations going on around us. It was a noticeable change, a somewhat awkward moment with the conversations stopping. I could see that he noticed it and he could see that I noticed it too. I asked him what he would like to drink. He chuckled and said to me without hesitation: 'A pint of your finest, and you better fucking run while you're at it, chicken wings'. I quickly responded by telling him to 'fuck off'. Everyone around the bar was listening to our quick exchange. The silence around the bar upon his entrance served as a prompt to have a barter with me. The way he spoke to me in his thick Manchester accent appeared effortless, as though he had already known me and knew what to pick on. It felt as though it was an opportunity for me to both perform that I belonged there and involve this new person in the group, as well as an opportunity for him to influence how he might be perceived in Starlings. After our quick exchange, the conversations that were happening around us recommenced after a brief bout of laughter. His performance had a profound impact on his acceptance in Starlings, and people who were eager to glean more information about who he was, where he came from and why he was in Starlings quickly surrounded him.

Knowledge and ideas are made available not simply through varieties of talk and text, but also through their absences (Hill 2008: 32). The brief moment of silence that occurred when the guest entered Starlings triggered a moment where inferences could be made about his awareness and understanding of the people in Starlings as well as his intentions with his insult directed towards me. Unlike what Back (1996) came to know in Riverdale about the 'duelling play' in youth clubs, people in Starlings social club only have a barter with people they perceive will not take offence. The social pressures surrounding individuals not presuming to know the intentions of others is regulated through the processes of having a barter. In other words, groups and social statuses in Starlings are regulated and checked through the expected acceptance of insults given; once returned, the insults indirectly place within a group context the status and the inclusion of the individual in a particular form of relating and understanding.

Significantly, this unfamiliar man approached the bar in silence. When he spoke, his accent and language were instantly familiar to those around him. His identification as a 'black', unfamiliar 'other' was interrupted by his accent, a socially indexical language form, and what he actually said, having a barter. The language he was using was at once the medium of the social production of familiarity but also its object (Bucholtz 2001: 229), and his accent was his performance of that familiarity. That this person was an unfamiliar black man who had never been in Starlings before, and the silence and unease his presence caused in Starlings, was trumped by his apparent knowledge of how to behave in a place like Starlings. He may or may not have known that what he instigated with me was 'having a barter', but that he performed a familiar exchange said more to the others in Starlings than the exchange itself.

As I mentioned above, Halleigh was a predominantly 'white' 'English' and 'working class' area of north Manchester. Over ten years ago, the National Front (NF) had a strong presence in Halleigh. Local concern with the history of Halleigh feeds the shock that most people feel when they are accused of being racist today (Smith 2012a; cf. Wieviorka 1997: 140). This history, of the local presence of the NF, is felt to have left residues of racial intolerance, which wrongly characterises the neighbourhood and its residents (Smith 2012b). Having a barter involves insults, slurs and other aspersions that might include racial and ethnic overtones and be perceived as offensive language in other social contexts, and so is highly monitored by people in Starlings. The brief exchange that the new guest and I performed in front of the bar that day in Starlings made explicit our interested positions in engaging in relationships beyond the two of us, including others in Starlings.

The tension between what the language appears to denote and the actual intentions of the speaker is a tension that linguistic anthropologist Jane Hill (2008) has argued feeds into a form of violence: 'words can wound' despite the personal intentions of the speaker. She explores in great depth the ways in which folk theories of race and racism are perpetuated by the notion that racism is entirely a matter of individual beliefs, intensions and actions, and that this ignorance can be 'cured by education'. If this were the case, she argues, racism should soon disappear entirely, except as a sign of mental derangement or disability (2008: 6). But since this is not the case, and since the problem of racism is persistent, she argues that there needs to be a move away from thinking of racism as entirely a matter of individual beliefs and psychological states, what she refers to briefly as 'personalism'. She does not deny that personalism figures in racism, but a crucial way to combat racism and its effects is a refiguring and awareness of the language and terms we use. She argues, 'racist effects can be produced in interaction, in an intersubjective space of discourse, without any single person in the interaction intending discrimination' (2008: 7). It is in and through the use and reappropriation of racist language that racism and discrimination persists because '[r]acist labels shape fundamental perceptions' (2008: 12). However, since such labels do 'shape perceptions', as opposed to being merely a level of verbal expression, then 'personal beliefs' do come into it. Since she argues that 'utterances are acts' (following Austin (1962) and Searle (1969)), she condemns the reappropriation of slurs, gaffes and slang terms, because they can be experienced as physical assaults, having the effect of genuine bodily pain (2008: 55).

Understanding injurious language as posing an ethical question about what kind of language we ought to use raises further questions about what it might mean when the one who uses it is not responsible for that usage. Judith Butler (1997) has pointed out that the circulation of derogatory terms also makes them continually available for reappropriation and that the one who reinvigorates such terms and hate speech re-establishes contexts of hate and injury. However, she raises the provocative question of whether a form of censorship is exercised when the intentions of the speaker are not taken into account. She asks: 'As we call for the regulation of injurious speech on the basis of "universally" accepted presuppositions, do we reiterate practices of exclusion and inclusion?' (1997: 90). If a 'community' is constituted through a particular kind of exclusionary language, how shall we trust it to deliberate on the question of that language? These are not rhetorical questions but ones that raise the issue of personalism, in terms of the human dignity of each person, and shifts the focus from speech to action, conversation and meaning, going beyond literary analysis to the dynamic dialectics within which levels of communication are (re)produced and maintained.

Having a barter is a 'performative contradiction' (Butler 1997: 89) in that the terms and language that a speaker may use in the context of Starlings are not meant to express their true beliefs. While they may point to actual events, aspects of an individual's appearance or behaviour, they are also pointing to what is normally silenced in wider social contexts and raises local frustrations with notions of politically correct language. What is interesting here is that the unfamiliar guest who came into Starlings established his right to 'belong' there precisely by engaging in (gender-biased) un-politically correct language. Subject positions are, of course, different from social positions. What having a barter points to is the tension between the two. Social positions are based on structural organisation such as class, race and gender, which circumscribe and access movement into certain subject positions (Skeggs 1997: 12). Taking into account what is expected from a person in Starlings reveals and challenges what is and is not expected of them in other contexts.

A departure from personalism may involve the 'baited indirectness' of what is said (Morgan 2001); the hearer must respond to the references made in an insult but respond to that insult in a particular way, establishing the meaning of the exchange. If we look at simply the terms that are spoken, taking into account what they are referring to themselves, meaning is still meaning, but not what is intended. What the unstructured interviews in Starlings with members of the ladies' darts team, and particularly with Bernice and Janet, show us is that having a barter is very much about the intentions of the speaker, the anticipated response and thus the transformation of what is normally perceived as insults in wider social usage.

There is a local fear of reaffirming a common local perception of the assertiveness of, and a sort of alliance between, the white middle classes and ethnic others in producing stereotypical assumptions about white, working-class groups of people who are from places such as Halleigh, which is talked of locally as 'political correctness gone mad', referring to a common perception that there is a sort of alliance between policy makers and the individuals they racialise through their policy that puts unnecessary restrictions on certain forms of communication and individual expression, such as having a barter. The effects of social categorisation were profoundly unsettling of people's own local understanding and expressions of who they were, where they 'belonged' and what their Englishness was all about (Smith 2012b). This crisis of confidence in local discourses of 'us' and 'them' was expressed through the monitoring and silencing of ways of relating that involve making a connection between circumstances and how one thinks, and expressing those thoughts in interaction.

To play with and transform the meanings of naturalised, taken-for-granted terms and ideas while at the same time maintaining exclusive relationships through the transformation of terms is why having a barter is so distinctive in Starlings. The distinctiveness of having a barter does not rely on 'formal' and 'informal' contexts, but on the awareness and understanding of the participants about one another (cf. Strathern 2004). That an unfamiliar guest in Starlings can break the silence by being aware of and initiating this kind of exchange reaffirmed to the regulars why they behave the way they do. My quick(ish) response to the guest's insult further demonstrated both his intentions and mine in not taking offence, and that there are boundaries there to be played with.

The unstructured interviews gave the game away. My own participation in having a barter was shaped and refined through both learning and practice in the context of the unstructured interview. The dense intersections of perception, performance and explanation were selectively made and made explicit in the interview context so that I could find my wit and participate in the expression of difference, distinctiveness and belonging through having a barter.

Conclusion

Unlike life stories, where we expect a degree of intimacy so that as we get to know a person we might expect more and more detailed life stories to be exchanged (see Staples, this volume; Linde 1993: 7), the ways in which what is already assumed about another person when having a barter determines levels of intimacy and demonstrates an awareness of the attitudes and intentions of others. Equally, there is an implicit understanding of wider social inclinations about political perspectives, and understandings about how one's social universe has and is changing over the years.

As Rapport has argued elsewhere, it is in 'the tension between form and content [that we can find] convenient ambiguities: one can always deny (to oneself and others) the content and the extent of what one has publicly asserted or claimed' (2008: 285). On the surface, these moments of conversational exchange in having a barter can be misleading, as participants necessarily evoke kinds of language that are provocative and essentialising. The social issues played with in having a barter are necessarily ones which can be taken with offence: one draws on insults to reaffirm and deepen interpersonal relationships (cf. Rapport 2008). The re-purposing of language in Starlings partly involves the acknowledgement that certain kinds of language can 'wound' and/or be perceived as offensive. The potentiality of this kind of language is what gives it its potency in having a barter. The problematics that Hill (2008) and Butler (1997) raise about the perpetuation of the historical legacies of injurious language and particular tropes, such as slurs and gaffes, are both reaffirmed and challenged through the directed exchange of having a barter. The language must be offensive in wider social contexts to have potency in having a barter in Starlings. What is significant in an understanding of what is actually happening in having a barter is in the direction that they take, as people direct insults at particular individuals, monitor the context in which it occurs and assess and maintain degrees of familiarity. When an unfamiliar guest in Starlings decided to evoke this kind of language and initiate an exchange of insults, he was making extra-discursive reference to the people around him and to himself as belonging there, in Starlings.

It is in the monitoring and the intended direction of the participants in having a barter that degrees of intentionality take shape. It was in and through the unstructured interview that I began to acquire an awareness of this practice and process. The unstructured interviews I had with members of the ladies' darts team and particularly Bernice and Janet were each a 'conversation with a purpose' (Robson 1993: 228; see also Skinner 2010). But it was during unstructured interviews in Starlings that I was instructed, to the bewilderment of my co-conversationalists, that 'all conversations have purposes' and that the significance of having a barter in Starlings is that the intentionalities of the speakers and listeners are necessarily unspoken but could then be made explicit in the unstructured interview context.

However, the unstructured interviews I would have with, particularly, Bernice and Janet about what having a barter is all about were marked and determined as separate from others within Starlings. The interview happened in a constructed space, set aside from other social gatherings. It was a privileged space, co-created, where I could become privy to insider, often unspoken, knowledge. And it was a space within which people could define themselves through explanations of the extra-discursive parts of themselves as particular kinds of people who do not take offence. Additionally, locally perceived social problems and frustrations were spoken about freely so that speakers could situate themselves along socially constructed boundaries. Explaining having a barter in this context of the unstructured interview became a conversation in a differentiated context and so an interruption from the flow of social life otherwise carrying on in Starlings – an interruption that would have particular inclusive outcomes for social life in Starlings.

Acknowledgements

This chapter has benefited from gracious and incisive comments from my colleagues Tony Simpson, Madeleine Reeves and Michelle Obeid at the University of Manchester and from my co-editors of this volume. I am especially grateful for the many conversations and experiences that the people in the social club that I have called 'Starlings' have shared with me, to all of whom I owe thanks.

Notes

1. Local imaginations of who would not take having a barter in the spirit that it is intended feed into local discourses of belonging and otherness, immigration, and nationalism, as issues of race and ethnicity become more and more contentious in having a barter. Exploring the ways in which people make assumptions about the intentions of others and the reception of having a barter is but one way to explore discourses of race and ethnicity more widely.

References

Austin, J.L. 1962. *How to Do Things with Words*. Oxford: Clarendon Press.

Back, L. 1996. *New Ethnicities and Urban Culture: Racisms and Multiculture in Young Lives*. London: UCL Press.

Boon, J.A. 1972. 'Further Operations of "Culture" in Anthropology: A Synthesis of and for Debate', *Social Sciences Quarterly* 53(2): 221–52.

Bucholtz, M. 2001. 'Play, Identity and Linguistic Representation in the Performance of Accent: Proceedings from the Ninth Annual Symposium of Language and Society', *Texas Linguistic Forum* 44(2): 227–51.

Butler, J. 1997. *Excitable Speech: A Politics of the Performative*. London: Routledge.

Chock, P.P. 1987. 'The Irony of Stereotypes: Toward an Anthropology of Ethnicity', *Cultural Anthropology* 2(3): 347–68.

Gluckman, M. 1960. 'Tribalism in Modern British Central Africa', *Cahiers d'Études Africaines* 1(1): 55–70.

Gottlieb, E.E. and T.J. La Belle. 1990. 'Ethnographic Contextualisation of Freire's Discourse: Conscious-Raising, Theory and Practice', *Anthropology and Education Quarterly* 21(1): 3–18.

Hendry, J. 1992. 'The Paradox of Friendship in the Field: Analysis of a Long-Term Anglo-Japanese Relationship', in J. Okely and H. Callaway (eds), *Anthropology and Autobiography*. New York: Routledge, pp. 163–74.

Hill, J. 2008. *The Everyday Language of White Racism*. Oxford: Blackwell Publishing.

Leveen, L. 1996. 'Only When I Laugh: Textual Dynamics of Ethnic Humour', *MELUS* 21(4): 29–55.

Linde, C. 1993. *Life Stories: The Creation of Coherence*. Oxford: Oxford University Press.

Morgan, M. 2001. 'Ain't Nothin' but a G Thang: Grammar, Variation and Language Ideology in Hip Hop Identity', in S. Lanhart (ed.), *African American Vernacular English*. Philadelphia: John Benjamins, pp. 185–207.

Radcliffe-Brown, A.R. 1940. 'On Joking Relationships', *Journal of the International African Institute* 13(3): 195–210.

Rapport, N. 2003. *I Am Dynamite: An Alternative Anthropology of Power*. London: Routledge.

———. 2006. 'An Anatomy of Humour: The Charismatic Repartee of Trevor Jeffries in The Mitre pub', in V. Amit and N. Dyck (eds), *Claiming Individuality*. London: Pluto Press, pp. 153–72.

———. 2008. *Of Orderlies and Men: Hospital Porters Achieving Wellness at Work*. Durham, NC: Carolina Academic Press.

Robson, C. 1993. *Real World Research: A Resource for Social Scientists and Practitioner-researchers*. Oxford: Blackwell.

Searle, J. 1969. *Speech Acts: An Essay on the Philosophy of Language*. Cambridge: Cambridge University Press.

Skeggs, B. 1997. *Formations of Class and Gender: Becoming Respectable*. Thousand Oaks, CA: Sage.

Skinner, J. 2010. 'Leading Questions and Body Memories: A Case of Phenomenology and Physical Ethnography in the Dance Interview', in P. Collins and A. Gallinat (eds), *The Ethnographic Self as Resource: Writing Memory and Experience into Ethnography*. Oxford: Berghahn, pp. 111–28.

Smith, K. 2012a. *Fairness, Class and Belonging in Contemporary England*. Basingstoke: Palgrave Macmillan.

———. 2012b. 'Anxieties of Englishness and Participation in Democracy,' in J. Edwards, G. Evans and K. Smith (eds), *Class, Community and Crisis in Post-Industrial Britain, Focaal: Journal of Global and Historical Anthropology* 62: 30–41. Oxford: Berghahn Journals.

Strathern, M. 2004. *Partial Connections*. Maryland: Altamira Press.

Wieviorka, M. 1997. 'Is it So Difficult to Be an Anti-Racist?', in P. Werbner and T. Modood (eds), *Debating Cultural Hybridity: Multi-Cultural Identities and the Politics of Anti-Racism*. London: Zed Books, pp. 139–53.

Chapter 5

'DIFFERENT TIMES' AND OTHER 'ALTERMODERN' POSSIBILITIES

FILMING INTERVIEWS WITH CHILDREN AS ETHNOGRAPHIC 'WANDERINGS'

Àngels Trias i Valls

Interviews

Emotive Performances and Composite Arrangements

Drawing upon ethnographic research on gift exchange in Catalonia,[1] this chapter reflects on the process of interviewing children. I will argue that interviews (oral and filmed) with children can be best described in terms of imagined spaces and as instances of 'wandering'. I will examine the different ways in which interviewing children allows the ethnographer to engage with different conceptions of temporality. I theorise concepts of time as a way of engaging with the ethnographic interview beyond the child/adult, oral/filmed, and other dichotomies. The chapter contends that the ethnographic interview can be best understood as 'what happens' when the fractures that naturally occur during our ethnographic encounters with informants are reconstructed.

During fieldwork I 'interviewed' children. It was not a preconceived aim to put children 'at the centre' of the research. The interviews were the outcome of ethnographically generated encounters to do with gift exchange. I found myself reflecting on my own practice of filming, recording, talking: on what Josephides (2012: 94) describes as doing 'maximal narratives' (life stories) and also 'minimal narratives' (talking and other exchanges). I did fieldwork[2] with children who had stories to tell about gift exchanges, and, as such, I went to their school, home, playgrounds. I observed, asked and engaged in 'minimal narratives' with them. I took pictures and filmed their exchanges and their gifts; I showed them my films and filmed interviews. I do not think any of my interviews could be classed as 'maximal narratives' (Josephides). However, I should question myself as to why I make a distinction between maximal and minimal narratives for this kind fieldwork primarily involving children. My child informants treated each exchange and each conversation about it as a 'maximal narrative' of their hopes and desires for gifts and commodities even though they were performed as 'minimal' ones. The interview was never a clear-cut event; it required many takes and breaks to be able to produce what we term a filmed 'interview'. Interviews were not special occasions per se; children and adults queried each other about gifts most of the time. My questions were one set of many that children had to answer about gift-giving.[3]

My position of being 'one of the many' adults had a profound impact on how I thought about my interviews and why I question what we mean by 'interview'. It had the effect of making the interview 'less important', less of a special (meaning different or structured) occasion. Conversations about gifts had a flow, and interviews were not particularly different within that series of talks, chats and narratives. At times, children were asked (by parents and others) about gifts in an 'interview fashion' and at other times, the conversations were just passing comments, repetitions of an earlier conversation, short queries. My interview moment, ethnographically speaking, was only one of these many occasions when children[4] elicited information, discussed and reflected on gifts. My interviews, as a strategy, mirrored what I witnessed happening around me. I reflected on the existing spaces of conversation and interview, and constructed – and imagined – my interviews along those lines. The result of this shift was that I was made to question the nature of the interview as I knew it.

Prior to fieldwork, I believed I had considered most academic views on interviews and filmed interviews, including postmodern discussions on fiction, the convergences of time and reality, the place of memory, authenticity, and how all these were bounded in the production of interviews (Pink 2001: 4, 11; Gell 1992: 328; Bourdieu 1977; Augé 1992: 77, 78; Tonkin 1992: 76–79; Spradley 1979; MacDougall 1978, 1995; Loizos 1992). After fieldwork I felt my earlier theoretical commitments[5] were not sufficient to resolve how I could respond to ethnographic interviews with children, hence I embarked on Bourriaud's commentary on what he terms 'that void beyond postmodernity', the 'altermodern' (2009: 2). This concept was a 'departure' from earlier postmodern ideas in that there was more focus on assemblages, fragmentation and clustering than was common in late twentieth-century discussions on representation and methodology.[6]

The altermodern, as a concept, is not without its problems (Hart et al. 2009), but it developed notions of 'composition', 'wandering' and 'heterochronia', as mutations of earlier postmodern ideas dealing with fractioned, globalised encounters. Within altermodern propositions the concepts of 'delay', 'mash-up',[7] 'non-accumulative temporalities', 'disorientation' and 'subtitling' appeared (to me) to speak for new possibilities. I wondered how methods such as interviewing and filmed documentaries could be imagined anew if we applied these concepts to them.

Bourriaud's (2009: 3–4) ideas on the composition and editing of interviews through ideas such as 'mash-up' seemed to give room for exploring the interview as a creative venue, one that was closer to ethnographic understanding of how narratives of gift exchange were taking place around me. Altermodern concepts gave me room to explore the possibility that interviews are different ethnographic modes in a composite arrangement.

This chapter is anchored in several questions that emerged during my fieldwork. As I conducted interviews with children, a nagging doubt emerged: my interviews did not always look like interviews. If I wanted to show my interviews to people I would have to make them recognisable as interviews (the ones I am showing below have been made recognisable on purpose) and in that transformation would they not lose some of their felt, emotive exceptionality? What do we recognise as an 'interview'? Could we think of interviews as composite arrangements: a form of wandering around imagined spaces that deal with different notions of time? I am proposing an altermodern approach to children's perceptions, experiences and expressions of time in the ethnographic interview, and I do this by focusing (below) on the delays, the fractures and the differently authored compositions that conversations with children bring about.

Interviewing Children

Moving Away from the Genres of Voice, Othering and Auditing

Interviewing children, with or without filming the interview, is often described as a distinctively challenging area of research practice in social sciences. Its 'difference' lies in the subject itself – children – and their relation to 'voice' as a muted group and as structurally vulnerable to exploitation (Christiansen and James 2008). These challenges are well illustrated in educational studies (Lewis and Porter 2007) and research methodology studies (Eder and Fingerson 2001) and regarding their implications in policy (Woodhead and Faulkner 2008). Anthropological accounts of these challenges are predicated on the centrality of children in research (Toren 1999), including a visual anthropology of childhood (Thomson 2008; Atkinson 2006; MacDougall 2001, 2006).

The suitability of children as interview subjects remains a challenge to research practice (Kyronlampi-Kylmanen, Taina and Maatta 2011), in particular concerning the 'good practice' of correct ethical engagement (Morrow and Richards 1996). Interviewing children becomes a process of trying to understand the distortion that children introduce to communicative practice, including long pauses, and challenges to adult logic. The literature assumes that engaging in 'structured conversations' with children represents a challenge: how should we rate 'confidence' in their expression and response? I agree with Alldred and Burman (2005: 175) that none of these approaches offer a conclusive resolution as to what 'interviews with children' are really like – or should be like – other than a phenomenology of difference that reifies their potential as 'other' actors.

Responses to this challenge vary: the creation of handbooks that reflect on the techniques we need to use to engage in new (and ethical) conversations with children (Christiansen and James 2008; Stamatoglou 2004), and treat subjective voices as ethnographic testimony (Pink 2001, 2004; Banks 1992; Hoskins 1998); filmic techniques that expand on the levels of collaboration with our subjects (Barbash and Taylor 1997: 87); the consideration of the filmed interview as 'reflective commentary' (Lydal 1996: 1–7) and as 'encounter' (MacDougall and Taylor 1998: 133); examinations of what is 'taken for granted' (Buchbinder 2010); shifting perspectives that include critiques to the pre-eminence of voice over image, and of the centrality of journalistic interviews in documentary practice (Barbash et al. 1996: 371).

Buchbinder argues that doing interviews with children leads to the emergence of a 'genre' (in her case a 'genre of complaint' of pain and injustice). She looks at the most radical case of interviewing children: children in pain and in hospital settings. In an argument not dissimilar to Foucault's on the relation between biomedicine and the genealogy of knowledge (Foucault 1963, 1969), Buchbinder argues that biomedical perspectives in hospitals prevent doctors from seeing how the medical child-interview becomes a 'genre' (children complain of pain) that obscures the internal discrepancies and tensions of the children's narratives – tensions that could be seen more openly if more attention was paid to the context of the ethnographic interview itself.

In interviewing children we are also dealing with the poignant issue of responsibility to children as subjects. Interviews with children are often about 'how' the encounter should be, and on providing assurances (Warming 2011). Here, however, I borrow from Strathern's (2000: 292) cautionary critique of auditing as 'good practice' in academic settings: I argue that, as with Buchbinder's case of the hospital interview, we need to pay close attention to our current intellectual fashions, and in particular how auditing processes may have filtered into our concerns as to what makes an interview with children 'adequate', 'recognisable', 'safe', 'fair', 'representative', 'inclusive' and 'participatory' (among many of the indexes of good practice) (Hill 2006).

I will argue that we should exercise caution when assessing the 'challenges' of interviewing children within our current academic contents. The first challenge, which I have already mentioned, is the emergence of genres of so-called 'childish' speech, thought and practice (Gubrium and Holstein 2003). Secondly, we should be cautious about the surreptitious 'othering' of children that occurs in the coevalness of time – as Fabian (2002) reminds us in the case of previously 'othered' groups – and its supporting belief that resolving coevalness can be achieved through reflexive debates that acknowledge the political nature of our encounters (Birth 2008: 19). Interviews with children can easily reproduce genres that specifically place children in a temporality of their own, and thus they end up being narrated (and filmed) as the 'other', even within discourses of empowerment and 'voice'. Birth calls this process 'homochronism', where the other is placed into a 'scholarly style history' that amounts to a distancing construction (Birth 2008: 18). Here, I will argue we should consider that our 'scholarly style history' is the history of our contemporary research methodologies. 'Homochronism' is very much a result of this distancing construction, as is our current period of poignant, heightened 'security alert' concerning how we should audit our research practices and exchanges with children.[8]

Doing interviews with children cannot be reduced to a series of polished techniques (helpful as they are); or to reflexive instances on how to reach the 'children's world' (the voice) whilst avoiding 'adult-centrality' (crucial as this is); or to acknowledgements of the nature of power relations, responsibility and ethics (essential as they are). I would argue that doing 'interviews' is less about technique, reflexivity and ethics – in an auditing sense – and more about the local temporality of children's responses to our shared world with them. I argue that doing interviews with children needs to transcend the predicament of our current auditing preoccupations, because they disguise the pervasiveness of homochronism. If children have a story to tell about their hopes and aspirations, about their orientations, we need ethnographic encounters that allow for this.

The challenge, I will argue, is not only about the nature of adult-child interaction and their differences in conceptualising and communicating ideas of the world, but how we manage to do 'good' interviews outside the constraints of auditing and policy-making processes. Our altermodern period is filled with new challenges that impact on how we interview; for example, changes in the material nature of cameras in social-networking exchanges, and new compositions of political disputes between creation and distribution of films, to name two. The challenge is about how we understand the interview itself, and, more precisely, the temporality of the interview. In this chapter, I am proposing 'a composition of understandings' about the interview that can help us tackle some of the predicaments I have outlined. In particular, I reflect on how children 'wander' (with delays, precipitations, excitement) in and out of interview times; and how their capacity for wandering suggests to us that beyond the shared experience and the disruptions of the shared 'interview' time, interviews are composed of different temporalities and modalities of tense, and of fragmentations.

What is an Interview Made Of?

Encounters, Fractures and Imagined Places

Rapport (2012) argues that the interview can be described by considering social exchange as comprising certain ideal types of interaction: the interview provides a 'kind of snapshot on the workings of everyday exchange' (2012: 67). Intrinsic to all interaction is the ambiguity of the meanings exchanged; and the interview is no exception. When faced with interviewing and doing interviews, Rapport asks, as I do, 'Is this an interview?' (2012: 57). When does one begin and end? When does it become non-viable? In particular, when do children and adults know that an interview is no longer possible as a form of exchange?

In trying to answer these questions, Rapport argues that what makes an interview special is that the interview is recognised as a non-routine interaction (2012: 58). The interview is bounded, and predisposes to a situation of enquiry (where both recognise that 'enquiry' is a valid a-temporal form of exchange). As my example below illustrates, in interviews with children the interview ceases to be possible when both adult and child recognise (often by the child first) that they are bored with the exchange or that there is no point in 'continuing' it, no matter how short the interaction has been. The interview becomes fractured[9] and delayed by moments of going back over the verbal exchange, and inside and outside the camera's frame. My evidence suggests that children do identify interviews as 'non-routine' events. I will argue, moreover, that it is children's approaches to the routine and non-routine that lie behind their fractured narratives during filming and interviewing.

Madelina Florescu discusses the kinds of interruptions inherent in interviews, and 'the register of imagination' that is initiated after we stop our recording devices (2012: 179). She argues for a 'quasi-simultaneity' of engagement in interviews: that an interview requires participants to be familiar with a plural environment, and for the memory of the interview to be embodied in the participants (2012: 192). Where I diverge from Florescu is that in my experience, the 'interview' did not have a 'beginning' or 'end' that were predicated on the tape 'running'. Children were familiar with an embodied memory of interviews through other non-routine and simultaneous conversations with other adults (and through social and visual media, TV and Internet). My interviews did not resemble a method: when doing interviews, the children and I met in an imagined place that simultaneously provided a commentary on other parts of the children's lives.

Possible Narratives

The interviews that I describe in this section were collected as part of research on gift exchange during the Christmas and New Year festivities in Catalonia (from 1 December to 6 January), my native region.[10] Nine children, aged from three to seven, participated in interviews over five years, in sibling groups and individually.[11] I used several digital cameras[12] and combined documentary techniques (that focused on narrative) with home movie techniques (that focus on the distortion of time and continuity (cf. Cotenas 2003: 81, 83)). My filmed interviews occurred in stairwells, halls and in streets as the children waited for events to take place. The parents and grandparents were usually not present, although in most cases they were within hearing distance. Both children and adults trusted me as a result of my returning over the years (what Josephides refers to as the ethnographic 'pull' (2012: 79)) and never quite leaving the field. Adults felt the children would be safe with me because we shared meanings on the 'boundaries' of what was adequate to do around children. The pervasiveness of adults making their home movies at this time of the year and my choice of digital cameras made my filming a fairly visually repetitive encounter rather than an exceptional one.

Interviews were one of the many approaches to fieldwork participation that ranged from conversations to debriefings, consultations, chats, informal and structured interviews. I started, intuitively, talking to children of all ages, often casually, using direct talk, questions and short conversations. Because the type of gift exchange I was looking at is often described as 'magical',[13] the children's carers assumed an unproblematic relation to the research. The only ethical concern raised by the parents was that the child should not be told about the nature of the 'magic' in the exchange.

To clarify what kind of exchange I am talking about here, the gift-giving practices during this period are about children receiving parental gifts indirectly in exchange for good behaviour.[14] The gifts are delivered through magical beings (not dissimilar to Father Christmas's delivery of gifts). There is *El Tio*, a woodland creature that scatologically rewards with presents by 'shitting' them out, and Three Kings (borrowing from the story of the Roman Catholic epiphany) and their emissary known as *Patge Faruk*, and their porters. It is these beings, not the parents, who know children's likes and profound hopes, and also their peccadilloes. Furthermore, they seem to be endowed with the capacity of 'seeing' children when they misbehave. Even though they do not live with the children, the Three Kings, in particular, have intimate details of what the children do and of the kind of naughtiness parents cannot do anything about.[15] Where parents fail to make a child stop using a dummy or pacifier, for example, the Three Kings have the power to challenge children to behave in exchange for the gifts they desire.

Secrecy, counter-direction and the mystification of the origin of the gift exchange are all effective strategies for parents to get their children to behave in certain ways without causing major issues of antagonism to parental will. Children are prevented from discovering who is who in the relationship of gift-giving for as long as possible. This is roughly up to the age of seven. Older brothers and sisters often 'tell the truth' – *diuen qui son els tres reis* – to their younger siblings in school, eventually. Such is the profound effect of the Three Kings in amending behaviour with their threats to withhold gifts, that Marc, an eight-year-old, who still 'didn't know' and had worked really hard to be 'a good boy', spent an evening crying in profound sadness when he was told, mistakenly, that one of the Three Kings was unhappy with him and had written him out of the 'good white book' that the Kings use. The mere invocation of the Three Kings is strong enough for children to modify their behaviour, a strategy used several times a day by parents during this period (*si no et portes be els reis no et portaran jugets* ('if you are not good, the Three Kings will not bring you toys')) to get their children to do things in certain ways.[16]

The effect of this mystification is short-lived. Children change their behaviour back to old practices with ease – as they gradually work out how to become more resilient to critique, and to deal with a threat and its consequences. Adults often say, and make the common assumption, that children eventually go back to their 'old ways' (to misbehaving). However, this is an adult-centred assumption. My fieldwork suggests that children actually strive for good behaviour both as an actual practice – as demonstrated during the interview – but also as a theoretical principle. An interesting outcome of children being exposed to constant public and domestic debating about 'being good' and 'getting gifts' is that they develop responses 'in theory' to what they are being asked. Adults struggle to understand these fine distinctions made by children because they are expecting a modification of behaviour that is tangible. Children, on the other hand, clearly show they understand how to navigate behaviour in theoretical as well as pragmatic ways (relative to their own hopes) as a distinctive narrative of their own.

What is Remembered and Imagined

The fifth of January is 'the night of nights', a large public and private event full of drama and promise. It is the night when the Three Kings are due to arrive. We prepare for an interview. Parents agree to any distraction that will keep children from what appears to them an endless wait. Children are emotionally charged. They are very excited, hopeful, a little bit fearful and nervous. They are also exhausted because it is past their bedtime. I remember feeling like this when I was a child myself – our memories are made of this emotional entanglement – and I am excited now too. I sit down with Gim, who is five years old, and Maria, who is three years old. I explain to them what I am going to do. I start with Maria who is a fast talker.

Maria's Interview [film strip name: CIMG3056.MOV – 1:12 (one minute, twelve seconds) 05.01.2009 – starting time 18:23]

[Maria looks up at me.]

Maria: My name is Maria
Àngels: How old are you?
Maria: I am three
Àngels: Three years old? And today, what did you tell me you were going to do?

[Maria gets closer to the camera.]

Maria: Today there will be (they will come to me) the Kings and the porters.
Àngels: Which ones do you like best?
Maria: Hmm ... the bronze one, the white one, the black one.
Àngels: What did you ask them?

[Maria looks away as she thinks. She holds her hands excitedly as she talks, looking intently at me and the camera when she describes which of the toys she likes best.]

Maria: A doll's pram, some high-heeled shoes of the snow white, [tongue roll and] and, and, a doll with a bed, that falls asleep, and, [clicks tongue] another doll, a pink handbag of, of the pram, that goes with the handbag, and some high heels.
Àngels: Good, and what do you have to do to get all this?

[Maria anxiously knocks her feet on the chair, smiling but rocking slightly.]

Maria: I have to be good (I have to behave good).

Àngels: What does it mean to behave good?
Maria: That, to listen to my dad and mum [she smiles] [Maria is
          renowned within the family for not listening to her parents].
Àngels: Yes, and what else?
Maria: And that the Kings and porters will come.
Àngels: If you are not good?
Maria: They will bring nothing.
Àngels: Will they bring you nothing?
Maria: They will bring charcoal.
Àngels: Charcoal? Do the Kings bring charcoal?
Maria: Yes [emphatically. Her mood has changed she is not playful
          but certain]. Yes.
Gim: Yes.

[Gim, her brother, who was listening quietly, nods his head off-camera
to agree with her; and although he knew he was not part of the
questioning, he felt he was able to answer and it related to him too.]

Àngels: Do they have a book, the Kings? Tell me about the book?
Gim: Yes.

[Maria nods, assent.]

Àngels: Tell me about the book they have.
Maria: The black one and that's it [Maria looks a bit tired and
          confused].
Àngels: Very good [aiming to close the interview].
Gim: [shouts in a correcting tone] And a white one.

[The Kings have two books, the black one and the white one. Maria
mentions the black one because she is, like her brother, worried she
will be in that book, and because black is the colour associated with her
favourite King.]

Àngels: Thank you.

[We take a two-minute break. Maria walks around while Gim and I
talk about the interview. He knows I will ask him about his name and
about the Three Kings. I put the camera on. He sits down readily, back
upright, prepared.]

Gim's Interview [film strip name: CIMG3057.MOV – 1:12 (one
minute, twelve seconds) 05.01.2009 – starting time 18:25]

Àngels: What's your name? You can start now.

[He looks and smiles at the camera.]

Gim: My name is Gim and I am five.

Àngels: What are you doing today?
Gim: Today the Three Kings will come.
Àngels: What happens when the 'Kings' come?

[He is looking down, looking for words, and thinking.]

Gim: Well, they bring gifts.
Àngels: What have you asked from them?
Gim: Hmm. Lots of things.
Àngels: So what kind of things? [Emotional pause.]
Gim: So many things that I can't remember.
Àngels: Do you remember one?
Gim: A Spiderman car.
Àngels: Do you like Spiderman? [He is very emotional at the thought
         of the gift he hopes to get. Children are told they will not get
         all the things they hope for and ask for.]
Gim: [moves his head to say 'Yes'].
Àngels: [emphatic reiteration] 'Yes'?!

[Gim nods in agreement.]

Àngels: How will that happen? [Interruption by his sister and a
         singing bird – their father is trying to stop the bird. Gim looks
         puzzled that I am suddenly stopping to look at the very noisy
         bird.]
Àngels: Sorry, go, go ahead.
Gim: I have to behave well.
Àngels: To behave well.

[Gim nods.]

Àngels: How will they bring the gifts – by car, plane?

[Gim looks puzzled.]

Àngels: What will the Kings do?

[He pauses to think.]

Gim: Hmm a car.

[Gim's sister, Maria, who was listening, speaks to their father nearby.]

Maria: What are you doing, Dad?
Àngels: Did you go last year to the Three Kings?
Gim: Yes.
Àngels: And what did you see?

[Gim and Maria speak simultaneously.]

Maria: I have [got] a skirt, [from last year] a dress, shoes.
Gim: They throw us sweets.
Àngels: What would you say to the Kings?
Gim: A kiss [blows a kiss].
Maria: Me too [blows a kiss].

[The camera pans out to Maria to include her.]

Àngels: Ok, tell me again.

[Maria blows a kiss.]

Àngels: Very good. [The interview stops and we take a two-minute
          break whilst Gim and Maria speak with their father, who
          leaves the room after speaking to them. I ask them to 'do a bit
          more', they agree. They walk around, move the swivel chair.]

[film strip name: CIMG3058.MOV – 0.49 (forty-nine seconds)
05.01.2009 – starting time 18:27] Elicitation using a film I took of
both of them making a Tio 'shit' for gifts.

[film strip name: CIMG3061.MOV – 1:16 (one minute, fifteen seconds)
05.01.2009 –starting time 18:29] Elicitation (same).

[film strip name: CIMG3062.MOV – 0:43 (forty-three seconds)
05.01.2009 – starting time 18:31] Interview on the *Tio* [a woodland
being[17]] from elicitation (we just looked at the computer screen). Their
earlier excitement is now lessened with the prospect of more questions.
Maria looks less interested but she joins in. She is (as she says in the
film) bored with it.

Àngels: What does the Tio do?
Gim: [thinks] Hmm ... it shits toys.
Àngels: And what does he shit?
Gim: Things.
Àngels: And what did it shit?
Gim: Thinking [he also looks more tired] ... Hmm, a bow [bow and
          arrows].

[Maria, who was swivelling the chair, perks up and intercepts whilst her
brother is thinking and looking away at the computer screen where the
earlier films are.]

Maria: Princess shoes with heels. [She rocks and moves the chair.]
Àngels: And what do you have to do for it to shit?
Gim: [He pauses to think.] To give him food. [He starts moving
          away.]
Maria: [Moves chair back and forth]

Àngels: And when do you give him food to eat?
Gim: All, all the days.
Àngels: And what do you give him to eat?

[Maria asks me a direct question on the theme, suddenly interviewing me.]

Maria: Where is your Tio?
Àngels: I don't know [of course I do, but I am not supposed to say it] ... in the woods. Do you know if the Tio comes from the woods [the forest]?
Gim and Maria: [nodding] Yes, yes.
Àngels: And what kind of food do you give to him?

[Maria is now swivelling back and forward, Gim also looks a bit more tired, less engaged with me, looking up and to the sides, but still attentive.]

Maria: I am bored.
Gim: Fruit, fruit. [He looks away, his sister listens.]
Maria: Look at Dad. [Both look amused.]

[I switch off the camera and turn my head. Their father is now back in the room, making a funny face and Gim and Maria laugh at the funny face. Their father leaves the room again. We take a five-minute break, they ask to watch a few more elicitations.]

Gim and Maria joint interview [film strip name: CIMG3066.MOV – 1:23 (one minute, twenty-three seconds) 05.01.2009 – starting time 18:37]

Maria: From ... I am bored. I don't want this. [Talking a bit more, she looks away, swivelling in her chair. Gim pulls a funny face to the camera, getting close to the lens and back. I laugh.]
Àngels: Tell me about the Kings, how they come. [Gim reacts immediately and is prompted to behave and respond.]
Gim: In chariots.
Àngels: What are the chariots like?
Gim: They are the colour ... colour grey. [He is pulling a face and appears to be struggling to engage. Grey is not what he means. He yawns but he goes on.]
Àngels: Is there a star? [He thinks carefully.]
Gim: Yes.
Àngels: Yes? Tell me, how is it?
Gim: It is yellow.
Àngels: Yes?

[I speak to Maria who is playing at the computer to include her.]

Àngels: Have you seen it, Maria? How is the star? How big is it?
Maria: Then, it is green and yellow.
Àngels: I see...

[Gim makes a face, responding to my sound. Like me he also knows the star is not green, but he lets his sister and me talk. He looks at me conspiratorially and shows surprise.]

Àngels: And the porters, which are your favourite porters?
Gim/Julia: The brown one
Maria: For me the black one, the white one, the blond/bronze one.

[Gim is now moving back and forward, looking at me whilst he gets close to the camera, accidentally.]

Àngels: Did you go to give your card to the Kings? I couldn't go. Will
          you explain it to me what happened?
Maria: Yes.
Gim: [pause] Yes.
Àngels: Tell me about it.
Gim: Yes, I will tell you. Then, they gave us sweets.

[They pick up the computer keyboard and are getting excited and distracted at the same time, but still in the interview, talking faster and playing with the keyboard harder.]

Maria: And, and, they gave us a balloon.
Àngels: And when you gave them your card (with the list of gifts),
          what did they tell you?
Gim: You have to listen to your mum and dad, and go to sleep late.
Àngels: Late or early?

[Gim laughs comically. Maria smiles, she realises she has made a mistake, she meant 'early'.]

Gim: Early.
Àngels: What did they say to you? [Gim looks talkative and willing to
          respond, but they are both looking for distractions.]
Gim: To listen to my mum.
Maria: I want to see these. [She points at more films from the
          computer.]

[Gim jumps towards the camera and points at the films. I have to move the camera as they take the camera's space.]

Àngels: Okay. [I switch the camera off and we conclude the interview.
          I continue the interview the following day, on the street and
          after they receive their gifts.]

Fractured Engagements and Delayed Reconstruction

I argue that disengaging, and breaking out of the interview, defined the above interview as a social exchange, and, moreover, that this will be the case for any ethnographic interview. Whether it be through boredom, different communication patterns, or how respondents understand 'what is needed' in exchange (short, span-mediated replies), fracture and delay are important features that we may take for granted in interviews.

In particular, the stories that children tell and perform for us are fractured and disengaged. However, unlike Rapport's theorisation of five 'modalities of interactional engagement' ('reciprocity, complementarity, collaboration, emergence and distortion' (2012: 62–65)), disengaging from the interview once it has been constituted (much harder to appreciate in adult interviews) becomes a constituent in the way the interview is constructed as a 'non-routine' event by children. I am not talking here of the time when the interview has 'finished'. We finished it many times, and restarted it many times with the camera on and off. Rather, there is a distinctive possibility that the interview that we recognise 'as such' actually does not have a specific beginning or end in the period of the interview. It is 're-engaged' now and then by the participants, reimagined as a possibility that can still continue. It is not the interview itself that is 'non-routine'. What are 'non-routine' are the breakages, fractures and disengagements during the interview.

Figure 5.1 Interviewing children

The interview is what happens in the reconstruction of the different breakages, fractures and disengagements of any given conversation. The reconstruction is both internal to each sequence (each minute and so on) and to those time-lapses that join the different sequences (the breaks in-between) and are imagined as such. The difference between a daily series of non-routine questions to children about their gifts and behaviour and an interview as non-routine concerns, then, how the individual actors involved reconstruct these differently.

Interviews with children are made of communicative and meta-communicative moments (including boredom) that are too short and fractured to figure in the representation of a conventional interview. In order for me to truly describe an 'ethnographic interview with children' I have to rethink what is meant by interview as a 'non-routine event' and how best to represent it. For this is not a 'normal' or adult-conventional space. The ethnographic interview with children is made of modalities of engagement and disengagement, fractures and breakages, and this is difficult to present. When discussing the ethnographic interview we need to identify its different modalities, and include not just 'the interview' proper but also conversations around it that are yet part of it. These include the possibility of there being delays in achieving the interview, fractures during its course, and the narrative of other conversations – still part of 'the interview'.

A further consideration must also challenge the assumption that the ethnographic encounter as a whole is more 'entire' (and satisfactory as a method or as a sum of approaches) than one of its 'parts' (the interview). Even when fraught and incomplete, ethnography is considered as standing as a unified and unifying experience. Yet, as Smith (2009: 2, 8) critically considers it, fieldwork is not necessarily a satisfactory endeavour, and perhaps the sum is not greater than its parts (cf. Strathern 1991). I would argue that both 'entire' ethnographies and interviews are fragmented, hard to attain and complex enough to be reduced to parts. Resolving these successfully requires a certain amount of fictionalising and re-engaging with the experience many times over. Why need we try to make interviews more successful than fieldwork itself? What we learn from interviewing children (and its unsuccessful moments, fragments and unattained answers) is that an interview has to be seen as more than simply engagement with a person who agrees to respond in a 'non-routine' fashion.

My filmed interviews eloquently show children moving 'in and out' of the interview very quickly, leaving through boredom, and stopping the interview, only to restart it again. Unsure as to what constitutes the boundaries of an interview – a practice adults take for granted through internal reflection on their audience – children are resolute in letting us know that interviews are different from other types of exchange.

From the filmed evidence of comparing how they answer the same question in different contexts, I believe children recognise the interview as a different kind of time, embodied in the attitude 'we are being asked something', and 'adults want to achieve something'. They distinguish this 'asking and answering' as a different interaction than the one they engage in with other actors. If Rapport is correct, as I believe he is, that an interview is a non-routine interaction, children appear to make subtle distinctions of their own between-routine interactions and non-routine interactions – even if the question, context and processes are very much the same. I believe interviews with children illustrate a feature of all interviews, whereby temporality needs not have an established pattern (it does not need to be structured, casual, open-ended or informal) for it to be constituted as non-routine, and recognisable as exceptional.

What I find interesting about Rapport's definition of the ethnographic interview is his understanding of distortion: in that the interview provides momentary (my use of time as moment here, not his) 'glimpses of tensions and distortions between forms and meanings' (Rapport 2012: 62–65). This is perhaps something that best reflects how interviews with children feel like. One gets a sense of what I call a 'delay': the tensions and distortions in the 'talking-partnership' that develops during the interview. Rapport's definition fills an important gap in the literature. His identification of interview moments as 'reciprocity, complementarity, collaboration, emergence and distortion' (2012: 62–65) is a very precise account of the kind of interviews one has with adults, who are less able to 'walk away' once the interview has started, and vice versa. Interviewing children offers further unambiguous glimpses concerning the 'distortions that can characterise relations between talking-partners' (Rapport 2012: 65), including distortions to children's internal conversations. I hope that my cases illustrate how interviews with children can transcend the predicament of the 'genre'. Children deal with the temporality of the interview by wandering between times: the 'time of the interview', a 'time of boredom', a 'time of distraction'. This wandering underpins our (later) reconstruction of the breakages that make the interview. This is what in altermodern prepositions is known as 'heterochronia' (a collection of different times).

I perhaps should clarify. I do not mean to say that there is no distinctiveness in children's narratives through interviews. To the contrary,

I borrow from Degnen's work (2007) with older people's narratives of temporality (2007: 230) and the understanding that certain combinations (in her case irrelevant information, in my case reiterations on good behaviour) mean the meeting of 'shifting temporal frameworks'. Conversations with children were fragmented. They were made of many reiterations, repetitions, shortened sequences, intonations and clarifications. The interviews were short, as short as one or two questions, with many different types of breakages in engagement. It often felt like the interview had not fully started or ended. The children and I 'wandered'. We moved in and out of the interview, in and out of conversations, short, cut, broken, delayed, without a definite direction. It was a kind of journeying in and out of the conversation and of the interview itself.

Journeying in Time

The Heterochronic Nature of Interviewing

Bourriaud's altermodern strategy for rethinking postmodern thought suggests a series of concepts in which contemporary social conditions thrive in a stage of fragmentation, in lives that are assumed to be chaotic, with 'fast changing lanes'.[18]

> Heterochronia describes work that can not be easily anchored to a specific times, where the artist traces lines and connections through time as space, differently than the modernist idea of time advancing in linear fashion, and the postmodern time advancing in loops, heterochronia, different or other time, changes in clusters together contemporary sings allowing an exploration of what is now. (Bourriaud 2009: 19)

My approach is an attempt to go 'beyond multi-temporality'. I find particularly useful Bourriaud's emphasis on looking at 'delays' in representation, because this is what I perceived the interview to do. In interviews that engage children, their answers are forms of delay rather than forms of the 'now' and the contemporary. They are 'parts assembled' of such delays (children assemble their behaviour through their engagements theoretically and in actual practice, in their hopes and nerves). Interviews, as methods of composition of tensions and breakages may share with the altermodern idea of heterochronic elements: 'Delay, analogous recordings, pre-recording coexisting with the immediate, live with the anticipated imagined ...

where temporalities and levels of reality are intertwined – rather than accumulated' (Bourriaud 2009: 21).

Here, then, I take on this understanding of interviews as possible heterochronic representations, where different elements and emotions, and pre-recorded and existing ideas of interview, are composed differently to other ethnographic moments. I argue that the interview is a different type of composition, one where performance, autonomy, extraordinariness and exceptionality coexist with fiction, rather than accumulating (as adults accumulate) intertwined levels of experiencing social realities. It unveils the specificity of all interviews alike, as all occurring at different times, and thus enabling the performance of imagined worlds (being a good boy/girl, getting the Spiderman car, wishing for high-heeled shoes, going to bed early, dealing with being bored, considering adult questions) to take place in assembled moments.[19] Interviews are, in this sense, assemblages of the different tension that children use to question the visit of the grandparent that sparks questions on the Three Kings; the comment from the mother to placate a tantrum; the teacher's question on their gift list; television reiterations of commodities; radio announcements of children's behaviour by the Three Kings emissaries; the words of the Three Kings to the children when they meet ... and so on.

The altermodern is a playful concept with which to re-narrate ethnographic encounters, and very particularly, the interview. Altermodern propositions emphasise 'journeying' and the reconfiguration of globalisation, in crisis, 'chaotic' cultural landscapes with a core preoccupation with 'docudramas' as places where one might imagine the connections between fragmented situations.

Using filmed interviews in order to locate children's participation in gift exchange allowed for a retelling of personal stories, and for children to 'give movement' to the interview whilst not necessarily engaging with it as such. The interviews with children, filmed or otherwise, highlight the capacity of the interview, as an ethnographic form, to challenge how we narrate what we imagine our participation in social spaces to be. In this context, I view the interview as a place of different positionalities of subjects amidst interactions of specific, albeit different, times and new communicative practices. I look at the interview as trespassing relationships between the people engaged in it, and inducing a sense of mobility, allowing for different ways of relating to and translating voice, and individual trajectories.

I want, finally, to consider the possibility of looking at the ethnographic interview (in general) as a way of anthropological reasoning about the temporality of our engagements. Fabian (2002) in his critique of anthropological writing and the way in which we place our subjects in time is particularly relevant to our enquiries as to how we construct and deny interviews as politicised encounters. Fabian's treatment of his two central ideas –'allochronism', the creation of different temporalities, and 'coevalness', where interlocutors coexist at the same time (2002: 30–31) – were meant to remind us that it is possible to articulate time and narrative as well as to point at the dangers of such articulations. Interviews 'serve as examples of the establishment of intersubjective time between researcher and research subjects' (Birth 2008: 4). As Birth critically comments on Fabian, it is the way in which we share temporality that makes 'communication intersubjectively significant' (2008: 4). Our informants can put us in 'their history' (Birth 2008: 18; cf. Rapport 2012: 68).

There is, then, a tension between an 'informant's history' and the interview as an imagined tense. Informants may put us in 'their history' but it is the interview that places us in the field. Josephides (2012: 91) is correct to describe the ontological and ethical preoccupations that surround placing oneself in the field, and the difficulty in achieving a balance between respect and distance. These, I feel, are the genuine ethical dimensions we face in interviews – rather than those found in more 'audited' practices I outlined earlier. However, as she also says, the 'interview is a flexible tool ... always transformed by the interviewees as something for their own use' (Josephides 2012: 103).

In being placed 'in the field' with a sense of permanency, Josephides alludes to something that is critical for our understanding of the interview: anthropologists 'listen and pursue knowledge in a particular way' (2012: 103) and not exclusively from interviews. If I understand Josephides correctly, the time of the interview is then pulled back (as the ethnographer herself) to the field that cannot be fully escaped (if the ethnography is to be written/filmed). In doing so, the time of fieldwork can be somehow 'paused' in the conventional ethnographic interview. In contrast to this 'pause', altermodern ideas of dubbing and mashing (and the use of domestic videos) are useful for me here in order to break away from earlier modern and postmodern epistemologies of interviewing as concerning 'voice' and 'narrative' and instead consider them as imagined instances. If we think of the interview beyond 'the pause' as a hypertextual-like practice in an imagined register, we can rethink the examples of Maria and Gim, above, as heterochronic places for children themselves (times where they get bored, times when they perform behaviour, times when they embody childhood, when they theorise, times when they feel nervous, times of remembering emotions, and so on, and where to imagine these times).

When looking at these extraordinary moments of filmed interviews, interviews with children helped me to think about some of the limits of interviews, as specific instances of imagined and felt conditions through which an ethnographic stance is to be developed, but which does not always preclude the interview as an ethnographic moment, but as I call it, a different time of ethnographic moment.

However, as a collection of 'askings' in a context of other extraordinary 'asking and listening' it is a process of inducing imagined narratives, and retellings, to be co-authored by all those involved in the interviews, including those imagined (i.e., an audience) in the interview. The interview brings together an intertwining of different types of knowledge and modalities of tense. The moment of the interview should not be deemed the only time or context in which the interview is constituted, then. What makes interviews with children extraordinary is that this kind of interview is intertwined with fictions of authenticity, at different times; the interview is an imagined composition, it is what happens during the reconstruction of fractures and delays, of wanderings in different times.

Notes

1. The research looked at a series of commodity exchanges that take place between 1 December and 6 January, mostly concentrated on 24 to 27 December, 28 December and 5 to 6 December. It involves nearly all families in every Catalan town. In the town of Igualada (39,639 inhabitants) it includes several large public occasions for gift display and gift-giving. The givers of these gifts tend to be adults, non-human beings and religious figures, with children reciprocating with non-commodity giving, such as poems and recitations and good behaviour. The largest public display includes the delivery of 2,339 parcels of toys and 5,000 kg of sweets, an equivalent of between 14 and 32 fully loaded trucks from the Three Kings (Roman Catholic figures) to children (adults may also be included).

2. I did fieldwork with different groups of children, neighbours, relatives, and friends of theirs. The children were already known to me, and vice versa, from past fieldwork experiences. Several of these children had previously seen me conducting interviews with adults and filming the several types of gift exchange that take place during this period. Children have their own stories to tell about these events, so this part of my research on gift exchange concentrated on getting to know these children's stories

in a way that was truthful to their experience and voice. However, this was not research about giving children a 'voice' but research that tried to understand interviewing outside the conventional paradigms on voice, and differences between adult/children that often render children as passive agents. I wanted to look at how children articulated the world of exchange around them.

3. On an average day, children may be asked by adults, parents, teachers and friends about what they want, what they hope to get, what they are asking for, what gifts they like, and why, what their tastes in gifts are, to make a list of their favourite commodities, list of alternative gifts (in case the gifts they want are not in stock in shops). During this month there is a daily, constant discussion and interjection between everybody about exchange.

4. I met the children in different contexts: at their home, school, play groups. I filmed them mostly at home, but we also filmed interviews on the street and in all the places (public and private) where gift-giving took place. The research was about gift-giving and my aim was to illustrate the instances of gift exchange during this period and how it related to current political discussions in Catalonia about inclusion and exclusion from communities and the state (Catalan/Spanish states). I noted that narratives of gift exchange in the literature and in social practice were often ignorant of what I perceived as the role of children as scapegoats of the political processes of inclusion of 'outsiders'. On my third return to this fieldwork location I wanted to examine what other narratives and practices were available – including those of children – outside the more hegemonic views of exchange. My consideration here, however, is not to focus on the issue of exchange – which I examine in another essay – but to use my experiences to rethink the interview.

5. I mean here postmodern commitments to reflexivity, positionality, the blurred lines between fiction and authenticity, the differences between authorial and representative anthropological voices and the role of audiences and editing in film making, among other things.

6. For me it was a departure from specific visual anthropological concepts on medium, author, authenticity that affect how we film and think of the interview.

7. Mash-ups are intuitive mappings of Internet applications that blend information from multiple sources. Mash-ups blur the nature of the relationship between authors and audience, and cast doubt on the authenticity of production, the certainty of the 'origin' of the production of any type of information. Often these include mixing pieces on YouTube, for example, or music mash-ups where different people contribute to produce a product that is not owned by anyone specifically, and where its composition may change or become 'liquid' as it is distributed and other people alter and change the original piece of music/art in compelling and innovative ways. Mash-ups are specifically altermodern in that they are a

new way of re-combining in digital contexts, although it is also applied to analogic, not only digital practices.

8. Other examples of the tension between homochronism and a wider understanding of the modalities of tense are better illustrated in ethnographic films (see MacDougall 2008, for example) than in other types of ethnographies. I am not directly discussing ethnographic film and the impasse between fiction, authorship and audience, because I was not making an ethnographic film – in its modern or postmodern sense, at least. I was doing visual anthropology, but I meant to film interviews with children because that was a reflection of the kind of social narratives that were being used by my informants. This gift-giving period consisted of adults asking children questions, creating different temporalities – to manage 'good behaviour' – which included direct daily questioning and home movies of children involved in gift exchange.

9. In postmodern thinking, fragmentation is thought of, largely, as an anti-dominant discourse (Harvey 1990: 239), and I agree with Harvey that temporal and spatial practices are never neutral. Here I look at fragmentations that do not aim at becoming a critique of existing discourses.

10. Although I grew up in this area, my relation to it is very much of a returning stranger. I have not lived there for more than twenty years, and most of my returns are an ethnographic necessity.

11. Two children were interviewed yearly, others only once or twice. The group of children I chose included family members, neighbours and acquaintances. The interviews were carried out at the children's homes and at their grandparents' homes where they spent most of their holidays during this period. It included filmed interviews that were 'fixed' (in an open room) and 'mobile' (following the child around the house).

12. JVC GR-DVP5; Casio Digital Exilim S10; Sony Ericsson K810i; X10i; Sony DSC-HX1, Flip Video UltraHD.

13. The magic of this event lies with the fact that children are made to believe that the gifts are given to them by out-of-this-world beings, and characters that live in faraway lands (the forest and the 'Orient'). This is an adult construct: I've never heard young children say it is 'magic/al'; the children believe in causality, they are given gifts because that is what these beings do. Adults also say it is 'magical', meaning children 'faithfully believe in it and behave well', implying an 'illusion' and being a 'special time during childhood when children still do not understand deception'.

14. Adults also receive gifts from other adults as well as from older children that 'know' about the deception and thus will understand it as an exchange of commodities from parents to children where children can reciprocate with a 'detail' (a non-expensive or handmade gift).

15. There is even a radio programme where Faruk, the emissary, talks to children (by name and surname) and publically discusses their behaviour.

16. The secret is part and parcel of a conceptualisation of childhood as a special time, full of beliefs, homochronistic, separate from the realities of life.

17. A Tio is described as a 'woodland thing': it is a tree log that has been altered with the addition of two front legs, a face with eyes and a mouth painted on, and two horns attached to it. It is covered with a blanket and a peasant's hat when at home and it is fed potato peel and orange peel daily (this food is 'removed' at night when children are in bed, and in the morning they are made to believe the 'Tio' has eaten it). As a result the Tio's stomach is full, and on 24 December it expels all the food in the form of gifts that it 'shits out' (*caga*). Twenty years ago it used to 'shit out' chocolate coins, chocolate cigarettes, chocolate in the form of 'poo', sweets and sweet coal (a type of sweet that signifies the child has not behaved well or that the Tio has finished – *ha acabat de cagar* ('has finished shitting'). Nowadays it also 'shits' toys. (Usually, there are no toys under the Christmas tree and there is no Santa Claus delivery on the following day.)

18. The eight central tenets of altermodernism are: energy, travel, viatorisation, borders, exiles, docufiction, archive and heterochronia. (Suggestively borrowing from social sciences and interpretative contemporary art, the term 'heterochronia' means existing within many times in order to question the notion of what is considered 'contemporary'. I use heterochronia to contest the interview as our imagined 'contemporary' tense during fieldwork.)

19. Ong and Collier (2005: 28) have a beautiful understanding of this idea in their altermodern (post-global) contextualisation of the shifts that decompose and rearrange 'new assemblages' that are the future localisation of power relations.

References

Alldred, P. and E. Burman. 2005. 'Analysing Children's Accounts using Discourse Analysis', in S. Green and D. Hogan (eds), *Researching Children's Experiences*. London: Sage.

Atkinson, A. 2006. 'From Play to Knowledge: From Visual to Verbal?', *Anthropology Matters Journal* 8(2).

Augé, M. 1992. *Non-Places*. London: Verso.

Banks, M. 1992. 'Which Films are Ethnographic Films?', in P. Crawford and D. Turton (eds), *Film as Ethnography*, Manchester: Manchester University Press.

Barbash, I., D. MacDougall, and J. MacDougall.1996. 'Reframing Ethnographic Film: A "Conversation" with David MacDougall and Judith MacDougall', *American Anthropologist* 98(2): 371–87.

Barbash, I. and L. Taylor.1997. *Cross-Cultural Filmmaking*. Berkeley: University of California Press.

Birth, K. 2008. 'The Creation of Coevalness and the Danger of Homochronism', *Journal of the Royal Anthropological Institute* 14: 3–20.

Bourdieu, P. 1977. *Towards a Theory of Practice*. Cambridge: Cambridge University Press.

Bourriaud, N. 2009. *Altermodern*. London: Tate.

Buchbinder, M. 2010. 'Giving an Account of One's Pain in the Anthropological Interview', *Culture, Medicine and Psychiatry* 34(1): 108–31.

Christiansen, P. and A. James (eds). 2008. *Research with Children*. London: Routledge.

Cotenas, E. 2003. *Ethnographic Film: Proposing an Alternative Critical Framework*. Sacramento: California State University.

Degnen, C. 2007. 'Temporality, Narrative and the Ageing-Self', in E. Hallam and T. Ingold (eds), *Creativity and Cultural Improvisation*. Oxford: Berg.

Eder, D. and L. Fingerson. 2001. 'Interviewing Children and Adolescents', in J. Gubrium and J. Holstein (eds), *Handbook of Interview Research*. London: Sage.

Fabian, J. 2002. *Time and the Other: How Anthropology Makes Its Object*. New York: Columbia University Press.

Florescu, M. 2012. '"Angola Calling": A Study of Registers of Imagination in the Interview in the Field', in J. Skinner (ed.), *The Interview: An Ethnographic Approach*. London: Berg.

Foucault, M. 2002 [1969]. *The Archaeology of Knowledge*. London: Routledge.

———. 2003 [1963]. *The Birth of the Clinic*. London: Routledge.

Gell, A. 1992. *The Anthropology of Time: Cultural Constructions of Temporal Maps and Images*. Oxford: Berg.

Gubrium, J. and J. Holstein. 2003. *Inside Interviewing*. London: Sage.

Hart, K. et al. 2009. 'Discussing the Altermodern', *Open Anthropology Co-operative*. Retrieved from http://openanthcoop.ning.com/

Harvey, D. 1990. *The Condition of Postmodernity*. Oxford: Blackwell.

Hill, M. 2006. 'Children's Voices on Ways of Having a Voice: Children's and young people's Perspectives on Methods Used in Research and Consultation', *Childhood* 13(1): 69–89.

Hoskins, J. 1998. *Biographical Objects. How Things Tell the Stories of People's Lives*. London: Routledge.

Josephides, L. 2012. 'Finding and Mining the Talk: Negotiating Knowledge and Knowledge Transfer in the Field', in J. Skinner (ed.), *The Interview*. London: Berg.

Kyronlampi-Kylmanen T. and K. Maatta. 2011. 'Using Children as Research Subjects: How to Interview a Child Aged 5 to 7 Years', *Educational Research and Reviews* 6(1): 87–93.

Lewis, A. and J. Porter. 2007. 'Research and Pupil Voice', in L. Florian (ed.), *Handbook of Special Education*. London: Sage.

Loizos, P. 1992. *Innovation in Ethnographic Film: From Innocence to Self-Consciousness, 1955–1985*. Chicago: University of Chicago Press.

Lydal, J. 1996 'Eliciting Reflective Commentary' in *Voices of Ethnographic Film at the Gottingen International Ethnographic Film Festival*. Gottingen, 20

May. Retrieved 25 August 2011 from http://www.unimainz.de/Organi-
sationen/SORC/fileadmin/texte_lydall/Reflective%20Voice.pdf.

MacDougall, D. 1978. 'Ethnographic Film: Failure and Promise', *Annual Review of Anthropology* 7: 405–25.

———. 1995. 'The Subjective Voice in Ethnographic Film', in L. Devereaux and R. Hillman (eds), *Fields of Vision: Essays in Film Studies, Visual Anthropology, and Photography*. Berkeley: University of California Press.

———. 2001, 'Visual Anthropology: Digital Video (The Author Replies)', *Anthropology Today* 17(5): 24–25.

———. 2006. *The Corporeal Image: Film, Ethnography and the Senses*. Princeton: Princeton University Press.

———. 2008 *Gandhi's Children*. Fieldwork Films, Prayas Institute of Juvenile Justice, New Delhi, & Centre for Cross-Cultural Research, Research School of Humanities, Australian National University.

MacDougall, D. and L. Taylor. 1998. *Transcultural Cinema*. Princeton: Princeton University Press.

Morrow, V. and M. Richards. 1996. 'The Ethics of Social Research with Children: An Overview', *Children and Society* 10: 90–105.

Ong, A. and Collier, S. 2005. *Global Assemblages: Technology, Politics and Ethics as Anthropological Problems*. Oxford: Blackwell.

Pink, S. 2001. *Doing Visual Ethnography*. London: Sage.

———. 2004. 'Performance, Self-Representation and Narrative: Interviewing with Video', in Christopher J. Pole (ed.), *Seeing is Believing? Approaches to Visual Research* (Studies in Qualitative Methodology, Vol. 7) Emerald Group Publishing Limited, pp. 61–77.

Rapport, N. 2012. 'The Interview as a Form of Talking-Partnership: Dialectical, Focussed, Ambiguous, Special', in J. Skinner (ed.), *The Interview*. London: Berg.

Smith, K. 2009. 'Is a Happy Anthropologist a Good Anthropologist?', *Anthropology Matters* 11(1).

Spradley, J. 1979. *The Ethnographic Interview*. Belmont, CA: Wadsworth.

Stamatoglou, M. 2004. 'Listening to Young Children's Voices: An Ethnographic Study on Nursery Play', *British Educational Research Association Annual Conference*, 18 September. Manchester: University of Manchester.

Strathern, M. (ed.). 2000. *Audit Cultures: Anthropological Studies in Accountability, Ethics and the Academy*. London: Routledge.

———. 2004 [1991]. *Partial Connections*. Lanham, MD: AltaMira.

Taina, K. and Mataa, K. 2011. 'Using Children as Research Subjects: How to Interview a Child aged 5 to 7 years', *Educational Research and Reviews* 6(1): 87–93.

Thomson, P. 2008 'Children and Young People. Voices in Visual Research', in P. Thomson (ed.), *Doing Visual Research with Children and Young People*. London: Routledge.

Tonkin, E. 1992. *Narrating Our Pasts: The Social Construction of Oral History*. Cambridge: Cambridge University Press.

Toren, C. 1999. 'Why Children Should Be Central To Anthropological Research', *Etnofoor* XII(1): 27–38.

Warming, H. 2011. 'Getting Under Their Skins? Accessing Young Children's Perspectives Through Ethnographic Fieldwork', *Childhood* 18(1): 39–53.

Woodhead, M. and D. Faulkner. 2008. 'Subjects, Objects or Participants?', in P. Christensen and A. James (eds), *Research with Children*. London: Routledge.

Chapter 6

DIALOGUES WITH ANTHROPOLOGISTS

WHERE INTERVIEWS BECOME RELEVANT

Judith Okely

Anthropologists have done brilliant and original fieldwork around the globe. A legacy of positivism has discouraged full exploration of the narratives of their experience as positioned researchers. This chapter outlines the context of fieldwork accounts elicited from over twenty anthropologists in informal interviews. The fieldwork ranges from Afghanistan in the late 1960s to Senegal from 2000. The anthropologists are of sixteen nationalities and varied ages. Fieldwork included locations in South and North America, India, throughout Europe and Africa and in South East Asia.[1]

The unexpected outcome was the extraordinary range of commonalities in the anthropologists' responses and research practices. Their experiences challenged the banality of formulaic methods; too often prioritised in other disciplines. The interviews were conducted not between strangers, but as trusting exchanges between fellow anthropologists where the interviewer intervened with similarities or contrasts. Some emergent examples from the dialogues are presented, although more space is devoted to the context and history of interview procedures for an anthropologist.

Regrettably, the ethnographic traditions from which interviews can emerge are largely unknown to the majority of other disciplines, whose outdated caricature of social science holds sway. Hegemonic multidisciplinary ethics committees have gained new powers to censor key approaches embedded in anthropological fieldwork, all in the name of constructed objectivity and invented contamination. Controversial presumptions about the interview as required detached encounter continue to prevail.

Participant Observation Sidelined

Paradoxically, while insisting that participant observation is the core of social anthropology, this chapter addresses both the unique insights gained through interviews in relevant contexts and their limitations, if not inbuilt errors. Social anthropology, as I was taught by Edmund Leach, a student of Malinowski, has participant observation as central – namely the aim to 'pitch one's tent in the centre of the village' (Malinowski 1922). This proved a crucial vindication when, after later being recruited by an independent Social Science Centre to examine Gypsies and government policy, I was eventually able to argue the need to live in a caravan on Gypsy sites. By contrast, my research manager, a seconded ministerial civil servant, prioritised interviews with mass questionnaires generating quantitative data. Thus my first major research entailed arguing for the necessity of intensive fieldwork in a limited number of locations (cf. Leach 1967).

Regrettably, despite the power of classical anthropological knowledge that has emerged from such field practice, and the continuing recognition of the unique insights from in-depth ethnography, pseudoscientific judgements continue to hold sway. This is often when anthropology is assessed alongside other disciplines in multidisciplinary committees. Quantitative criteria blend with naive scientised, positivist notions. Objectivity is conflated with distance. Seemingly, the ideal social science researcher should remain a detached alien and refrain from humane rapport with their 'objects', rarely recognised as subjects of research. This constructed ideal dominates other disciplines' ill-informed regulation of social anthropology. Stephen Rose has brilliantly outlined how all disciplines, both science and social sciences, came to have an inappropriate 'physics envy' (1997) in contrast to all other sciences. Elsewhere I have pointed out how the earliest field anthropologists were trained biologists keen on the total context (Okely 2012: 18).

Decades ago, the sociologist, Anne Oakley, in her now classic and most cited article 'Interviewing Women' (1981), confronted and challenged the presumptions with which social anthropologists also have to contend. She, the sociologist, examined established textbook guidelines for interviewing; many she exposed not only as ludicrous but unethical in that the interviewer was expected to withhold crucial health information from the interviewee. The guidelines prioritised distance, censoring all reciprocal exchange. Oakley exposes the absurdity of procedures that demand that the interviewer must in turn refuse to be questioned but divert any questions from the interviewee, regardless of risks to health, if basic information is withheld. A misplaced notion of contamination reigns supreme. For example, when interviewing pregnant women, Oakley was asked if it was 'dangerous to smoke' or poignantly 'which hole' might the baby come out of. Observing correct procedures, the interviewer was expected to answer 'that's an interesting one' or 'I'll think about that'. Otherwise, it was asserted, this would affect the scientific objectivity of the project.

The research potential in shared perspectives, rather than performed detachment, was instead endorsed by Oakley. She described (1986, personal communication) in significant detail her rapport when interviewing women about housework. She discovered that if she arrived with a basket of shopping and on which, instead of a table, she then placed the tape recorder, the interviewees' replies became more relaxed, therefore expansive. Thus her women interviewees could empathise with the female interviewer through shared gendered responsibilities. Similarly, the sociologist Janet Finch deliberately exploited her shared identity as a clergyman's wife with her interviewees (1984). Elsewhere, I have explored the knowledge gained by non-verbal, vicarious, identification in interactions with the rural aged in France (Okely 1994a).

Regrettably, today the prioritising of distancing, parading as scientific universal lives on, and with greater hegemony. A younger generation of researchers can be intimidated and confused. Additionally, the presumed predominance of the interview in most social sciences puts at risk both the practice of participant observation and the creative potential in the interview as method. If not subject to constraints, semi-structured interviews tend to be discredited because they are not easily 'controlled'. Such is the judgement by self-anointed 'experts'. Yet, as this chapter contests, it is the free-ranging narratives of interviews, moving into dialogues, which bring new knowledge, precisely because unpredicted.

Ethnocentric Ethics Committees

The revival of presumed discredited notions of social science re-emerged after ethics committees were imposed on UK universities in recent years. This imposition was triggered by the exposure of a medical (not a social science) scandal in several UK research hospitals, namely those at Bristol and Alder Hey. Years after the deaths and burials of vulnerable babies, often after heart surgery, bereaved parents first learned that the inner organs of their loved ones had been removed and retained. Stomachs, intestines and brains had been secretly stored in hospital jars for decades, ostensibly for research.

Yet social anthropologists have never 'gutted' babies, let alone adults. We have respected and deferred to peoples' differing mortuary beliefs and rituals. Nevertheless, despite our profound respect for humanity across all cultures, anthropologists are now being subjected to ethnocentric diktat. After a 2001 official enquiry into the 'baby hearts', together with law suits, medically driven notions of legal consent have subsequently been imposed also on the social sciences and humanities. No allowance is made for the fact that in such disciplines the researcher's interaction with speaking humans is ever-changing. A legalistic form to be signed as a one-off is a diversion, not a solution. So-called 'informants' are not patients whose identity as bodies is prioritised. The medical blueprint of 'informed consent' for bodily intervention is transposed for all contexts. No matter if the people are non-literate where official forms are perceived as evidence of the researcher as spy, police or another all-powerful official.

Proof of anthropologists' prior ethical self-regulation is found as follows. Louise de la Gorgendière, an anthropologist, not a medical practitioner, had in the early 1990s exposed the unethical behaviour of a UK university government and charity-funded medical research project. African mothers and babies were unwittingly treated as laboratory objects when the UK medics tracked the possibility of HIV transmission through breastfeeding. The mothers were not informed that they were HIV-positive. De la Gorgendière exposed the scandal, while anonymising the university in her subsequent publication (2005).

Ignorance of Ethnographic Practice

Cross-national ignorance of ethnographic fieldwork that might entail months, indeed years, of co-residence and shared day-to-day experience is confirmed in even more disturbing directives beyond the UK. An anthropology professor informs me of her recent attempts to introduce a doctoral programme at her distinguished Canadian university. Although the undergraduates and postgraduates are familiar with anthropological approaches in university courses, the official doctoral proposal has to be passed via multiple formalities – through committees whose members have no anthropology qualifications. Such 'experts' may have never read a single text in the discipline.

This Canadian anthropologist, with a Cambridge doctorate, recounted how prospective doctoral anthropology students would be required to present for the committee's approval an advance list of questions to be asked of individuals. Once in 'the field', the anthropologist would have to obtain from everyone encountered a signed 'informed consent' to such advance, formatted questions.

Thus fieldwork is reduced to pre-planned interrogation, where diversion and innovation are forbidden as unethical (cf. Macdonald 2010). Such approaches risk undermining the creative routes to cross-cultural knowledge around the world. Paradoxically, although I critique here any presumption that the interview is the core to the discipline, I explore key instances where this mode of research proves rewarding and crucial in the appropriate context. But first the mistaken dependence on the interview format will be addressed.

Pre-ordained Questionnaires and Questioning

Before completing a postgraduate anthropology 'conversion' course, immediately after graduating in P.P.E. (Politics, Philosophy and Economics), my experience as a research assistant to an economist provided stark insights into the limitations of a questionnaire. The advance construction of questions often proved absurd and counter-productive, even when focused on the apparently simple topic of shopping habits. The project was subsidised by commercial companies interested in what would become the Templars shopping centre in east Oxford. My employer was a Nuffield College doctoral student who had personally devised the questionnaire. This I had to administer, knocking on random doors along working-class streets of Oxford.

I, the interviewer, was given just three options to tick box as answer to each question: Yes, No or Don't Know. One question was: 'Do you buy your Sunday roast joint on Friday or Saturday?' Many of the doorstep interviewees were bemused. Poverty-stricken, widowed pensioners pointed out they ate alone on Sundays and waited until late Saturday to pick up the last discounted meat chop. There was only half a page at the end of the schedule for 'Comments'. This space, to the potential ethnographer, provided the richest material. Sometimes, I was invited in for a chat and given rare insights into working-class lives hitherto hidden from a relatively privileged Oxford graduate. Interviewees giggled at the absurd presumptions in the questions. Even the choice of beef, let alone the idea of a family meal, alerted me to age and cultural bias.

But my employer was less interested in the volunteered insights and details in the comments section, just so long as the tick box answers were there to be quantified. He confessed that, after several attempts at himself administering the questionnaires, he abandoned this because he felt 'too shy'. Thus even limited face-to-face interaction was delegated to females (Okely 1987). More constructively, this future anthropologist learned through practice that interviews, based on pre-formed, presumptive questions and answers, had confirmed disturbing limitations.

Trial and Error Scepticism of Questioning

Again, before my postgraduate anthropology 'conversion' course, it was thanks to the experience with my ex-partner Hugh that I learned about ethnographic fieldwork, in this case, in the west of Ireland (Brody 1973). We soon confronted problems when attempting to question the rural residents, faced with us, intrusive, outsider 'Anglos' (Okely 2009). We could be given elaborate answers, but ones that seemed to reflect the presumed values of us the interrogators. Deutscher (1970) documented the contrast between what people, in answer to formal interviews, said they believed and what they actually did.

All this was excellent preparation for subsequent fieldwork with the Gypsies for whom the very question mode was associated with persecuting Gorgio (non-Gypsy) officials. It was culturally unacceptable to ask questions, even among the Gypsies themselves. Years earlier, Lévi-Strauss had learned that when first asking Amazonian Indians whether they ate koro grubs, they repeatedly denied this, knowing outsiders' stigmatising of such food. The only way was for Lévi-Strauss to express an interest in eating them (1973 [1955]: 160; Okely 2012: 80–81). Thus participation rather than detached interrogation brought proof.

My previously well-grounded scepticism of the questionnaire mode was revived when recruited for the Gypsy project. The research director, trained in social administration and survey techniques, requested that I administer a multi-page questionnaire for Gypsies nationwide (Okely 1987).

To her great credit she had previously organised and devised the questions for the first official Census of Gypsies and Travellers throughout England and Wales (MHLG 1967). However, one question asked mainly by the police or local officials of each Gypsy 'head of household' [sic], was 'Why do you travel?' This was addressed to nomads for whom, by definition, travel was their core lifestyle. When living on Gypsy camps, I faced a parallel confusion when Gypsy children would ask me, 'Judith, what's it like living in a house?' How could I begin to convey this taken-for-granted lifestyle? In contrast to the disingenuous census question, an anthropologist's grounded analysis of nomads' varying movement was by accumulative, detailed observations of multiple incidents. All this would emerge from the wider context of shared residence and participant observation (Okely 1983: Chapter 3).

I delegated the questionnaires to a social worker who found that many of the answers contradicted what she knew through months of acquaintance. The director recognised the inconsistencies. It was eventually conceded that questionnaires would be inappropriate, apparently because the Gypsies were non-literate. But the director insisted that such methods would be adequate for literate, allegedly 'rational' officials. So a representative from every local authority that had provided a Gypsy site would be formally interviewed. However, the powerful skilfully block access to information (Nader 1974) – something I would witness first-hand when obliged to administer the questionnaire to officials myself.

When, in one such interview, I asked the reason why a local authority Gypsy site had eventually been bulldozed, the official declared this was because the land was 'liable to flooding and therefore unhealthy'. This was, coincidentally, the site where I had first lived. The interview over, this same public official, now relaxed, invited me to join him for lunch. He then casually revealed that the site had to be closed because it gave 'a bad impression on the main route to our beautiful cathedral city'. Flooding was irrelevant but politically correct. Thus ethnographic participant observation was proven to contradict, indeed falsify, formal question/answer techniques.

Participation Sidelined

With a few notable exceptions (Agar 1980 [1967]; Hammersley and Atkinson 1983, among others), methods textbooks favoured just one sociological tradition out of many. Formalised interviews emerging from massive quantitative surveys had become central, invariably conducted by people who were not those who wrote up the results. Named authors of such treatises found no problem in never having encountered the hundreds of surveyed individuals. The great Chicago sociology tradition (Whyte 1955 [1943] /1955) which developed the practice labelled 'participant observation', had by the 1980s in the UK been subsumed into what other sociologists labelled, if not dismissed, as symbolic interactionism.

Some sociology colleagues at Essex University, where I lectured in the 1980s, bizarrely asserted that researchers, such as myself, who engaged in participant observation fieldwork were 'anti-structure': apparently face-to-face interaction was incompatible with the study of the larger economic and political structures and contexts. Apart from a few welcoming allies in this celebrated department (including social historians), I was branded 'anti-structure', it seems, because I actually lived alongside the people I studied. Empirical research, I was to discover, prioritised the interview as survey. Such ignorance of anthropological fieldwork among some social scientists continues today, but with even more negative consequences for research. In the 1970s and 1980s, no ethics committee existed to block our anthropological fieldwork in ways that are imposed today.

Hegemonic Committee Controls

Unfortunately, continuing ignorance has had potential problems for a younger generation of anthropologists. Bureaucratised managerialism has intervened where previously the lack of formal-methods training had paradoxically facilitated creative advantages for anthropologists, who were then freer to pursue independent enquiries. Subsequently, university multidisciplinary ethics committees, claiming hegemonic expertise, have risked damaging social anthropology research proposals. Here are some examples linked to the use of interviews by anthropologists.

One anthropologist, a UK university lecturer, had published his anthropology doctorate based on unique long-term experience as teacher, then ethnographer, of an elite boys' boarding school in Zambia (Simpson 2003). Through the years, he maintained contact with his ex-pupils, many of whom had joined the political elite. After discovering that a considerable number had tragically became victims of HIV Aids, he determined on a follow-up study of his ex-pupils' life trajectory. This would clearly include interviewing the survivors and family.

By good fortune, he had already recorded interviews with his ex-pupils about their expectations on the threshold of leaving school. Masculinity, linked mainly to heterosexual mores, would, he proposed, be problematised in what would be a pioneering study (given the near absence of such research). Nevertheless, when he applied for research funding, this project risked being blocked before it began. His university's multidisciplinary research committee, initially lacking any anthropologist, argued that such research would be scientifically 'contaminated'. This was because the researcher already knew the individuals he proposed to interview. Such a judgement from a leading UK university defies belief.

As obvious to any anthropological practice, the proposed research had the potential to reveal hitherto crucial hidden insights unavailable to strangers. It was precisely because the researcher knew his subjects, through years of mutual respect, that it would be revelatory and highly original. Fortunately, the lecturer's head of department and professor of anthropology, intervened to reverse the committee's shockingly 'scientistic' judgements. Thus another book emerged, *Boys to Men in the Shadow of Aids: Masculinities and HIV Risk in Zambia* (Simpson 2009).

Similar outdated interventions by so-called ethics committees are a continuing threat to the discipline (Macdonald 2010). Even before such committees, in the early 1990s, my doctoral student, Clive Foster, faced similar scepticism from the chief scientist's committee at the Scottish Office. Foster had been head of a Borstal School before these institutions for 'young delinquents' were abolished. By chance, while completing an MA in Social Anthropology at Edinburgh, he encountered several of these ex-borstal boys, now adults, but poignantly victims of heroin addiction and now HIV-positive. Imaginatively, he proposed, as his doctorate, a follow-up study of individuals he had once known. They spontaneously asked him to record their life experiences, in contrast to 'all those researchers pestering us with questions'. Edinburgh had, in the early 1990s, been labelled the 'Aids capital of Europe' and thus attracted multiple research projects, but far from ethnographic ones and instead favouring questionnaires between strangers.

Hoping to receive some minor funding, Foster was interviewed at the Scottish Office. Innocently unprepared for the aggressive ignorance of anthropology, he was lambasted because his emphasis on informal dialogues in the individuals' home space was 'unscientific'. Foster had not offered a 'control group' of previously unknown residents.

It was considered irrelevant, indeed highly suspect, that the ex-borstal boys, now adults, had first approached Foster, a respected individual from their past. As with Simpson, above, his authoritative departmental head intervened, arguing that ethnographic research had a different history. Money was awarded on condition the doctoral title claimed to be studying only the 'carers'. Thus the medical experts claimed a monopoly of the sick.

Thankfully, medical anthropology, pioneered at Brunel, is increasingly taken seriously in several universities. Foster's day-to-day informal ethnography and dialogues were later to explain the concentration of HIV as mainly due to multiple on-site needle sharing in Edinburgh (Foster 1995). In contrast, Glasgow had an explicit policy of issuing free, clean needles, so HIV was not passed on. Foster's research produced poignant insights into marginalised lives.

In both these examples, the anthropologists built on long-term acquaintance and shared knowledge. Follow-up research would include the asking of questions, sometimes in semi-structured interviews, verging on dialogue, and where long-term trust was crucial for access and revelation. But other disciplinary experts, seeped in differing traditions, would have blocked access. It is also ironic that these projects had vital potential for the enhancement of medical research.

Interviewing after Participation

These examples of the value of prior acquaintance already had resonances with my 1980s fieldwork among the aged in rural France (Okely 1994a, 2001). Given my 1970s dissatisfaction with the very act of asking questions among the Gypsies, by contrast, in another context, after extended fieldwork in Normandy, I found the semi-structured interview mode exceptionally rewarding. Welcomed as a French speaking Anglaise, I established trust through shared participation. I learned to hand-milk cows under the tutelage of Jacqueline Grégoire, to local astonishment that 'une professeur' would engage in manual labour.

To make her acquaintance, as a strategically authentic means of access, I requested an interview. Jacqueline was president of the local club for the aged. This would demonstrate my genuine respect and interest in the clubs. The answers to my very basic questions were banal because I hardly knew what to ask at this stage, before long-term immersion and because we were complete strangers; each acting with caution and restraint.

Anticipated or not, the mechanical act of interrogation would demonstrate the limits in learning about her unprecedented world view, towards which she would later lead me (Okely 2001). After about forty minutes of Q and A, throughout which she plucked a chicken, she announced she had 'work to do'. To her surprise, I asked to join her in the barn where she would embark on milking her cows (Okely 2009: 55).

It was only after knowing Jacqueline over a few years of intermittent fieldwork that I could most constructively interview her; complete with tape recorder. By then, I knew what questions to ask. In many instances, I anticipated the central themes in potential answers. I wanted to give her the opportunity to express everything in her own words and to range in unexpected directions, all under her control (Okely 1996: Chapter 10).

As in our first encounter, she insisted on not 'wasting time' during the interview, which she agreed to only while milking. The most poignant sound for any archive is the milk spurting into each bucket as I recorded our exchanges. Again her labour and my presence as apprentice milkmaid added to the emergent, shared knowledge.

Interviewing after Extended Friendship

In another instance, I found the introduction of a tape recorder for interviewing proved poignantly revealing. This was when, in the late 1970s, I interviewed Harold Busby, an octogenarian and deserter from the First World War. I had known him for a decade having once lived in a neighbouring Oxfordshire village. Again, mutual trust and affection ensured an in-depth self-narration; in this case, a unique record for oral history. During my intermittent visits in later years, Harold tended to ramble and repeat himself. But the introduction of this alien machine dramatically focused his attention. All repetition ceased, as he seemed to recognise this was the last chance to record his testimony (Okely 1996: Chapter 10). This has special significance given the huge media and political focus on the centenary of 2014.

He mentioned that some historians had visited in a one-off interview project, but he was deeply critical of their simplistic questioning.

Thus, in contrast to fieldwork among the Gypsies, in other forms of research, the interviewing device, complete with recorder, was productive, but only after a relationship of trust. Just as important was the accrued knowledge of what questions to ask. As with Jacqueline Grégoire later, sometimes I knew the very answers. But I wanted Harold Busby's individual voice, including his rural working-class Oxfordshire accent, which linguists might treasure. I was rewarded by magically unexpected passages.

The success of this type of recorded interview left its mark. When 'methods training' was made compulsory under The Economic and Social Research Council (ESRC) diktat in the early 1990s, I had long noted the absence of convincing textbooks. Thus I planned a book on ethnographic methods in anthropology; expanding on years of lecture notes. Unexpectedly, I was drawn to tape recording multiple dialogic interviews, and with a creative focus never pre-planned.

Reversal of Scepticism

The compulsory methods courses were a consequence of prime minister Margaret Thatcher's unsuccessful attempt to abolish the then Social Science Research Council in the 1980s (Okely 2012: 8). The surviving, newly named Economic and Social Research Council responded to government pressure to provide 'transferable skills', especially after Thatcher had decreed that the word Science be deleted from the original SSRC. Social science departments rushed to introduce postgraduate methods courses. Ironically, I had already smuggled methods into my anthropological theory lectures at Durham University (Okely 2007a). I challenged the assertion that the publication of Malinowski's diary (1967) was irrelevant (Okely 1975).

By the early 1990s, my anthropology postgraduates at Edinburgh University were increasingly demoralised by the compulsory methods course, convened by a sociology professor. He ridiculed anthropologists because they had 'no hypotheses'. Apparently they just 'made it up as they went along'. Right up to the mid 1990s, bewildered anthropology applicants for ESRC doctoral grants were also asked what hypothesis they were testing. I repeatedly protested to the ESRC and was relieved that, eventually, applicants were asked to outline the more general, free-ranging 'research questions'.

Open-ended Inspiration

Already I had been inspired by *The Professional Stranger* (Agar 1980
[1967]: 16) where Agar, as anthropologist, had once faced similar critiques from other social scientists. When repeatedly asked what 'tool'
he was using, he silenced them with the brilliant 'funnel method',
namely, being open to everything at the start before refining the approach, topic and focus (Okely 2012: 20–22). This resonated with the
holistic approach I had acquired via Leach's Cambridge postgraduate
course on Malinowski. The anthropologist should be open to every
aspect of a group or society.

Long-vindicated during open-ended fieldwork among the Gypsies, and sceptical of formal question and answer interrogations, my
methods lectures at Essex, Edinburgh and then Hull, drew on the full
range of anthropological practice through existing publications. My
transcribed lectures were ready, after minor adjustments, for a methods book to reassure the demoralised postgraduates. In a publication
proposal, I suggested, merely in passing, that I would add some examples of anthropologists' fieldwork, naively believing these were easily
found in prefaces and footnotes, if not in the main texts.

Questions for Other Anthropologists

I was seeking answers to questions that had, for years, been circu-
lating in my intellectual consciousness. Here I had learned what to
ask but could not locate the answers. Anthropologists had done very
different fieldworks across space and time. The edited volume *Anthropology and Autobiography* (Okely and Callaway 1992) had begun to address the positionality of individual anthropologists. The trope of the
lone male hero I had already disrupted when confronting my shared
Ireland field experience as accompanying 'wife' who was not refer-
enced in the ensuing monograph (Brody 1973; Okely 2009).

There were, however, many more questions beyond the
problematising of gender, age, ethnicity and nationality, given the
very different fieldworks anthropologists had undertaken across
space and time. For example, what initial ideas or plans, if any, did
the anthropologists have when first embarking on fieldwork? Could
this contradict the obligation to outline advance 'aims and objectives'
– the emergent bureaucratic blueprint for research proposals? Did
the original research questions remain fixed, once immersed in the

field? How did the anthropologists come to choose a specific region and locality? In what way did they depend on participant observation?

Mauss's pioneering essay on bodily habitus (1935; cf. Douglas 1966; Foucault 1977) with its emphasis on cross-cultural differences in bodily practice (including the gaze and regimentation (Okely 1996: Chapter 7 and 8)) had been inspirational. It would be illuminating to discover how other anthropologists made bodily adaptations across taken-for-granted cultural familiarities.

The role of local associates has also proved crucial. Long ago, Whyte in *Street Corner Society* (1955 [1943]) noted the intermediary 'Doc', who moreover advised Whyte not to ask questions, but to 'hang around'. This indigenous member appreciated the greater rewards in participant observation over interrogation. Likewise I had depended on crucial individuals or intermediaries, especially among the Gypsies, facilitating my integration. From examples scattered in the literature, these seemed to resonate with the gender, age and even personality of the fieldworker; thus the specificity of the fieldworker had consequences for choice of key associates.[2]

Serendipity and Revelatory Mistakes

The concept of serendipity in Powdermaker's *Stranger and Friend* (1967) had long seemed persuasive. In occasional discussions or readings, it emerged as crucial in the research process. Serendipity challenged the parody of science found in methods textbooks and application forms. These invariably demanded that researchers' have pre-formulated hypotheses to 'operationalise', in crude, mechanistic mode. Even more ironic is that serendipity is legendary in scientific discovery. The role of chance was, indeed, crucial in all types of my fieldwork, but such concerns were rarely, if ever, addressed in ethnographic teaching and other publications. Exceptionally, the sociologist Law has acknowledged 'mess' in social science research (2004). Research cannot be tidily planned.

Sudden 'breakthroughs' have been crucial in discovery and analysis: one so-called 'anecdote' can throw light on an entire system. We do not need accumulated quantitative 'data' to find explanations and theoretical underpinning. Again in much social science research the very concept 'anecdotal' is used as put-down rather than crucial insight. By contrast, Needham's 'Blood, Thunder and the Animals' (1967) is inspirational. Needham only learned about the indigenous classification systems when, following his embodied cultural habit, he removed a tick from his foot and threw it into the fire. He only then learned of his major mistake when reprimanded by his companions for in effect throwing his blood onto flames. This would have dire consequences according to the people he was with. One seemingly trivial gesture led to the unfolding of their cosmology.

Similarly, I learned the subtleties of Gypsy pollution rules only when I innocently broke them and was instructed as to the correct behaviour. Such acquired knowledge I searched for in other anthropologists' existing publications; but this was either unrecorded or marginalised with insufficient detail.

Seized Chance Changes All

My transcribed lectures were near publication in the late 1990s when I was visiting the anthropologist Brian Morris. We found ourselves exchanging extended narratives on our respective fieldworks, he among nomads in India (1982), among other groups in Malawi, then I in England and France. Here, in this 'eureka' impromptu discussion, were the very details I had neither found nor could disentangle from prefaces and footnotes. I asked if Brian had a tape recorder, and as he was locating it, then setting it up, I scribbled down questions arising from those very intellectual problems outlined above and later to be fully noted (Okely 2012: 155). Although the original questions were metaphorically scribbled on the back of an envelope, they emerged from decades of intellectual curiosity. Four hours later we turned off the recorder. He had given me extended answers along circuitous paths, signposted only vaguely by the broad, open-ended questions.[3]

After this serendipitous discovery, competing with administrative and teaching commitments, I was to accumulate similar recorded, then transcribed, exchanges with over twenty anthropologists of some sixteen nationalities (see note 1). Their words and magnificent articulation of experiences across the globe, all to be selected and edited for each themed chapter, inevitably transformed the text. Hence the extended delay in finalising *Anthropological Practice: Fieldwork and the Ethnographic Method* (Okely 2012). An advance article appeared as 'Fieldwork Embodied' (Okely 2007b).

The interviews followed a trajectory of the research practice from initial ideas to choice of region, location and topic, confronting possible changes. The process included entry, encounters with key associates, specificities of the fieldworker, participant observation, bodily knowledge, breakthroughs and mistakes, as well as note-taking.

Thus my initial proposal to complete a methods textbook, during a one year's ESRC Senior Research Fellowship awarded in the mid 1990s, was utterly transformed – all through the chance inspiration of interviewing one anthropologist, followed by many others. That year, largely freed of bureaucratic obligations and teaching, enabled creative, by definition, unplanned innovations. Unfortunately, having been obliged to outline advance rigid 'aims and objectives' in the application, I was subsequently awarded the second-lowest rating by the chairman of the 'End of Grant Committee'.[4] Thus the punishment for innovation and changed focus ensured that any future grant applications would be prejudiced.

Other Interviews Filmed

Sometime after my project on methods dialogues commenced, I realised that Alan Macfarlane had already embarked on filming interviews with anthropologists. He has accumulated an impressive online collection. He notes:

> it may seem strange that anthropologists have devoted so much energy to investigating other people's tribes (including filming them), and so little time on their own. When the 'ancestors' are encouraged to talk, they do so with a frankness and insight which it is a pleasure to be involved in preserving. This modest project, done in odd moments and with little funding, will ideally enable our descendants in a hundred years time to catch a glimpse of a rich period of anthropological research. (Macfarlane 2004)

Interview Strategies, Not Techniques

My self-initiated project of refocusing on interview-dialogues, contradicting past experiences, revived a questioning of the positivist orthodoxies, which repress creative, original research. Unfortunately, some discussions of interviews are imbued with mechanistic procedures. When engaging in, or 'conducting', an interview, the notion of 'techniques' is, I argue, inappropriate. The pioneering article by Anne Oakley (1981) stands as a lasting critique of positivist formulae, which, as the examples above confirm, remain embedded in multidisciplinary research committees.

Such issues were alive and well in one of the most famous sociology departments in the late 1980s. A superb undergraduate who gained a distinction by the examiners for the dissertation I had supervised, subsequently came guilt-stricken to my office. His imaginatively chosen topic entailed recording views about ageing among older non-academic staff on the campus, e.g., porters, janitors and cleaners. He confessed to having 'cheated' because one evening he had invited many of the interviewees for an informal gathering, complete with drinks in a common room. He recorded, then transcribed, the group's shared discussions on the topic of ageing.

This new graduate was concerned because, according to what he had been taught in some sociologists' methods courses, the interviewees had 'contaminated' each other's testimony through such interaction. The problem was that the evidence had not arisen solely from a one-to-one formal exchange between researcher and interviewee. He confessed that he had cut and pasted each individual's quotes, as if acquired entirely in isolation.

But on the contrary, I reassured him that if he had described in a methods section his initiative for the group discussion, he should have been praised for imagination and ingenuity. The interaction between usually lone employees revealed perspectives that the novice ethnographer could not have anticipated. Thanks to these ideas, newly generated from grass-roots level, this graduate won a convincing doctoral grant to study ageing among retired miners (Dawson 1990), and is now a professor of anthropology.

The Leading Question

Instead of notions of objectivity and detachment, alternative and provocative interview strategies were already outlined in Omvedt's 'On the Participant Study of Women's Movements' (1979). Here she explores 'the methodology of the leading question' (ibid.: 384). She argued that the gender and ethnicity would affect the responses in her research in India. A perceived representative of the powerful, namely a white male middle-class interviewer, questioning poor Indian women was more likely to elicit what they perceived as his values and the status quo. Here were echoes of the Gypsies' responses to questioning by intrusive, powerful outsiders. By contrast, Omvedt contested that if the interviewer was female and openly critical in her questioning, very different answers would be elicited.

One sociology colleague, specialising in quantitative surveys del-egated to part-time employees, was infuriated when co-marking my course scripts, which cited Omvedt. It broke all the rules of detachment. Yet in his own reading list for qualitative methods that I inherited, his main advice had been to 'read a few novels'. Presumably, qualitative methods were mere fiction, although Clifford and Marcus (1986) were to validate literary styles.

The notion of interviewing in one-to-one isolation has some history within U.S. anthropological research, as revealed in a Durham University anthropology research seminar in the late 1970s. Two American anthropologists, a married couple, described their fieldwork among Amazonian Indians. They set up a tiny 'interview hut' in the woods with just enough room for one anthropologist and a 'captive native' seated face-to-face in uncontaminated enclosure. But these anthropologists complained in their seminar presentation that other Indians kept interrupting the formal procedure by knocking and trying to enter this alien, restricted space. These attempts at 'data collection' through 'objective' procedures were eventually abandoned. But the anthropologists never recognised the claustrophobic ethnocentricity in their approach.

Interviews as Reciprocal Exchange, Not Interrogation

By contrast, as developed in the emergent book *Anthropological Practice* (Okely 2012), my approach to exchanges, interviews or dialogues with anthropologists subverted any ideals of contamination. The interviews were dialogues rather than any formal interrogations. In a study of school children, the sociologist Burgess innovatively redefined the notion of interviews as 'conversations' (1984). However, he does not address the power imbalance confirmed by the absence of any reciprocal information from him, the adult; surely the essence of conversation.

My dialogues with the anthropologists were not one-way transmissions, but reciprocal exchanges of experience, helping make the implicit explicit. If the interviewer was prepared to reveal mistakes and vulnerability, then so might have the interviewee. I spontaneously interjected with examples of my own; sometimes contrasts, other times parallels that eased trust.

For instance, Mohammed Talib revealed that, when first outlining a research topic in the 1980s at his Indian university, he had been told that it was not academically relevant to study stonebreakers near Delhi. This was because allegedly they did not fit into his colleagues' interpretations of the Marxist class system. Stonebreakers could not be classified as 'working class'. They were non-unionised.

Indeed, they had come to the fore precisely because they were indentured labourers. We laughed as I reciprocated with a memory of my
own concerning the 'radical' researchers at the London Centre for
Environmental Studies, who had, in the early 1970s, protested to the
director that 'their' money might be funding Gypsies; members of
a mere lumpenproletariat. A geographer, now a celebrated professor, to my astonishment, protested to me that 'after all Gypsies were
only a minority'. Fortunately, the Rowntree Memorial Trust agreed
to finance the Gypsy research, and the Centre's Ford Foundation and
government funding was not called upon. The Rowntree Trust also
agreed to fund research into hypothermia among the aged by a gentle,
future colleague, Malcolm Wicks. The generalised aged brought no
controversy. But Gypsies, as an ethnic minority, remained scapegoats
on the margins. These examples from Talib and myself reveal how the
very choice of topic and group selected by the anthropologist can be a
source of controversy.

In my dialogues, it was informative to swap experiences, triggering
and elucidating hitherto unexplored debates. I, the interviewer, deliberately voiced contrasts or commonalities. Nevertheless, in the view
of multidisciplinary ethics committees, I deliberately broke the rules
of an outmoded positivism that decrees that shared exchanges, let
alone prior friendship or acquaintance, 'contaminate' and therefore
invalidate ensuing research and knowledge outcomes. On the contrary, such strategies evoke critical perspectives on research contexts
and process.

Interviewees Selected

In defiance of positivist orthodoxy, I found it constructive to conduct
these interview-conversations only with anthropologists whom I had
already come to know. The exchange was founded on mutual trust
arising from previous in-depth acquaintance and, in some cases, long-
term friendship. One interview, after only casual contact, proved to
be an utter failure. The interviewee remained rigid, seemingly pressurised to come up with rehearsed formulae rather than relax into
what might be feared as a confessional.

Some interviewees are of my generation, others younger. The interviewees' nationalities include persons of African, Asian, North and
South American ancestry, as well as from all over Europe, namely
Swedish, Norwegian, Polish, Dutch, Basque, English, Scottish, Maltese
and French.

I did not interview any students because I was concerned about a power imbalance, but not the myth of contamination. Another factor in the choice of interviewees was to select anthropologists who had both completed their doctorates and published widely, preferably with one or more monographs. They were sufficiently confident to reveal what less-established academics might wish to conceal for 'an imagined fear' of jeopardising their careers. Entirely relaxed in self-revelatory narratives, we laughed together at past naiveties and, crucially, informative blunders in our exchange. (Paradoxically, one eminent anthropologist was at first very uptight at the start of the interview, saying, 'I don't know why you want to ask me about field methods. I never attended any courses nor followed the correct formulae'. But through four hours of spellbinding exchange, he recounted multiple recognisable trajectories echoing what I heard among so many others.)

Interview Location

In all but two cases, I recorded these dialogues either in my own house or the anthropologists' houses. In the latter case, some could produce their field notes and give life to the discussion. In just two cases, I recorded in a public space. Michael Herzfeld, passing through Denmark where I was visiting professor, chose the slot after checking in at Copenhagen Airport where we sat in a noisy lobby. Helena Wulff and I met up in a Stockholm café. The problem was a non-functioning tape recorder: I hand-wrote her answers. Every now and then she told me to turn off the phantom recorder and then I held my pen aloft. Indeed many of the anthropologists wanted to explain some aspects but in confidence. So in reality I did turn off the recorder.

In one case, I interviewed a married couple, Roy Gigengack and Raquel Alonso, while their three-year-old son explored every touchable object in my sitting room. Helene Neveu Kringelbach also brought her youngest daughter, then at the crawling stage. When I asked if I should produce some toys, Helene reassured me the baby would find plenty in an academic's space!

The Stranger's Arrival

Bodily Impressions and Lessons

The details of participant observation became apparent through many of the questions. Some wonderful revelations, told merely as comic anecdote, were ripe for placing in wider context. When Pratt (1986) problematised the literary trope of arrival, she limited this to the impact on the arriving anthropologists, but was not concerned with how the 'others' viewed the stranger's arrival. My interviewees provided some choice examples where the stranger's external appearance was crucial.

Louise de la Gorgendière (1993), a white French-Canadian, arriving in a Ghanaian village, was classified as a 'confused ancestor' born in the wrong (white) body returning home. Signe Howell (1984), a Norwegian arriving in tropical forest Malaysia, was seen as a tall, ungendered body, until a man saw her discretely bathing in the river. He ran back to the villagers shouting, 'It's a woman. It's got breasts'. She was thus classified as an unthreatening female (Okely 2012: 109–10).

There were continuing bodily consequences for the anthropologist who was expected to adapt to unfamiliar ways of walking, dressing or working. These revelations were articulated as answers to my question on learning through the body, in contrast to any demands for detached observation. Participation brings new knowledge. This may only later be articulated in answer to a fellow anthropologist who also learned difference through the body unspoken (Okely 1992 and photograph p. 18).

Choice and Change of Topic

The anthropologists of my generation have not been 'contaminated' by research-methods training. They have indeed had to 'make it up as they go along'. This is where the commonalities emergent in the dialogue material proved so exciting and often unpredicted. These interviewees, as intellectuals, driven by scientific curiosity, pursued knowledge through innovative ways (Silverman 2012). The vast majority had had to adjust their topic(s) after immersion in the field. Some even, through technical problems of access, had had to change continents. All this emerged from my opening questions about their original aims and plans.

Part of the biographical trajectory thus included not only choice of topic, but also choice of location. This could be a matter of hit or miss, requiring ingenuity. Joanna Overing was all set to study in New Guinea but discovered that anthropologists had carved up territories as their own intellectual property. She and her husband switched at the last moment to Venezuela, South America, and a locality that could be reached before the seasonal flooding. Overing had wanted to study large gatherings, but such events were rare. Before anything, she had to study the complex kinship system (1975). But she hated kinship and perforce found herself labelled a kinship expert.

Starting with the choice of country, area or topic, the route was not usually linear. Often the anthropologist was drawn by a puzzle, i.e., political, intellectual or even autobiographical. For example, Paul Clough, originally of U.S. citizenship, revealed that he deliberately chose Nigeria, which, in the 1980s, did not have U.S. colonial legacies. Originally a sociologist supervised by a celebrated Marxist, he eventually found that the dominant theories did not fit. Influenced by Polly Hill, he was transformed into an anthropologist; open to what he learned at village level, i.e., what the people themselves taught him.

Mohammed Talib was by chance drawn towards a media storm concerning indentured labour: a political scandal in a celebrated democracy. He was not to predict that his study would also embrace the Hindu temple in honour of the monkey god, erected by the quarry workers (2010). Suzette Heald had prepared to study bilingualism in a border zone in Uganda. But a few weeks before departure, her accompanying husband was redirected to a teaching post in a different locality. Here bilingualism did not feature. Within the first week Heald serendipitously switched to violence and masculinity, after encountering two men with weapons saying they were off to kill someone (Heald 1998 [1989]; Okely 2012: 61–62).

Helena Wulff and Helene Neveu-Kringelbach, who researched dance (2007), drew, in part, on their prior dance experience (Okely 2012). Such expertise assisted rapport in the field. The peoples appreciated both anthropologists' bodily empathy and knowledge. Additionally, Neveu-Kringelbach, of Franco-Senegalese parentage, was returning to Senegal to her childhood location. Joseba Zulaika, of Basque nationality, had wanted to go to Africa, but his supervisor at Princeton advised him to return to the Basque country. Encouraged to study metaphors, his focus was transformed by an ETA (*Euskadi Ta Askatasuna* – Basque Homeland and Freedom) assassination on a bus where his mother had been a passenger. Years before governments thought it relevant, Zulaika decided to study terrorism in his own village (1982, 1995).

Akira Okazaki went, as a young man, far from Japan to live among the Maasai in Africa. Propelled in his French literature studies by the debate '*Qu'est-ce-qu'est la literature?*', he was keen to live with non-literate peoples. Upon arrival, Okazaki described how he completely changed his original focus. Only in his early forties did he accumulate sufficient funding to return in pursuit of an anthropology doctorate, this time in the Sudan (1997, 2002).

Johnny Parry went first to northern India expecting to study micro-politics. But no one in his chosen field locality was interested. They seemed obsessed with discussing marriages of women from a lower to a higher caste. After his first Delhi seminar presentation about his findings, a professor declared: 'What you are talking about is hypergamy'. Parry unabashedly revealed his response in my interview, namely that he asked, 'What is that?' He had been studying a well-documented category, without even knowing it (1979).

The most dramatic role of accident is in Malcolm Mcleod's case. He recounted how, wanting to study witchcraft he was advised by a French anthropologist, visiting Oxford, to select the Asante in Ghana. He duly went (Okely 2010). But within weeks, he was utterly inspired by the material culture, and sidelined his interest in witchcraft. He was eventually to become the Keeper of the Museum of Mankind, then Curator, in Glasgow. On returning to Oxford after a few years' fieldwork in Ghana, he encountered the same French anthropologist, who by chance was again visiting the university. Mcleod informed him of his change from witchcraft among the Asante to material culture. The Frenchman immediately remonstrated that he had not advised the Asante in Ghana but the Azande in east Africa, already famously studied by Mcleod's mentor Evans-Pritchard.

Grounded Curiosities

Thus from the outset, my dialogues exposed the absurdity of funding bodies, insisting on advance formulations of well-honed research plans, let alone hypotheses. The anthropologists' critical quests, intellectually grounded, and holistic passions for knowledge should be trusted. Since the very topics have to change, it is clear that current committee demands for advance questions are an absurd straight-jacket on discovery and knowledge.

I recall the late and inspirational David Brooks, my colleague at Durham University, being mocked in the mid 1970s by our economistic colleagues for his charismatic lectures on cross-cultural ritual and religion (Okely 2007a). During and after fieldwork among the Bahktiari nomads in Iran, curiosity drove him to study, in depth, the significance of Islam, both at local and state level. No advance questions submitted to a committee could have embraced what he was to discover through participation. David predicted, a year or more in advance, the overthrow of the Shah and the crucial political role of Islam. But he was a prophet in the political and academic wilderness. After the Iranian revolution, books on Iran were rushed out, including one by a professor of international relations (Halliday 1978). One perceptive critic of this early book noted that Islam was not even in the index (Okely 1994b).

Key Individuals, Influence and Intellectual Curiosity

Another question my dialogues addressed was the encounter with, and role of, specific associates. In a number of cases the meeting of the outsider anthropologist and the insider depended on matching opposites; in other cases they were fellow intellectuals (Sanjek 1993), or else the same gender and age, or the associate acted as surrogate parent.

Again the encounters were a matter of chance. The notion of the flâneur, who strolls without premeditated aim might be said to be integral to anthropological practice and explored in other contexts (Tester 1994). Encounters with potentially key individuals might be accidental but it was important the anthropologists seized the chance. In some cases, the associates' experience and advice changed the anthropologists' focus and even research locality.

The seemingly aimless flâneur again subverts the bureaucratic prioritising of 'aims and objectives', which have so infected university and research committees (Okely 2006). In short, the advance prioritising of what government ministers define as 'useful' and 'income generating' is scandalously counterproductive. If David Owen, as Foreign Secretary in 1978, had listened to the likes of David Brooks, instead of continuing officially to support the Shah, British/Iranian relations would not have left such a toxic legacy.

Conclusion

One question I regret never asking, and which a postgraduate at a Glasgow seminar asked me, was, 'Did the fieldwork change you? If so, in what way?' In many instances, transformation is implicit in the transcripts. But it would be inappropriate to guess what each individual considered most relevant. There are always unexpected answers to emerge from dialogues between colleagues, not just between strangers. Exploring differences through anthropology gives life to prior difference or consolidates escape from ethnocentrism.

Interviews as dialogues between persons with shared anthropological commitment reveal ever-unfolding ethnographic narratives. Often sidelined as 'mere anecdote', detailed analysis of scattered material systematises knowledge into how anthropologists discover and convey the full range of human possibilities.

Notes

1. The anthropologists included: Paul Clough, Roy Gigengack, Louise de La Gorgendière, Suzette Heald, Michael Herzfeld, Signe Howell, Felicia Hughes-Freeland, Ignacy-Marek Kaminski, Margaret Kenna, Raquel Alonso Lopez, Malcolm Mcleod, Brian Morris, Helene Neveu-Kringelbach, Akira Okazaki, Joanna Overing, Jonathan Parry, Carol Silverman, Mohammad Talib, Nancy Lindisfarne-Tapper, Sue Wright, Helena Wulff, Joseba Zulaika.
2. I resist the label 'informants', as if mere objects of interrogation.
3. Questions to Interviewees:
   1. What were, if any, your initial ideas? In what way, if any, were they changed in the field?
   2. How did you establish connections?
   3. Were there any key events/encounters?
   4. Did serendipity play a part?
   5. How did you go about your research?
   6. What were the most successful approaches?
   7. What were the least successful approaches?
   8. Did you learn by mistakes?
   9. In what ways did you use a) participant observation, b) interviewing; either structured or semi-structured?
   10. Did you learn with your body and all your senses?
   11. What, if at all, was the importance of memory?
   12. Who were your main informants or associates?
   13. What, if any, were the effects for rapport and your approach of your gender/age/'race'/ethnicity/nationality and personality?

14. How did you record and make use of field notes?
15. Did photography or other images feature in your research?
16. What was the role of memory in analysis?
4. This was because the final manuscript had not been submitted within the minute time frame (Okely 2012: footnote 1). Yet I had completed a backlog of other publications, including an edited volume (Okely 1996) alongside follow-up fieldwork (Okely 2001).

References

Agar, M. 1980 [1967]. *The Professional Stranger: An Informal Introduction to Ethnography*. London: Academic Press.

Brody, H. 1973. *Inishkillane: Change and Decline in the West of Ireland*. London: Allen Lane, Penguin.

Burgess, R. 1984. *In the Field: An Introduction to Field Research*. London: Allen and Unwin.

Dawson, A. 1990. 'Ageing and Community in a Post-Mining Town, N.E. England', Ph.D. dissertation. Essex University.

De la Gorgendière, L. 1993. 'Education and Development in Ghana: An Asante Village Study', Ph.D. dissertation. Cambridge University.

———. 2005. 'Rights and Wrongs: HIV/AIDS Research in Africa', *Human Organisation, the Journal of the Society for Applied Anthropology* 64(2): 166–78.

Deutscher, I. 1970. 'Words and Deeds', in W. Filstead (ed.), *Qualitative Methodology: Firsthand Involvement with the Social World*. Chicago: Markham, pp. 27–51.

Douglas, M. 1966. *Purity and Danger*. London: Routledge & Kegan Paul.

Finch, J. 1984. '"It's great to have someone to talk to": The Ethics and Politics of Interviewing Women', in C. Bell and H. Roberts (eds), *Social Researching: Politics, Problems and Practice*. London: Routledge, pp. 70–87.

Foster, C. H. 1995. 'Drug Users in a Therapeutic Cul-De-Sac', Ph.D. dissertation. Edinburgh University.

Foucault, M. 1977. *Discipline and Punish* (trans. A. Sheridan). London: Allen Lane.

Halliday, F. 1978. *Iran: Dictatorship and Development*. London: Penguin.

Hammersley, M. and P. Atkinson. 1983. *Ethnography: Principles in Practice*. London: Tavistock.

Heald, S. 1998 [1989]. *Controlling Anger: The Anthropology of Gisu Violence*. Oxford: James Currey.

Howell, S. 1984. *Society and Cosmos: Chewong of Peninsular Malaysia*. Oxford: Oxford University Press.

Law, J. 2004. *After Method: Mess in Social Science Research*. London: Routledge.

Leach, E. 1967. 'An Anthropologist's Reflections on a Social Survey', in D. Jongmans and P. Gutkind (eds), *Anthropologists in the Field*. Assen: Van Gorcum, pp. 75–88.

Lévi-Strauss, C. 1973 [1955]. *Tristes Tropiques* (trans. J. Weightman and D. Weightman). London: Jonathan Cape.

Macdonald, S. 2010. 'Making Ethics', in M. Melhuss, J. Mitchell and H. Wulff (eds), *Ethnographic Practice in the Present*. Oxford: Berghahn, pp. 80–94.

Macfarlane, A. 2004. 'Anthropological and Other "Ancestors": Notes on Setting up a Visual Archive'. Retrieved on 7 September 2014 from http://www.alanmacfarlane.com/TEXTS/ancestors.pdf.

Malinowski, B. 1922. *The Argonauts of the Western Pacific*. London: Routledge & Kegan Paul.

———. 1967. *A Diary in the Strict Sense of the Term*. London: Routledge & Kegan Paul.

Mauss, M. 1935. 'Les Techniques du Corps', *Journal de Psychologie Normale et Pathologique* 35: 271–93.

MHLG. Ministry of Housing and Local Government. 1967. *Gypsies and Other Travellers*. London: Her Majesty's Stationery Office.

Morris, B. 1982. *Forest Traders: A Socio-Economic Life of the Hill Pandaram*, LSE Monographs. London: Athlone Press.

Nader, L. 1974. 'Up the Anthropologists: Perspectives from Studying Up', in D. Hymes (ed.), *Reinventing Anthropology*. New York: Vintage, pp. 284–311.

Needham, R. 1967. 'Blood, Thunder, and Mockery of Animals', in J. Middleton (ed.), *Myth and Cosmos: Readings in Mythology and Symbolism*. New York: American Museum Sourcebooks in Anthropology, pp. 271–85.

Neveu-Kringelbach, H. 2007. 'Le Poids du Succès: Construction du Corps, Danse et Carrière à Dakar', *Politique Africaine* 107(3): 81–101.

Oakley, A. 1981. 'Interviewing Women: A Contradiction in Terms', in H. Roberts (ed.), *Doing Feminist Research*. London: Routledge & Kegan Paul, pp. 30–61.

Okazaki, A. 1997. 'Dreams, Histories and Selves in a Borderland Village in Sudan', Ph.D. dissertation. SOAS, University of London.

———. 2002. 'The Making and Unmaking of Consciousness: Two Strategies for Survival in a Sudanese Borderland', in R. Werbner (ed.), *Postcolonial Subjectivities*. London: Zed Books, pp. 63–83.

Okely, J. 1975. 'The Self and Scientism', *Journal of the Anthropology Society of Oxford*, republished in Okely (1996), *Own or Other Culture*. London: Routledge, pp. 27–44.

———. 1983. *The Traveller-Gypsies*. Cambridge: Cambridge University Press.

———. 1987. 'Fieldwork up the M1: Policy and Political Aspects', in A. Jackson (ed.), *Anthropology at Home*. London: Tavistock, pp. 55–73.

———. 1992. 'Anthropology and Autobiography: Participatory Experience and Embodied Knowledge', in J. Okely and H. Callaway (eds), *Anthropology and Autobiography*. London: Routledge, pp. 1–28.

———. 1994a. 'Vicarious and Sensory Knowledge of Chronology and Change: Ageing in Rural France', in K. Hastrup and P. Hervik (eds), *Social Experience and Anthropological Knowledge*. London: Routledge, pp. 45–64.

———. 1994b. 'Dancing with the Bakhtiari: Obituary for David Brooks'. *The Guardian*, May 13.

———. 1996. *Own or Other Culture*. London: Routledge.

———. 2001. 'Visualism and Landscape: Looking and Seeing in Normandy'. *Ethnos* 66(1): 99–120.

———. 2006. 'The Bureaucratization of Knowledge: Or What are Universities For?', in D. Carter and M. Lord (eds), *Engagements with Learning and Teaching in Higher Education*. C-Sap, Birmingham University, pp. 127–37.

———. 2007a. 'Gendered Lessons in Ivory Towers', in D. Fahy Bryceson, J. Okely and J. Webber (eds), *Identity and Networks: Fashioning Gender and Ethnicity across Cultures*. Oxford: Berghahn, pp. 228–46.

———. 2007b. 'Fieldwork Embodied', in C. Shilling (ed.), *Embodying Sociology: Retrospect, Progress and Prospects*. Oxford: Blackwell, pp. 65–79.

———. 2009. 'Written Out and Written In: Inishkillane Remembered', *Irish Journal of Anthropology* 12(2): 50–55.

———. 2010. 'Fieldwork as Free Association and Free Passage', in M. Melhuus, J. Mitchell and H. Wulff (eds), *Ethnographic Practice in the Present*. Oxford: Berghahn, pp. 28–41.

———. 2012. *Anthropological Practice: Fieldwork and the Ethnographic Method*. London: Berg/Bloomsbury.

Okely, J. and H. Callaway (eds). 1992. *Anthropology and Autobiography*. London: Routledge.

Omvedt, G. 1979. 'On the Participant Study of Women's Movements: Methodological Definitional and Action Considerations', in G. Huizer and B. Mannheim (eds), *The Politics of Anthropology*. The Hague: Mouton, pp. 373–93.

Overing, J. 1975. *The Piaroa: A People of the Orinoco Basin: A Study in Kinship and Marriage*. Oxford: Clarendon Press.

Parry, J. 1979. *Caste and Kinship in Kangra*. London: Routledge.

Powdermaker, H. 1967. *Stranger and Friend: The Way of an Anthropologist*. London: Secker & Warburg.

Pratt, M.L. 1986. 'Fieldwork in Common Places', in J. Clifford and G. Marcus (eds), *Writing Culture*. Berkeley: University of California Press, pp. 27–50.

Rose, S. 1997. *Lifelines: Biology, Freedom and Determinism*. London: Allen Lane, Penguin Press.

Sanjek, R. 1993. 'Anthropology's Hidden Colonialism: Assistants and Their Ethnographers', *Anthropology Today* 9(2): 13–18.

Silverman, C. 2012. *Romani Routes: Cultural Politics and Balkan Music in Diaspora*. Oxford: Oxford University Press.

Simpson, A. 2003. *'Half-London' in Zambia: Contested Identities in a Catholic Mission School*. Edinburgh: International African Library.

———. 2009. *Boys to Men in the Shadow of AIDS: Masculinities and HIV Risk in Zambia*. London: Palgrave Macmillan.

Talib, M. 2010. *Writing Labour: Stone Quarry Workers in Delhi.* Delhi and Oxford: Oxford University Press.

Tester, K. (ed.). 1994. *The Flâneur.* London: Routledge.

Whyte, W.F. 1955 [1943]. *Street Corner Society: The Social Structure of an Italian Slum.* Chicago: University of Chicago Press.

Wulff, H. 1998. *Ballet Across Borders, Career and Culture in the World of Dancers.* Oxford: Berg.

Zulaika, J. 1982. *Basque Violence: Metaphor and Sacrament.* Reno: University of Nevada Press.

———. 1995. 'The Anthropologist as Terrorist', in C. Nordstrom and A. Robben (eds), *Fieldwork under Fire: Contemporary Studies of Violence and Survival.* Berkeley: University of California Press, pp. 205–22.

Chapter 7

TALKING AND ACTING FOR OUR RIGHTS

THE INTERVIEW IN AN ACTION-RESEARCH SETTING

Ana Lopes

This chapter draws upon an action-research project in which the ethnographer became a participant and facilitator of a collective effort that led to the unionisation of sex workers in the UK. It is within this context that I will explore the way in which the interview in action-research settings can be used as a tool for action planning and action generation, as well as 'authentic' data generation. As I turned from ethnographer to action researcher, I became a co-producer or co-generator of knowledge that is relevant for action. I ask, in this chapter, to what extent can the agenda of the interview be appropriated by those being interviewed, as a tool to critically understand structures of power and seek social change?

In addition, within the action-research context, where power relations are challenged, and interviewer and interviewees share a practical/political agenda, the interviewer sometimes becomes the interviewee. What happens then? Can the interview in this context be used as a tool for the development of a 'bottom-up' anthropology?

This chapter will contextualise the unionisation of sex workers in the UK within an action-research project. To do so, I must begin by briefly outlining the development of the sex workers' rights movement.

The research project explored here had a practical result, leading to the first successful attempt at unionising sex workers in the UK. This initiative, however, appears as part of a wider movement for sex workers' rights. I will now outline the key moments of this movement that underpin the unionisation of sex workers in the UK.

The Sex Workers' Rights Movement

The sex workers' rights movement is usually understood as having started in the 1970s in Europe and the United States. It is important, however, to note that sex workers have mobilised, more or less formally, in many different parts of the world for more than a century (Doezema and Kempadoo 1998). In Europe, the sex workers' rights movement became visible in 1975 – as prostitutes occupied a church in Lyons, France, in order to draw public attention to police harassment and the injustice of existing laws. Shortly after, Claude Jaget (1980) published a key work on prostitutes' rights: *Prostitutes: Our Life*.

In the United States (San Francisco), Margot St James, who was a former prostitute, formed COYOTE (Call Off Your Old Tired Ethics) in 1973. She is widely viewed as the founder of the modern sex workers' movement, as COYOTE was the first organisation in the Western world to call for sex workers' agency in the struggle for their rights – rather than relying heavily on allies, usually feminist campaigners or theorists.

Sex workers in the state of New South Wales, Australia, were the first to get recognition within the trades union movement, as they were officially recognised by the Australian Liquor, Hospitality and Miscellaneous Workers' Union. This achievement by Australian sex workers was followed by the establishment of a closed-shop union in a peep show club in San Francisco, the Lusty Lady.

Nowadays, sex workers are officially unionised in countries such as Argentina, the Netherlands and Greece, as well as in the United Kingdom. In Argentina, the association of female sex workers AMMAR (Asociación de Mujeres Meretrices Argentinas), founded in 1995, is officially affiliated to the National Workers' Union CTA (Central de Trabajadores Argentinos). This national union counts 1.5 million members. AMMAR has nine branches across Argentina (see Hardy 2010).

In the UK, sex workers have entered the mainstream union movement through an affiliation of the collective International Union of

Sex Workers into the general union GMB. Before discussing this de-velopment, I will briefly sketch out the history of sex workers' formal organising in this country.

In the mid 1970s, Helen Buckingham established herself as the main spokesperson for prostitutes in Britain. She was a high-class es-cort, bankrupted in 1975 by the Inland Revenue after they demanded tax payments based on her earnings from prostitution. Buckingham claimed that if the government wanted to tax her, it must also allow her to work legally. She became a researcher and one of the main subjects for Jeremy Sandford's (1975) book *Prostitutes*. Subsequently, Buckingham and others involved in Sandford's research launched PUSSI (Prostitutes United for Social and Sexual Integration). The group later changed its name to PLAN (Prostitution Laws Are Non-sense). She later allied herself to Selma James to form the ECP (English Collective of Prostitutes).

The ECP emerged from within the Wages for Housework Cam-paign, and it follows a class-based analysis, from which their aboli-tionist stance follows. Moreover, their position is contradictory insofar as they call for unpaid labour (housework) to become paid labour, while simultaneously calling for a form of paid labour (sex work) to be abolished – therefore, to become unpaid. Together with its sister US-based organisation, the US_PROStitutes Collective, it forms the In-ternational Collective of Prostitutes (English Collective of Prostitutes 1997: 83).

The most successful campaign for the repeal of prostitution laws was led by PROS, Programme for the Reform of Laws on Soliciting. This loose national alliance was first established in Birmingham in 1976 by a group of sex workers, social workers and a lawyer. Later, PROS groups would be set up in different cities in the UK. The organisation's objective was to campaign on behalf of street prostitutes and to abolish imprisonment for loitering and soliciting. Its far-reaching achievement was to repeal the law that prohibited sex workers to solicit clients on the streets. Due to a shift in public opinion that had begun to see sex workers as victims rather than criminals, PROS was successful in repealing the legislation that allowed imprisonment for soliciting in the early 1980s. Thus, although the non-payment of fines for soliciting and new pieces of legislation might result in imprisonment, sex workers now had time to make arrangements for themselves and their children, before they are effectively arrested.

PROS was also responsible for starting the debate about unionisation of sex workers in the UK. Their discussion raised both negative and positive reactions from the general public and union officers. In fact,

in 1981, PROS received an encouraging letter from a local branch of
the Union of Shop Distributive and Allied Workers (USDAW) that read:

> At our branch meeting the question of PROS was raised and surprisingly
> received a very sympathetic hearing. It certainly showed how public
> opinion has changed. Could you tell us what you think we should aim
> for? The total remission of all laws relating to prostitution or were you
> thinking of putting some act in to control it? If we start at branch
> level now, we should be able to raise the matter at the [19]82 Labour
> Party Conference, the trouble with democracy is it works slow. (cited in
> McLeod 1982: 144)

Sex workers would only finally gain membership of an official union
some twenty years later. By the time that happened, PROS was no
longer active as an organisation. Unionisation and an emphasis on labour rights is only one possible way for sex workers' organisation and
self-empowerment. In this case, it was facilitated by an academically
framed action-research project. In the following section I will outline
how the unionisation of sex workers in the UK came about in the context of an action research project.

The International Union of Sex Workers
and Action Research

The action-research project I am discussing here can be understood as
going through three distinct phases: a pilot phase, unofficial organisation and official unionisation. The first phase – the pilot phase – was
based on participant observation and ethnographic interviews.

When I first planned my Ph.D. research project I began by
collecting a sample of pilot interviews in which I consulted potential
participants on what topics they thought were useful to research. I
planned to carry out orthodox anthropological research, making use
of the traditional ethnographic methods: observation, ethnographic
interviews and field notes (e.g., Spradley 1979).

In order to meet potential participants I approached The Sexual
Freedom Coalition (SFC), a group established in London in 1996
that campaigns for the abolition of laws that limit people's freedom
of expression of sexuality. This group was relevant to my research
because many of its members were sex workers and they were actively
campaigning for the legalisation of prostitution. It was through SFC
coordinators and at SFC meetings that I met and talked to sex workers
who were members of this group. I interviewed three sex-worker

members of the SFC and observed and accompanied one of them in her work as a striptease dancer.

The aim of this pilot phase was to try to coordinate the needs of sex workers and the goals of the ethnography: to gain an understanding of the sex industry through the perspective of sex workers themselves. However, what I found from my pilot interviews was more than a research topic. I found that urgent action was needed. Sex workers needed to organise. In the words of a dancer I interviewed at the time:

> What we need is a platform. The problem is not with the work itself, but our lives could be better. The public has to understand that we're not seedy, we do this for a living.

In order to address this, I called a meeting or focus group to which all interviewees were invited as well as potential allies: mostly activists and fellow students. The result of this meeting was the emergence of an association called the 'International Union of Sex Workers'. From that moment, I took on the role of catalyst for action and was a resource for the group. As a researcher, my 'mandate' was one of facilitating the establishment of a platform from which sex workers could demand their rights.

During this second phase of the action-research project, this informal organisation campaigned for labour rights, especially the right to join a recognised union and the mainstream trades union movement. A basic website was set up, which in itself triggered international interest and links with sex-worker organisations all over the world. An electronic discussion list to which sex workers and supporters could sign up contributed to strengthening those links, and became an important strategising, communication and planning tool. A magazine, *R.E.S.P.E.C.T. (Rights and Equality for Sex Professionals and Employees in Connected Trades)* featuring articles by sex workers and directed at sex workers was also published and distributed both nationally and internationally.

The first issue, which came out in June 2000, featured an article written by Rona, one of the group's members. In the article Rona expresses her views on why sex workers should unionise.

> Yes it is a profession – I believe a perfectly respectable profession, and should be viewed as such in the same way as a teacher, accountant or anyone else. I believe that the first step is to obtain recognition for sex-workers as legitimate workers in a legitimate industry and profession. The first move is to form a union and then press for the same rights as other workers enjoy. (Rona 2000: 4)

Writing and publishing this first issue helped us establish some important links, nationally as well as internationally. Participating and reporting on the May Day demonstration that took place in London in 2000 made us reflect on issues of pride and ways to break up the stigma attached to sex workers. The editorial of the second issue of *Respect* reads:

> In this number, we reinforce the theme of pride. For as long as we are made to feel ashamed of the work we do, there is no way sex-workers can assert our rights. (International Union of Sex Workers [IUSW], 2002)

During this developmental phase, the IUSW had a marked presence in several demonstrations and parades in London. Such participation signalled support for the events or causes they represented and also aimed at building up visibility for sex-worker activism.

In a third phase, and after several attempts to gain official union recognition, negotiations began between the IUSW and the GMB with the view to forming the first officially recognised sex-workers' union branch in Britain. Gaining official recognition as a union had always been a priority of the IUSW. In July 2001, the Labour Campaign for Lesbian and Gay Rights invited us to the Gay and Lesbian TUC (Trades Union Congress) Conference that took place in London. I took this opportunity to meet with the several gay and lesbian union officers and discuss the possibility of TUC recognition for our recently created sex workers' union.

The rationale behind the move was the belief that gay and lesbian officers would be more sympathetic to the sex workers' cause than other union officers. We drew parallels between the sex worker and gay population: both groups had a history of social stigma; homosexual acts had been illegal until the 1960s and the removal of its illegality had greatly aided the decrease of stigma and the establishment of rights. Sex workers look to the decriminalisation of their work as key to eradicating the discrimination they are victims of.

Although the conference was fruitful in terms of networking with different unions, no signs of TUC recognition resulted from it. Most officers I approached were interested in our case and sympathetic on an individual level, but no headway was made in terms of getting unions interested in representing our group of workers.

In November 2001, I attended the No Sweat annual conference. No Sweat is a worldwide organisation that campaigns against sweatshop labour. The term sweatshop refers to unsafe working places where workers labour for very long hours and for very low pay. No Sweat aims to publicise, expose and eradicate sweatshop employment. They claim that the way forward is to help unionise sweatshops and that joining a union is the way to enforce existing laws and extend labour rights.

At the conference, a GMB (British general union) London region officer presented a new GMB campaign to unionise sweatshop labourers working in East London. The GMB started as the General and Municipal Boilermakers union but after a series of amalgamations it sees itself as a general union and represents workers from a diversity of industries and sectors. It is the third largest union in the UK, with around 600, 000 members. The campaign presented at the conference counted on the support of No Sweat. The officer argued that it was the duty and responsibility of a general union like the GMB to organise sweatshop workers and to play an important role in helping to minimise their exploitation and improve their working conditions. The similarities with the sex industry became obvious to me.

The GMB were proposing to empower sweatshop workers – not to simply close down the factories and let the workers face unemployment. Likewise, the IUSW campaigns for the establishment of labour rights in the sex industry, protection from exploitation and the eradication of violence and harassment – not the eradication of the whole sex industry.

At the end of the conference I approached the GMB officer, introduced the IUSW and requested the GMB's help in bringing our organisation onto an official footing. I was impressed by the seriousness of his response. Later, he would confess that, at first, he thought he was being filmed for 'Candid Camera'![1]

Given the opportunity to join one of the biggest mainstream unions in the UK, the IUSW organised a general meeting to which sex workers and allies were invited in order to discuss whether this was desirable and beneficial for sex workers in general. This meeting was intended to be an open meeting – the IUSW felt that it was a small and relatively new organisation, and could not therefore claim to represent the whole sex-worker community. A great effort was put into publicising the meeting.

This historic meeting took place on 2 March 2002 and was attended by over seventy people. There were representatives of most sectors of the sex industry – from prostitution, to striptease, pornography and phone-sex workers. Although most sex workers present were women, there were also three male sex workers who took part. There were several representatives of service-providing agencies, as well as clients of sex workers. After presentations from a representative of Red Thread, a sex workers' collective based in Amsterdam that had recently affiliated to a Dutch union, and GMB officers and a general discussion, there was a unanimous vote that the sex workers' branch should be formed.

In joining the GMB, a basic labour right was attained for all sex workers in the UK: the right to join and be represented by a recognised union. Much was to be learned by both sides. IUSW activists knew little about union organisation and structure; on the other hand, the GMB officers who helped get the branch off the ground knew little about the realities of the sex industry and the needs of different groups of sex workers.

Branch membership fluctuated over the years. Nowadays it counts over eighty members. They are men and women, biological or transgender, who work in several sectors of the industry. Over the years, the branch has made significant achievements: it has gained union recognition in two different table dancing clubs; it has won a court case on behalf of an unfairly dismissed sex worker; it has given legal help to many sex workers throughout the country; it has offered training (including for exiting the industry) to many sex workers; it has created a safe space for sex workers to organise, meet and talk; and it has given sex workers an organised voice through which to reach the public and the government. Since its inception, other groups and organisations that campaign for sex workers' rights have been founded and developed.

Action Research

Origins and Processes

The term 'action research' was coined by social psychologist Kurt Lewin in 1946 to describe research leading to social action. Lewin (1946) attempted to improve industrial relations and minimise hostility between different racial groups in the United States in the 1940s. He described his problem-solving perspective on research as a spiral of steps, each one comprising the stages of planning, acting, observing and reflecting.

This 'action research spiral' is Lewin's main legacy to action researchers.

Action research is also linked to the work of Paulo Freire and his seminal work *Pedagogy of the Oppressed* (1972), which emphasises dialogue, informed action, and educational activity based on the lived experiences of the participants, community enhancement and consciencialização – a process by which individuals perform in-depth analysis of their own realities. He insisted that knowledge must be created with people and not imparted to them. Freire was a founder of what is now known as critical pedagogy.

Action research has also been influenced by critical theory, which argues for the recognition of the role of values and beliefs. Critical theory asks how a situation can be understood in order to change it. Action research goes further by asking how it can be changed (McNiff and Whitehead 2006).

Feminist theories, epistemologies and methodologies have also inspired many action-research projects. The metaphor of 'giving a voice' to those who have been marginalised and silenced in knowledge-creation is common to feminist and action research, as is the idea of embracing experience as a source of legitimate knowledge (Maguire 2001).

The action-research process is cyclical and it is usually visually represented as a circle or spiral (Lewin 1948; Stringer 1999). However, these visual representations fail to convey the nature of the action-research process, as they erroneously imply that those involved in the action-research process 'return to the point of departure'. They are unable to convey the idea of the process as dynamic and progressive.

Instead, I see the action-research process as a wave: action research embodies a pattern (observation – planning – action), but it is one that moves the situation forward. In fact, action researchers and participants never find themselves back at the starting point, as they are necessarily changing their own situation in the process. Within this process, we start by observing and reflecting on the situation and the possibilities available then collaboratively plan our action. Following action and its evaluation, we are ready to, again, observe and reflect on the new situation we find ourselves in, starting a new wave, rippling outwards from the first.

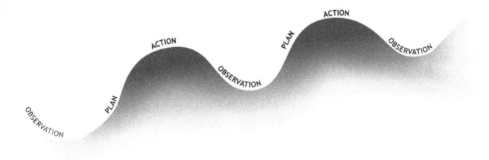

Figure 7.1 Action-research process as a wave

In our common struggle for unionisation of sex workers, we found ourselves going through a wave-like process. We would observe and meditate on the situation and the possibilities available; consequently we would plan our action then act and evaluate our action. This would be the starting point for new observation and reflection on the situation and we would follow the same process again, this time on a different level, starting a new wave.

The lack of labour rights within the sex industry was the initial problem (that was highlighted in all my pilot interviews) that triggered the action-research project described in this chapter. That observation led to the awareness of the lack of union representation for sex workers. Thus, the plan designed by the initial group of participants led to the action of setting up a union to represent those who work in the sex industry.

The second major wave of action in this project was triggered by the important realisation that, although the initial problem had been 'solved' – that is, there was now a union to represent sex workers' interests – there was a significant limitation to the effectiveness of such a union, since it was an informal organisation, not recognised by the appropriate body, the Trades Union Congress (TUC). One of the strategies developed by the group of participants was to seek membership in official, existing unions, which led to the emergence of a sex-worker branch in the GMB.

This process necessarily gains a life of its own, independent of the action researcher. Since the activities prompted by action research are fully integrated in the group's activities, they are likely to be ongoing after the research has been 'written up'. In fact, although I and other original project participants are no longer involved in the sex workers' rights movement in this country, the union that resulted from this action-research project continues to grow and develop.

Nevertheless, it is clear that action research is not a neat, orderly activity that allows participants to proceed step-by-step to the end of a process (Oja and Smulyan 1989: 176; Stringer 1999). As the project developed, the participants and I found ourselves working backwards through the stages, rethinking interpretations, skipping steps and sometimes making radical changes in direction.

As an action researcher my role was not one of a detached observer, however, but that of an 'experiencing subject' (Paget 1993) embarking on a systematic knowledge quest for social change. While not aspiring to objectivity, action-research approaches demand that those involved are reflexive and explicit about the perspective from which knowledge is created (Reason and Bradbury 2001). The notion of validity in action research challenges mainstream research cultures. In fact, action research values the process of research, as much as its products and its 'success' is based to a large degree on how much participants' knowledge and capacities are developed within the process (Kindon, Pain and Kesby 2007).

Action research, which at its core contains a vision of transformation for social justice, represents an epistemological challenge to mainstream research traditions. By assuming that those who have been most systematically excluded carry the most valuable wisdom about themselves and their own lives, action research is a counter-hegemonic approach that fundamentally challenges the role and value of the expert in knowledge production.

What is Action Research?

Action research evades simple definition, since there are so many strands and traditions within this methodological approach. Although it has been used in the sex industry before, this project is the first application of action research to the movement for sex workers' rights.

There are many traditions within action research, and in fact there is no consensus as to what exactly action research is. However, the tradition that I have followed in the course of my research project derives from the tradition of community-based, emancipatory action research. Within the context of community-based action research, the role of the researcher is not that of an expert who does research but that of a resource person who acts as a catalyst, who stimulates people to change. I have been a catalyst for action and a resource person, available to, and at the service of, a group of sex worker activists and advocates – rather than an outsider/observer.

In *Handbook of Action Research*, Reason and Bradbury (2001: 1) define action research as 'a participatory, democratic process concerned with developing practical knowing in the pursuit of worthwhile human purposes'. Action research is based on the assumption that the mere recording of events and formulation of explanations is inadequate (Stringer 1999); and that those who are designated as 'subjects' or 'informants' in other types of approaches to research should actually participate directly in research processes. Moreover, those research processes should be applied in ways that benefit all participants directly.

Action research has three major distinctive elements: people, power and praxis. It is people-centred, as it is informed by, and responds to, the needs of the (oppressed or disenfranchised) people. It therefore promotes empowerment of the research participants, and it is about praxis – it recognises the inseparability of theory and practice. Action research challenges the power relation between researcher and 'objects', since the action researcher is a peer of other research participants. Its key methodological feature is dialogue (Sohng 1995: 6). Sohng further argues that ideally, dialogue within action or participatory research empowers by bringing 'isolated people together around common problems and needs' (ibid.: 6). This process has been clear within the context of my project. Indeed, the action-research project and the organisations it has resulted in (IUSW and GMB branch) have become a forum for a group of workers who – due to heavy competition within a clandestine and stigmatised industry – have few other opportunities to collectively reflect on their own practice, problems and needs. From the process of creating opportunities for collective reflection, empowerment has flowed.

Action research, rather than a method per se, is an orientation towards research that rests on an ontology that attributes to human beings the capability of reflexivity and self-change, and on an epistemology that embraces that capability within the research process (Kindon, Pain and Kesby 2007).

Action researchers work with communities and groups that have traditionally been marginalised or oppressed, and through dialogue facilitate the process by which those groups identify issues of concern to them, gather relevant information, and test and implement possible solutions (Brydon-Miller 2002). Thus, action research is explicitly political and demands that the researcher play a dual role – that of scholar and activist.

The Interview in an Action-Research Setting

During the course of this project, I carried out participant observation, working in the sex industry myself for five years, as a part-time telephone operator on an adult chat line. Although the nature of sex work per se has not been the focus of the action-research project, this has enabled me to experience first-hand some of the problems and vulnerabilities faced by sex workers: mainly, stigmatisation and lack of labour rights.

The core of my participant observation, however, took place within the movement for sex workers' rights: meetings, conferences, actions and demonstrations. I collected numerous documents, including meeting minutes and notes, newsletters, reports, position statements, motions and resolutions, newspaper clippings, correspondence and other documents. I also kept a personal journal in which summaries of daily research activities, observations and reflections on research and action were recorded.

The ideal method for data generation in an action-research setting is dialogical. Focus groups, therefore, are a popular method. Although several focus-group discussions were organised throughout this research, I also carried out semi-structured ethnographic interviews with activists and advocates I met or worked with in the course of my involvement in the sex workers' rights movement. The interview sample reflects my own experience within the international sex workers' rights movement. Normally, I met people in their homes or workplaces, though some interviews took place in hotels – as conferences were privileged places to meet activists from different countries.

Within the context of this action-research project, reaching out or recruiting sex workers to be interviewed, both nationally and internationally, was not problematic, bar logistical issues related to international travel. Being aware of the aims and action element of the research project, sex workers were forthcoming. In fact, some were proactive in initiating the process and requesting to be heard.

This contrasts with Gall's (2006) research on sex-worker unionisation based on secondary sources, as he admits to having failed at interviewing sex workers from all countries studied except Britain. Gall points to the difficulties in contacting sex workers as a reason for not having conducted interviews. Sex workers, he says, are a 'hard-to-reach (research) population' (Gall 2006: 14). Thus, he gathered his data from websites, activists publications, and mostly newspaper clippings and television documentaries. This is highly controversial, as sex workers have often complained about the ways in which the mainstream media represents them. My own research work pointed at this misrepresentation as one of the reasons why sex workers engage in activism (Lopes 2006). Sex workers have good reasons to be suspicious about academic research that does not take into account their own agendas. It is not surprising, then, that they were not cooperative with Gall and other researchers.

Within an action-research setting, research is guided by action needs. Those needs were discussed collectively with project participants. The aim of interviewing sex-worker activists was to find out

what works and does not work in sex-worker organising efforts. Interviewees were aware of the role of the researcher and the aims of
the project. However, the same interviewees also knew the researcher
in her role as sex-worker activist. Many had previous experience of
collaborating in political activities with the researcher – such as organising meetings, demonstrations, etc.

It was therefore also of interest to the interviewees to find out about
the researcher's (and the group she was working with) experiences
of organising within the sex industry. This interest may have been
conscious or not; it may have taken place previously or may have been
triggered by the interview itself. This often triggered return questioning. So interviews took directions sought after by the interviewee, becoming what I would like to term a bottom-up ethnography.

Occasionally, the return questioning went further. Roles became
reversed when I was asked to take the place of the respondent. Below
I explore these cases in more detail.

The Reverse Interviews

Sarah

Sarah was a very active member of the IUSW. I interviewed her at her
own request, at the flat where she saw her clients. In the interview I
asked her about her work and also about the political organisation we
were both part of: What should our future strategy be? What needed
to be done? What could we do? At the end of the interview, I was ener-
gised with a sense of hope, optimism and camaraderie. But I also felt
the pressure of taking up her time and was concerned that I might be
responsible for her loss of earnings. I was therefore relieved to hear
Sarah say:

> I love talking about my work and there's always more I can say about it.
> It's really interesting. One of the things I like is that every time I talk to
> people it keeps unfolding itself to me.

But when I said that what I had found really 'useful' had been the second part of the interview, where we reflected about the course of the
political campaigns we were involved in and how to proceed, I saw a
light appearing in her eyes. Sarah then said that she thought it would
be really 'useful' for the organisation (the action part of the project)
if I were to be interviewed as well, and that she would like to conduct

the interview. We arranged a date and time to meet in Sarah's work flat again.

As we sat at her table, Sarah produced a list of typed questions and a tape recorder. The questions were mostly about the history of the organisation, its set up (Sarah had not been a founding member) and my ideas about the future of the organisation. She also gave me an opportunity to reflect upon and discuss the difficulty of combining the role of researcher with that of activist, as well as ethical issues in action-research settings. This is an excerpt of my response to her (Sarah transcribed the interview and subsequently emailed it to me):

> Individually it has been very difficult at times to balance the activist versus researcher roles, mostly in terms of being fair and open and honest. Because everybody who comes regularly to the meetings knows that I am doing a study. But I don't tell people immediately because there are other issues that I feel are more important and immediate. If I'm trying to recruit someone, the important thing is to let them know about the group, how it works, etc., and deal with their worries. And it's only after I've spent some time with them that I will talk about the research. But that creates ethical problems for myself.

What was it is about this type of research – action research as opposed to a more regular form of research (whatever that might be!) – that made it possible or likely for interviewees to turn the tables on the interviewer? The answer is that they had a stake in the research from the outset. They were not merely contributing to someone else's academic research and career but could see the direct benefits that would accrue from the project.

Michelle

Michelle and I had met at a conference on sex work. She was the founder and leader of a sex workers' rights organisation in a European country. The organisation had been set up in the 1980s. I saw her as a senior leader in the movement. A few years later, we met at another conference. This was a much smaller event, organised by a German trades union that had begun to organise sex workers. We were staying in a small hotel where the conference also took place. I was eager to use the time left after the sessions for networking and interviewing. Michelle was happy to be interviewed, but she made it quite clear from the outset that the 'price' would be that she would also interview me. So when I had finished asking her about her organisation, the state and future of the sex workers' movement, we turned the tape recorder around and swapped places as interviewer and respondent. Michelle asked me about my motivations, the history of the IUSW, the benefits of unionisation for sex workers and to what extent I thought society was ready to accept sex work as labour, and sex workers as recipients of labour rights.

Michelle seemed to have a clear agenda – to understand how UK sex workers achieved unionisation, whether it was a good thing and whether it would be something for sex workers based in her country to pursue. Some of her questions were the same as mine. I had asked:

> Could you tell me how you became involved in sex-worker activism?

Michelle asked me:

> Can you tell me a bit about your personal story, how you became involved in sex workers' rights?

The cases I described here were atypical, in the sense that the questioning back became 'formalised' and framed as an interview. The sex workers who 'turned the tables' on me as an interviewer were not more 'enlightened' than other sex workers I interviewed. They were, however, like other people I interviewed in the course of this project, activists for sex workers' rights. The possibility for this kind of role-swapping had more to do with the particular setting of the research (the sex workers' rights movement) than with the type of research itself (action research).

Conclusion

When one carries out an action-research investigation one does not investigate a theory to be applied. Rather, one investigates methods for the 'implementation of a political idea' (Sohng 1995), and those most concerned with the results of one's investigation are the research participants themselves.

Action research relies heavily on relational approaches (Coghlan and Brannick 2010: 29), that is, on interpersonal relations and communal processes. However, when traditional semi-structured interviews are used, the power structure that underpins traditional, non-participatory and non-action-oriented research is maintained. Two ways of challenging such power structures have been firstly to see the interviews as part and parcel of the action – as well as the research; and secondly, by alternating the roles of interviewer and respondent. Turning the tables and swapping places shorten the distance between the researcher and those 'researched'. Power relations are challenged.

Since my aim was to contribute to the sex workers' rights movement, this approach was the more useful, since often sex workers challenge the value of being part of research projects from which they get no benefits. Sue Metzenrath (1998), a representative of the Scarlett Alliance (Australian national forum for sex-worker rights organisations), puts it succinctly when she writes:

> research [on sex work] should not only be driven by the personal and academic interests of researchers alone but they should try to support the research needs of sex-workers and their supporters...For far too long researchers have been using sex-workers as guinea pigs without any benefit accruing to sex-workers as the result of research. (Metzenrath 1998: 11)

Although it would be naive to believe that reciprocity is ever fully achieved or that privileges and hierarchies are ever completely absent, the notion of reciprocity – the ongoing process of exchange aiming at establishing and maintaining equality between parties – is part of the basis of ethical practice in action research (Maiter, Simich, Jacobson and Wise 2008). It is ideally a type of 'bottom-up' research, which is in tune with the aims of action research.

Notes

1. Old reality TV programme in which people were put in awkward or ridiculous situations and their reactions secretly filmed.

References

Brydon-Miller, M. 2002. 'What is Participatory Action Research and What's a Nice Person Like Me Doing in A Field Like This?' *SPSSI Convention, Toronto Canada, 28–30 June 2002*. Retrieved 21 October 2012 from http://ebookbrowse.com/brydon-miller-pdf-d338656940

Coghlan, D. and T. Brannick. 2010. *Doing Action Research in Your Own Organization*. London: Sage.

Doezema, J. and K. Kempadoo (eds). 1998. *Global Sex-Workers: Rights, Resistance, and Redefinition*. London: Routledge.

English Collective of Prostitutes, 1997. 'Campaigning for Legal Change', in G. Scambler and A. Scambler (eds), *Rethinking Prostitution: Purchasing Sex in the 1990s*. London and New York: Routledge.

Freire, P. 1972. *Pedagogy of the Oppressed*. Harmondsworth: Penguin.

Gall, G. 2006. *Sex Worker Union Organising: An International Study*. London: Palgrave Macmillan.

Hardy, K. 2010. 'Incorporating Sex-workers into the Argentine Labor Movement', *International Labor and Working Class History*, 77(1): 89–108.

International Union of Sex Workers. 2002. 'Editorial', *Respect 2*, October 2002.

Jaget, C. 1980. *Prostitutes: Our Life*. Bristol: Falling Wall Press.

Kindon, S., R. Pain and M. Kesby. 2007. 'Participatory Action Research – Origins, Approaches and Methods', in S. Kindon, R. Pain and M. Kesby (eds), *Participatory Action Research Approaches and Methods*. London: Routledge.

Lewin, K. 1946. 'Action Research and Minority Problems', *Journal of Social Issues* 2(4): 34–36.

———. (ed.). 1948. *Resolving Social Conflicts: Selected Papers on Group Dynamics*. New York: Harper and Row.

Lopes, A. 2006. *Trabalhadores do Sexo, Uni-vos! Organização Laboral na Indústria do Sexo*. Lisbon: Dom Quixote.

Maguire, P. 2001. 'Uneven Ground: Feminisms and Action research', in P. Reason and H. Bradbury (eds), *Handbook of Action Research: Participative Inquiry and Practice*. London: Sage.

Maiter, S., L. Simich, N. Jacobson and J. Wise. 2008. 'Reciprocity: An Ethic for Community-Based Participatory Action Research', *Action Research* 6(3): 305–25.

McLeod, E. 1982. *Women Working: Prostitution Now*. London and Canberra: Croom Helm.

McNiff, J. and J. Whitehead. 2006. *All You Need to Know about Action Research*. London: Sage.

Metzenrath, S. 1998. 'In Touch with the Needs of Sex-Workers'. *Research for Sex Work* 1 June 1998.

Oja, S. and L. Smulyan. 1989 *Collaborative Action Research: A Developmental Approach*. London: Falmer Press.

Paget, M. 1993. *A Complex Sorrow: Reflexions on Cancer and an Abbreviated Life*. Philadelphia: Temple University Press.

Reason, P. and H. Bradbury (eds). 2001. *Handbook of Action Research: Participative Inquiry and Practice*. London: Sage.

Rona. 2000. 'Why We Need a Union', *Respect 1*, July.

Sandford, J. 1975. *Prostitutes*. London: Martin Secker & Warburg.

Sohng, S.S.L. 1995. 'Participatory Research and Community Organizing', *The New Social Movement and Community Organizing Conference, 1–3 November 1995*. Seattle: University of Washington.

Spradley, J.P. 1979. *The Ethnographic Interview*. New York and London: Harcourt Brace Jovanovich College Publishers.

Stringer, E.T. 1999. *Action Research*. London: Sage.

Epilogue

EXTRAORDINARY ENCOUNTER?
THE INTERVIEW AS AN IRONICAL MOMENT

Nigel Rapport

The argument of this book has been that the interview should be seen as a special, productive site of ethnographic encounter. It is less to be distinguished from participant observation than appreciated as a site of a very particular and important kind of knowing. The contributions to this volume, in their distinct settings, speak alike to the added value that might be gained from incorporating the interview into the process of gathering ethnographic data.

'Specially productive?' It has been argued that the interview embodies a particular kind of interactional and experiential context. Contributors have been concerned to show how the interview is a kind of space within which personal, biographic and social cues and norms might be explored and interrogated. There is an 'extraordinariness' to the interview insofar as perspective may be gained on the ordinary flow of experience and immersion within it; information derived from the interview may be non-structural or anti-structural, non-conventional and counter-intuitive, something not open for discussion, not discernible, in 'ordinary', everyday, social interaction.

The ordinary as against the extraordinary is thus an important conceptual distinction for the volume. And there are others. The interview, we have urged, should be appreciated both as an analytical category, a significant component in the methodological toolbox of human science, and as a way of being in the world: a modality of human experience, a kind of consciousness and a kind of relationality.

In addition, the interview represents a point of tension between remembering and re-authoring. That is, the interview ushers in both a retrospective and introspective space within which to reflect on (past) experience, and a prospective space within which to imagine a transformation of (future) experience. Both past and future are at stake in the present moment of the interview. Lastly, we have examined how the interview may be both a site of important insight into specific persons and locales and at the same time give on to perspectives concerning global and generalised contexts. The interview elicits information that is at once specific and universalisable, personal and social, pragmatic and conceptual, transformational and insightful of the everyday.

While anointing the interview with this ambitious and 'extraordinary' potential, we have at the same time wished to ground it in the complexities and specificities – the 'ordinariness'– of anthropological fieldwork. Our interview is a 'contaminated' phenomenon, part and parcel of ongoing and longer-term relations. The 'interviewer' and 'interviewee' are more properly to be known as 'talking-partners' (Rapport 1987: 170–85), party to an environing 'talking-relationship' of which the interview is but a moment – albeit a distinctive one. In other words, the interviews examined and vaunted in this volume are not between strangers. And the gifts they bring, the insights they afford, are epiphenomenal upon pre-existing relations of trust, or senses of mutual knowledge.

The Volume

Let me recap, briefly. Pat Caplan presents the biography of a man from Mafia Island, Tanzania, whom she knew for nearly four decades, from her first visit as a Ph.D. student in 1965–67 until his death in 2002. Caplan's interaction with Mikidadi took a variety of forms over the years, spanning an arc from the more formal recounting of a life to the informal and less self-conscious exchanges 'within' that life. It is from this variety of modalities of Mikidadi's expression that the complex appreciation of his life emerges. Here is the personal story of someone who wanted to 'be someone', who had a great desire for more education, but whose chances were largely obstructed by happenstance. Here, too, is a view upon the history of a local community (Mafia Island) and of a whole country (Tanzania) from the immediate postcolonial period, through the Revolution in Zanzibar and its union with Tanganyika, to the period of 'African socialism' (*ujamaa*), the rise of neo-liberalism in the late 1980s and the switch to multi-party-ism. Also from Mikidadi's life emerges an understanding of Islam and what it means to be a good Muslim. Finally, however, the personal relationship that is evinced between anthropologist and informant is one that exceeds conventional terms and contexts, proceeding against the grain of gendered, familial and financial norms (cf. Caplan 1997).

As Isak Niehaus elaborates, the biographical perspective obtained from in-depth engagement with one person in a variety of interactional formats over time potentially offers unique insights. While foregrounding personal subjective experience and historicity, such engagement has the capacity to capture the interplay of structures and events, institutions and practices, public and private domains, as well as of diverse, sometimes discordant and contradictory, discourses. Also revealed are the disjunctions between different levels of experience, such as representational models, normative notions, and concrete acts; how people's ideals do not match the actuality of their lives. Niehaus's own work on Reggie Ngobeni's life – its unfolding, shifting, indeterminate and contradictory meanings – is set against the broader and public context of HIV/AIDS in South Africa. Might not an empathetic understanding of the factors that influence the life of one individual sufferer make an extremely valuable addition to the study of the pandemic: be of vital importance to making therapeutic interventions more effective?

James Staples, in recounting his fieldwork experiences among leprosy sufferers in Anandapuram Colony, on India's south-east coast, and in colonies in Hyderabad and Haryana, makes a distinction between life-history accounts that are 'synoptic' and those that are more 'organic' and nuanced. In other words, Indian sufferers of leprosy are practised in giving public testimonies (such as to representatives of donor agencies and other potential patrons), in conventionalised narrative forms, wherein the onset of leprosy causes a violent rupture in otherwise positively construed life-courses. Such narratives – powerful in effecting access to succouring funding – may be analytically informative concerning the politics of representation and identity formation, but may still obscure sufferers' authentic lived experience. Ironically, a focus on leprosy as the central element of a narrative of a life story detracts from its organic complexity and wholeness. It may also deflect the gaze from broader sociopolitical and economic contexts within which leprosy exists. If life before and after the disease (in synoptic accounts) is presented as uniformly good, then those charged with the management of leprosy can more easily frame solutions without reference to the wider problematic (sickening) conditions of

people's existence: the 'structural violence' that shapes the lives of
the Indian poor. In his detailed life-story account of 'Das', Staples endeavours to capture both a life and a time to illustrate how the onset
of leprosy was one of a range of factors that shaped Das's life. Das
experienced and responded to leprosy against a backdrop of pre-existing poverty and social exclusion, and in relation to dominant social
categories of caste and gender.

Katherine Smith immerses the reader in the niceties of fieldwork in
a marginalised, poor and working-class white community in north-
west England. We see her interacting with her informants as a barmaid in the community's social club, 'Starlings'. More significantly,
we follow her 'behind the scenes' in her persona as a naive American
researcher where she is given privileged access to the traditions and
norms of local verbal exchange – how talking-relationships work in
the public space of the club, and what they portend, how they are to
be interpreted – by way of retrospective post-mortems in semi-structured interviews with key informants. 'Having a barter' in Starlings,
confronting other community insiders with humorous insults and
challenges in public, is a many-levelled discourse. By way of interviews with members of the ladies' darts team, in particular Bernice
and Janet, Smith becomes privy to bartering purposes, and becomes
initiated herself into the local interpretative community: becomes
herself bartered to and about. Cursing one another in sexist, racist,
ageist and generally politically incorrect terms plays with the stigma
generally accorded to this chapter of the so-called British lumpenproletariat (or 'white trash'). One pretends to own the stereotype. But
this stereotypification is more a flag of convenience (Rapport 1995):
it keeps dismayed outsiders at bay. But insiders too are chastened: one
may not take offence as one suffers public deprecations of one's character and behaviour; friends and neighbours are challenged to remain
friends and neighbours amid the tensions of poor and confined lives.
While 'having a barter', intentions of speakers and listeners remain
unspoken: what do one's fellows truly think and feel? To fellow members of Starlings, of the local interpretive community, one gives the
benefit of the doubt: one trusts. In interviews outside the bartering
context, Smith is taken within this circle of trust.

For Àngels Trias i Valls, too, the interview provides a means to join
with local respondents in reflecting upon the norms of ordinary social
life. More than this, however, it also leads to a reconsideration of the
analytical norms that the anthropologist might deploy in understanding local social exchange 'as a whole'. That is, the interview serves
as an 'altermodern' trigger, drawing attention to the way in which

social life per se concerns an existential 'presentism': a temporal now-
ness that continuously fragments time and structure and system.
Trias i Valls's research subjects are children in Catalonia, being interviewed, in particular, for their views on Christmas gift-giving. These
are wholly 'ethnographic' interactions, Trias i Valls insists, part and
parcel of ongoing talking-relationships that make single-focused approaches to 'the interview as technique', 'the interview as voice-giv-
ing' and 'the interview as site of power and responsibility' beside the
point. Conducting interviews with child informants as pure ethnographic encounters transcends our auditing preoccupations and
predicaments, and affords a potential vantage point upon authentic
accounts of orientations, hopes and aspirations in multilayered social
worlds. Interviewing children also introduces a challenge concerning
the temporality of children's responses, the temporality of their being
with another in interaction (such as the interviewer). For, interviewing children casts doubt on the homogeneity of time (on a supposed
coevalness) and the continuity of time. The way that children wander
in and out of 'the interview time' (disrupting, delaying, precipitating,
in their excitement and their boredom) suggests that beyond the seemingly shared experience of the interview, social exchange is composed
of different temporalities, and should anyway be analysed in terms of
modalities of tense. In other words, differences in child-interviewees'
approaches to routines of interaction throw light upon fracture as a
social phenomenon in its own right. Disengaging and breaking and
re-engaging did not only define her child-interviews but enabled Trias
i Valls to extrapolate more broadly so as to appreciate how boredom,
different communicational patterns, fracture and delay are significant
features of any social interaction and any talking-relationship.

Judith Okely, in interviewing anthropological colleagues about
their experience, builds upon a prior-existing trust. She conducted
interviews, deliberately, not with strangers, but as exchanges undertaken to deepen trust and mutual knowledge between a number
of fellow anthropologists already known to her. Here are interviews
between members of the same interpretive community, for purposes
that are as personal as they are professional. The anthropologist, after
all, must know themselves so that they can know others (Okely 1996).
The outcome, Okely reveals, was the extraordinary range of commonalities discovered among her respondents' experiences and research
practices – common to one another and also to herself; during the
interviews she frequently intervened, offering similarities or contrasts
from her own life. The interview project challenges the banality of
formulaic methodologies that are too often prioritised in the social sci-

ences, Okely concludes. It is regrettable that the ethnographic tradition of participant observation from which such incisive interviews can emerge is largely unknown or underappreciated outside sociocultural anthropology and in the multidisciplinary ethics committees that today hold such sway. Here an outdated, scientistic caricature of social science still obtains. Yet such a misprision has the hegemonic power to censor key approaches embedded in anthropological fieldwork, in the name of so-called objectivity and the avoidance of 'contamination' with research subjects. It is not the interview as a supposed detached encounter that is authentic but the extent to which it can throw light upon existing relations and common knowledge.

Ana Lopes takes the idea of involvement even further. In her 'action research', she endeavours to combine the role of researcher with that of activist. An action-research context, she elaborates, is one where 'ordinary' power relations are challenged, and interviewer and research subjects share a practical and political agenda; the anthropologist's primary aim here is to find ways to implement a political idea. The chapter explores, therefore, how the interview in an action-research setting might become a tool for 'action planning and generation', and not merely data-gathering. Here, the ethnographer becomes a co-generator of relevant knowledge – is interviewee as well as interviewer – as the agenda of the interview is appropriated by the research subjects as a tool to further their own understandings of structures of power and routes to social change. Dialogue is the key methodological feature of this action research, whose key ontological orientation concerns all human beings' capacity for reflexivity and 'self-change'. The anthropologist's involvement is part of a wave-like pattern: from observation to planning to action. More precisely, Lopes describes being participant and facilitator in a collective effort to unionise sex workers in the UK; she serves as 'catalyst for action' and 'resource' in establishing a platform from which sex workers can demand rights as members of The International Union of Sex Workers. The erstwhile marginalised and oppressed sex workers thus identify issues of concern to them, gather relevant information, and test and implement possible solutions – in collaboration with the purportedly interviewing anthropologist. The interviews – conducted with those who had previous experience of collaborating in political activities with Lopes – served to sharpen an awareness of 'action needs': what might work and what might not in organising efforts. For Lopes, the interview is a research process deployed in order to directly benefit her 'research subjects' – though even this term is to be now avoided.

Together, the case studies demonstrate two things of importance. First, as a form of gathering data, it can be profitable to insert the interview into on-going relations with research subjects, so that the interview assumes a metonymic status, pointing to a relationship beyond itself that possesses different modalities, and is elucidatory of the shifting nature of identity between these modalities. Second, the content of the interview, the kind of data it elicits, can be particular to itself: distinctive in its irony, its self-consciousness. For research subject and researcher alike, it is the possible occasion of insight into the 'ordinary', the normal and normative, the habitual and conventional that is extraordinary.

An Ironising Moment

I would elaborate upon this image of the interview as a cusp, a cuspidal moment. From the vantage point of the interview one looks forward and back, one critiques and affirms, one plans and takes stock: one gains purchase on a life, both as it is lived on the inside and as it might be espied from the outside. I do not mean that the interview is unique in this way, offering a unique opportunity – far from it. I take the 'ironic' capacity and the ironising practice to stand aside from the flux, the normativities and the mundanities of life to be a human universal. It is a ubiquitous human practice to oscillate between being in the middle of a life and spectating upon that life, wondering how it came to be, where it will next lead and how it might be wished to be (Rapport 2003: 42–50, 2005). As Victor Turner memorably phrased it: '[T]here were never any innocent, unconscious savages, living in a time of unreflective and instinctive harmony. We human beings are all and always sophisticated, conscious, capable of laughter at our own institutions' (cited in Ashley 1990: xix). What is special in the interview, 'extraordinary', is that the anthropologist is given insight of a particularly personal, privileged kind into the interviewee's ironising practice. The anthropologist is witness.

Of course, layers of ambiguity remain. This is the burden of Katherine Smith's chapter; elsewhere she refers to the 'palimpsest' of interpretation (Smith 2012: 34). The interviewee is enacting an introspective, critical, usually private practice before an anthropological witness. Whatever the level of trust, one can never be certain of the intentionality of another, of the purpose behind their expression, of the meanings of their words. 'All communication is translation' in George Steiner's pithy summation (1975: 238). Whether in interview or in 'ordinary' conversation, to ascertain the contents of symbolic forms – words and intonations and gestures – is to interpret. Again to borrow from Steiner, while language (or culture as a whole) might possess a common surface – is in the possession of an interpretive community of fellow competents – it retains a private base: 'The language of a community, however uniform its social contour, is an inexhaustibly multiple aggregate of speech-atoms, of finally irreducible personal meanings' (Steiner 1975: 46). As a piece of informational exchange, the interview retains all the uncertainties of every human symbolic exchange (Rapport 2012a).

And yet, the anthropologist is witness nevertheless to an ironising moment of another. It can be a privilege. To borrow terms from James Staples' work among vagrants, beggars and lepers, one is offered insight into the 'amazing' quality of lives, as lived possessions and objects of will, however apparently marginal and 'peculiar' (Staples 2007).

With Rickey Hirsch

I felt privileged in 2007 when I met Rickey Hirsch in Montreal and was allowed to hear and record his life story (see Rapport 2012b: 77–120). Rickey was then 84 years old. Born in 1924 in Bucharest, his life-course had intercepted with a number of the defining events of the century, it seemed to me: the Depression of the 1930s, the rise of Nazism, the Second World War, the Holocaust, the founding of the State of Israel, mass migration to the New World. Rickey had been a Romanian, a 'Jew', a displaced person and an Israeli, before becoming a Canadian. Coming from a broken home and being passed (with his sister) from parent to parent and grandparent to grandparent, Rickey had, at fifteen, been sentenced by Romanian fascists to a life of hard labour (for his Jewish ethnicity), then escaped and lived rough, then joined up with the advancing Russian army, then met up with the American army of occupation in Austria, then joined the French Foreign Legion, then smuggled people and contraband in Italy, then fought in the Israeli War of Independence, then emigrated to Canada with a young family, then worked his way up from waitering to running a driving school, then heading an association of all the driving schools in Quebec, then retirement and widowhood and extramural university courses. I found the helter-skelter of imperilling details – his being there amid risky uncertainties and his capacity always to secure himself and to move on – stupendous. But I want to extract from my transcription of the recording one moment in which Rickey breaks the flow of his narration, and moves from an account of episodes and details to a present feeling about them. The extract below begins when I ask Rickey about the signature he places on his paintings; we are seated in his apartment high above downtown Montreal (and have been for some hours) and the walls are covered with framed scenes he has himself composed:

Nigel	Often you sign your artwork 'Rickey' and not 'Hirsh'. And sometimes it's 'Rickey Hirsh' and sometimes it's 'R'?
Rickey	Yeah, because ... I started first 'Rickey', then someone else said, 'Do your whole name, or let me make you a name so that you work under this name'. So I suggest this to other people – to do this ... and they say, 'No'. It was an art dealer and an auctioneer who said, 'I'll make you a name'. But what I think, they mostly are Jew [i.e., the art dealer's intended audience for the work was mostly ('merely') Montreal Jews]. 'Put your full name as it is, and I will promote you, I'll make you a CV and all kinds of things like that'... That's why you see different signatures.
Nigel	But you feel ambivalent about 'Hirsh', then?
Rickey	I was to begin, because even to your pronunciation, the name is 'Hirsh'. But in German pronunciation it's '*Heersh*'. But you have to spell it with two Es instead of an I. So the people call you 'Hirsh', you feel insulted because it's not your name; but that's it. And even 'Rickey' is not my name, my name is 'Rudy'. But when I came here in Canada, my wife said because I had a German name and because I came to Canada, not to have again the suffering that comes with the name, so call yourself 'Rickey'. And she even spelled it for me. So I went and I changed legally the name, from 'Rudy' to 'Rickey'. And most of the people knew me only by the name 'Rickey': 'Mr Rickey'.
Nigel	Was it 'Rudolph'? It wasn't short for 'Rudolph'?
Rickey	No, 'Rudy'. R-U-D-Y.
Nigel	'Cause 'Rudolph': there's lots of British or American 'Rudys'.
Rickey	So this was the transformation of my name too.
Nigel	And your mother's name? Her maiden name?
Rickey	'Braun'.
Nigel	'Rudy Braun', possibly ...?
Rickey	... A name doesn't mean a thing. I don't know your name. I know your face, I feel your character. It's not important to me.
	[...]
Nigel	Can we come another day to hear the second part of the story?
Rickey	Yeah, of course. I don't know if it will be the second part, maybe another part.
Nigel	But you seem to have it at your fingertips ...
Rickey	Yeah, but we are jumping from one to another.

Nigel   Not really ...
Rickey   Yes, there are many years difference. When I was telling you
           that story in Constanza [a major Romanian port-city in World
           War Two], I need to tell you the four years in elementary
           school, and the four years in high school.
Nigel   But it was pretty understandable.
Rickey   I think that's thanks to your intelligence that you can
           understand it. Some people may not. I can talk to them and
           tell them the same story and they'll make something different
           out of it.
                                    [...]
Nigel   I suppose when you went back [to Romania and Constanza]
           with your son, you told this story? You've told the story before:
           besides telling it to yourself, you told it to your son. So it has a
           kind of life of its own as a story, because you've told it already
           a few times.
Rickey   Yeah, but not too many people. Because if you tell them your
           story, they have another story to tell you, so ... I want to forget
           all these things. You just made me remember all of it!
Nigel   Because it's painful?
Rickey   My age. I don't want to live with the past, I just want to live
           in the moment. I have a different philosophy now, thinking
           about myself. Because who knows when the time comes. So
           why ... I walk every day in the mountain [in the middle of
           the city of Montreal]. And in the summer, when you walk
           there, you see some of the people, they sit on the benches
           there, and they contemplate whatever ... And you see with
           the long faces, like this [Rickey puts on a long sad face] and
           you wonder why. Because they live with the past: everything
           that they regret, it shows on their faces. I don't want to be one
           of them. So I'm looking ahead.
Nigel   But it's an amazing story of intelligence and strength and
           survival.
Rickey   Survival the most.
Nigel   And ingenuity, stamina.
Rickey   I think stamina you get physically just because you're young.
           But ingenuity: it's a part of the intelligence.
Nigel   But emotional stamina. For instance when you're seventeen
           and your father ... and you're with the policeman and your
           father pretends not to know you ... That's a cataclysmic
           moment.
Rickey   And when you reach your mother and you see those other
           people ... I remember my father's father, he was, I don't think
           he had a good relation with my father's mother. So when
           everybody else was at the table eating he was given a plate
           and a piece of bread and dripping, and he was eating this.
           I remember that. I never questioned why he was not with
           everybody else at the table. Once when I was a little kid, I
           went up with some friends in the field, and I find a turkey. It

was winter, and the turkey was frozen and dead. So I drag it
home with me, and I bring it home to my grandmother, and
she says, 'What is this?' I say, 'My mother sent it to you that
you should cook it for Friday'. And my grandmother did! My
mother didn't know, nobody knew! But somebody I knew told
me that you can die, and the people can die, because you don't
know what kind of sickness ... I don't know, it was frozen. But
I remember I had a torture in my mind that night there until
I see everybody getting up the next morning. Ha ha!

We stop the tape recording at this point and agree to meet again. It has
been exhausting for Rickey and his energetic recounting of episodes
has slowed and stopped. He has roused himself for one final humorous incident remembered – his grandmother cooking and serving the
dead turkey he had found in a field, amid the poverty and confusion
of familial entanglements and strife – but this has been preceded by a
momentary realisation that he has had enough. It is that outburst I
would focus upon here, when Rickey says: 'I want to forget all these
things. You just made me remember all of it! ... My age. I don't want to
live with the past; I just want to live in the moment. I have a different
philosophy now, thinking about myself ... [People] live with the past:
everything that they regret, it shows on their faces. I don't want to
be one of them. So I'm looking ahead'. It is clear to me that Rickey
is struggling with himself here. He has dwelled upon the past eighty
years for a number of hours. The memories are harrowing, very often,
as well as sometimes humorous in an anomic way. The remembering
has seemed easy and fluid, the memories following one another in a
rapid and unforced flow. I did not have the impression that although
he claims he has been 'made to remember it all' by our meeting, that
Rickey did not process these memories regularly himself – to himself
and for himself. But at the same time he had obviously made himself a
resolution: that he would 'look ahead' and 'live in the moment'. This
is what he wants. But it would also seem to represent something of
a 'want', something he is at present without. I feel I am witness to a
kind of moment where Rickey considers the habituality of his being
and reminds himself of a determination to alter course. It is difficult
because habits of mind – memories – are resources deployed towards
a comforting continuity of selfhood. But Rickey has determined that
the next stage of his life-project will represent something of a break:
his 'philosophy' concerning himself is now to occupy a more futurist
and momentary awareness. The emotional cadence of Rickey's voice
changes – momentarily – and I am brought to an awareness myself
that Rickey is alive to himself, true to himself, at this moment, and de-

ciding how (and who) he will be. It is an insight into the authenticity of another and I am privileged that Rickey has let me witness it.

Faye Ginsburg writes of the interview that it is: 'part of an ongoing reconstruction of experience, providing continuity between the past and current action and belief' (1989: 137). With the caveat that the 'continuities' of selfhood also include radical ruptures in life-project and world views, and re-beginnings, this would seem a good summary of an encounter with Rickey Hirsch.

The Ordinary and Extraordinary

To return to the key conceptual distinctions of this volume, it has been argued that lives possess an 'ordinary' habituality punctuated by 'extraordinary' moments of ironic self-awareness and self-accounting. The interview would appear able to insinuate itself productively amid this oscillation and bear witness to its authenticity: there are moments of being when we can and do stand outside the experiential flow of our lives and call ourselves honestly to account. The interview can be appreciated not only as a significant 'analytical category', then, a way to know another, but also as a 'modality of human being': a kind of way in which we know ourselves, interviewing ourselves as it were. This self-interviewing can deliver any number of outcomes, but a key tension would appear to be between 'remembering' and 're-authoring': the cognitive space of the interview can entail both retrospective and prospective modalities, and we can decide both to carry on along an existing path and to effect a determined break, and any number of gradations between; we can decide that the past is to be re-authored as well as that the future is to be negated. Lastly, for the interviewer and the interviewee, the interview may afford insight into a setting as well as a life: in learning of individual intentionalities one gains perspective on the wider social and cultural structurations that those individual intentionalities feed into, influence, create, critique, respond to and face up to. The interview elicits information that is at once 'local' and 'global'. I shall give Rickey the final word:

> I'll make your life so bitter with all these stories of mine! Ha ha ... And then I didn't live with my mother, I didn't live with my father, at one point during the wartime I didn't sleep with my grandmother either, I was sleeping wherever ... these hiding places that I could stay in. I sleep in a bordello; I was covered up by some of those girls there who were sleeping with German soldiers in there, one of them brought me a Parabellum, and I say, 'With this one I'm going to kill my father'. And

I wanted to. I didn't find him. Maybe it was his luck and mine as well, because my conscience was gonna be even worse! But like this now, I'm happy the way I am. I went through all this ... Ehhhhh, when I take you back now, then I grow up!

References

Ashley, K. 1990. 'Introduction', in K. Ashley (ed.), *Victor Turner and the Construction of Cultural Criticism*. Bloomington: Indiana University Press, pp. ix–xxii.

Caplan, P. 1997. *African Voices, African Lives: Personal Narratives from a Swahili Village*. London: Routledge.

Ginsburg, F. 1989. *Contested Lives*. Berkeley: University of California Press.

Okely, J. 1996. *Own or Other Culture*. Routledge: London.

Rapport, N. 1987. *Talking Violence: An Anthropological Interpretation of Conversation in the City*. St. John's, Newfoundland: I.S.E.R. Press, Memorial University.

———. 1995. 'Migrant Selves and Stereotypes: Personal Context in a Postmodern World', in S. Pile and N. Thrift (eds), *Mapping the Subject: Geographies of Cultural Transformation*. London: Routledge, pp. 267–82.

———. 2003. *I am Dynamite: An Alternative Anthropology of Power*. London: Routledge.

———. 2005. 'Nietzsche's Pendulum: Oscillations of Humankind', *The Australian Journal of Anthropology* 16(2): 1–17.

———. 2012a. 'The Interview as a Form: Dialectical, Focussed, Ambiguous, Special', in J. Skinner (ed.), *The Interview: An Ethnographic Approach*. Oxford: Berg, pp. 53–68.

———. 2012b. *Anyone: The Cosmopolitan Subject of Anthropology*. Oxford: Berghahn Books.

Smith, K. 2012. *Fairness, Class and Belonging in Contemporary England*. Basingstoke: Palgrave Macmillan.

Staples, J. 2007. *Peculiar People, Amazing Lives: Leprosy, Social Exclusion and Community Making in South India*. Delhi: Orient Longman.

Steiner, G. 1975. *After Babel*. Oxford: Oxford University Press.

NOTES ON CONTRIBUTORS

Pat Caplan is Emeritus Professor of Anthropology at Goldsmiths, University of London. She has carried out research on Mafia Island, Tanzania since the mid 1960s, focusing on kinship, gender relations, food security, political change, spirit possession and personal narratives. Her second area of interest is Chennai (Madras) where she has worked since the mid 1970s, researching women's organisations and changing food practices among the middle classes. More recently, she has been involved in research in the UK, especially west Wales, on food, risk, and the effect of animal diseases. She is the author or editor of more than a dozen books and numerous articles, and the biography discussed here is due to be published in both Swahili and English later this year.

Ana Lopes is currently a research fellow at the Centre for Employment Studies Research (University of the West of England, Bristol) and an elected executive member of the British Universities Industrial Relations Association. She was previously a lecturer at the University of East London. She has written on a variety of topics, including sex work, migrant labour and community organising, and is currently researching casualisation in Higher Education. She is committed to the values of interdisciplinary research that does not shy away from sensitive and controversial issues, applying research to empower disadvantaged groups in society.

Isak Niehaus teaches Social Anthropology at Brunel University in London and has done extensive research in South African rural areas. He is the author of *Witchcraft, Power and Politics: Exploring the Occult in the South African Lowveld* (with Eliazaar Mohlala and Kally Shokane, Pluto, 2001) and of *Witchcraft and a Life in the New South Africa* (Cambridge University Press, 2013).

Judith Okely is Emeritus Professor of Social Anthropology, Hull University and Research Associate, School of Anthropology, Oxford

University. Her books include: *The Traveller-Gypsies*; *Simone de Beauvoir: A Re-Reading*; *Anthropology and Autobiography* (co-edited); *Own or Other Culture*; *Knowing How to Know* (co-edited) and *Anthropological Practice: Fieldwork and the Ethnographic Method*. She has done fieldwork in Western Ireland, England and France. As a 'World Scholar', she was awarded the seal of Pilsen City and an honorary medal of West Bohemia University, Czech Republic. She was selected as a Pioneer of Qualitative Social Research ESDA UK.

Nigel Rapport is Professor of Anthropological, Philosophical and Film Studies at the University of St Andrews, where he directs the Centre for Cosmopolitan Studies. Among his recent publications are *Of Orderlies and Men: Hospital Porters Achieving Wellness at Work* (Carolina Academic, 2008) and, as editor, *Human Nature as Capacity: Transcending Discourse and Classification* (Berghahn, 2010) and *Reveries of Home: Nostalgia, Authenticity and the Performance of Place* (Cambridge Scholars, 2010).

Katherine Smith lectures in Social Anthropology at the University of Manchester. She has carried out ethnographic fieldwork in the north of England. Her research interests include fairness and equality, social policy, social class, political correctness and humour. She is author of *Fairness, Class and Belonging in Contemporary England* (Palgrave Macmillan, 2012).

James Staples is a Senior Lecturer in Anthropology at Brunel University. He is author of *Peculiar People, Amazing Lives* (Orient Longman, 2007) and *Leprosy and a Life in South India* (Lexington Books, 2014), as well as editor of *Livelihoods at the Margins* (Left Coast Press, 2007) and two recent volumes on suicide, and has published numerous journal articles and chapters on his work in South India.

Àngels Trias i Valls is a Senior Lecturer in Anthropology and Research Methods at Regent's University London. She has carried out ethnographic fieldwork in Japan and Europe. Her research interests include economic and visual anthropology, gender and sexuality, and virtual communication technologies, relatedness and power in social and virtual contexts and relations of inequality and cosmopolitanism. She is editor of the journal *Anthropology Review: Dissent and Cultural Politics*, and is working on a project on sensorial relatedness in ethnographic research.

INDEX

CPSIA information can be obtained
at www.ICGtesting.com
Printed in the USA
LVHW01s2038190318
570411LV00004B/4/P